Paris Sewers and Sewermen

Paris Sewers and Sewermen

Realities and Representations

DONALD REID

Harvard University Press
Cambridge, Massachusetts, and London, England

Library of Congress Cataloging-in-Publication Data

Reid, Donald. Paris sewers and sewermen: realities and representations
/ Donald Reid.
p.   cm.
Includes index.
ISBN 0-674-65462-5 (cloth)
ISBN 0-674-65463-3 (paper)
1. Sanitation workers—France—Paris—History.
2. Sewerage—France—Paris—History.
I. Title.
HD8039.S2572F87   1991
305.9'628—dc20   90-40617
CIP

Acknowledgments

This book has been fun to research and write. It would have been less so without the assistance of a number of people. The sewerman Lucien Gauchet adopted me, saw to it that my boots fitted, and took me along with his crew as they went on their rounds. The present leadership of the sewermen's union and the past union leader M. Sarrazin shared with me their materials and memories. Jacques Chèze of the Paris sanitation department helped me understand current developments in the sewers.

I benefited greatly from the readings I got at various stages of writing. Joan Scott and the Triangle History and Politics group commented on very early versions and encouraged me to open the sluice gates. I am especially grateful to the friends who took the time to give my completed manuscript the critical scrutiny it required: Patrice Higonnet, Lloyd Kramer, Catherine Kudlick, Patricia O'Brien, Holly Russell, Charles Tilly, and Steve Vincent. I would also like to thank my editor Elizabeth Suttell for her advice; my copy editor Anita Safran has my special appreciation for her encouragement and forbearance.

The National Humanities Center provided the time and a welcoming environment in which to work on the manuscript. The University of North Carolina at Chapel Hill's University Research Council funded a trip to Paris; the University's Endowment Committee of the College of Arts and Sciences for Scholarly Publications, Artistic Exhibitions, and Performances subsidized the cost of illustrations. Above all I want to thank Holly Russell—not, as they say, because this book would not have been written without her, but because her love offers so much more than books.

Contents

Introduction   1

I • The Sewers

1   The Old Regime   9

2   Sewers and Social Order   18

3   Engineering and Empire   25

4   The Visit   37

5   The Irrigation Fields   53

6   Montfaucon Liquidated   71

II • Representations of Labor

7   Cesspool Cleaners and Sewermen   87

8   Disorder Above and Order Below   107

9   The World Turned Upside Down   121

III • The Sewermen and Their Union

10   In the Public Service   137

11   The Body of Sewermen   149

12   Sewermen Today   169

Conclusion   179

Notes   183

Index   231

Illustrations

1. A sewerman with his *rabot* over the shoulder. Drawing by Henry Monnier in Emile de La Bédollière, *Les Industriels* (1842).   28
2. Two sewermen in a *petite ligne* (early twentieth century).   31
3. Sewermen operating a sluice-cart in a collector sewer. Collection Roger-Viollet.   33
4. Sewermen lift the lid of the ball used to clean the syphon. Collection Roger-Viollet.   34
5. The line to visit the sewers (c. 1910). Collection Roger-Viollet.   40
6. Sewermen walk *wagons* of visitors through the sewers. From *The Illustrated London News* (1870).   42
7. The boat trip through the sewers. Engraving by Méaulle after a drawing by Tofani (1896). Collection Roger-Viollet.   43
8. The Paris sewers; photograph by Félix Nadar (1865). Reproduction permission granted by the Archives photographiques de Paris /S.P.A.D.E.M.   45
9. A mannequin dressed as a sewerman; photograph by Félix Nadar (1865). Reproduction permission granted by the Archives, photographiques de Paris /S.P.A.D.E.M.   46
10. Sewage farming at Gennevilliers in the 1870s. Engraving from *L'Illustration* (1877).   61
11. Work in the Paris municipal sewage farm at Haute-Bourne. Collection Roger-Viollet.   64
12. Sewermen put on their boots in a *chambre de rendez-vous* (early twentieth century). Collection Roger-Viollet.   142
13. The death of two sewermen by asphyxiation at the Boulevard Rochechouart in 1880. Drawing by Henri Meyer. Collection Roger-Viollet.   150
14. A sewerman poses; photograph by Boyer (1911). Collection Roger-Viollet.   151
15. A sewerman ascends with a box of rats; photograph by Boyer (1911). Collection Roger-Viollet.   152

Paris Sewers and Sewermen

Introduction

Persons who undertake to pry into, or cleanse out all the filth of a common sewer, either cannot have very nice noses, or will soon lose them.
  —William Hazlitt, "On the Clerical Character," in *Political Essays*

I don't preserve the sewerman's stench for its own sake. The sewerman is only the path, the vehicle, the load.
  —Antoine de Saint-Exupéry, *Citadelle*

The urban physiology of excretion constitutes one of the privileged means of access to social mentalities.
  —Alain Corbin, "L'Hygiène publique et les 'excréta' de la ville préhaussmannienne"

AFTER the French Revolution, European elites had new reason to fear a social world turned upside down. That trauma had confirmed that disruption of the social order could lead to anarchy and unloose the people's basest passions: the old social vessels had split apart, their contents spilling out into the streets. In the nineteenth century, classical liberalism replaced Old Regime inculcations of obedience with an explanation of social hierarchy in terms of the continual, self-regulating exchanges of the market. This world view embodied a dynamic stasis, in which human action continually reinforced an ever-changing, yet stratified social structure. However, the idea that the upper classes "created" the lower classes in the very process of carrying out their market activities and that in turn the continuous generation of the lower classes was necessary to sustain the upper classes in their privileged position contained a barely concealed threat to the social order.

At mid-century, Karl Marx and Friedrich Engels subjected liberal economic theory to the torture of dialectical philosophy. This inquisition revealed capitalist progress to be based on proletarian regression: "Man reverts once more to living in a cave, but the cave is now polluted by the mephitic and pestilential breath of civilization."[1] Marx and Engels argued that the propertyless class spewed forth by capitalism could be held down for a shorter or longer period of time, but eventually the return of the oppressed would overthrow capitalist society. In the words of *The Communist Manifesto,* the bourgeoisie resembles "the sorcerer, who is no longer able to control the powers of the netherworld whom he has called up by his spells."[2]

The myriad analogies to this trope endowed one another with meanings. The dangerous potential of much that comes from below was crucial to Sigmund Freud's interpretation of civilization and its discontents. Repression of instincts is necessary for the development of civilization, yet repression also presents the greatest threat to civilization. Freud himself certainly wavered in his faith in society's ability to control and direct instincts which, given free rein, could destroy civilization.[3]

From another angle, the anthropologist Mary Douglas has brilliantly dissected the very different dialectic of the pure and the impure, and the logic behind the dangers of defilement. She argues that societies identify dirt—matter out of place—in situations of apparent disorder: particular concern over pollution arises when the rules which determine relationships are threatened or contradictions appear in the moral codes operating in a culture.[4] For the bourgeoisie, the nineteenth century was an era of social disorder fraught with challenges to cultural boundaries and moral principles. In this era, the confluence of a growing revulsion for dirt and a new concern for public hygiene and its medical consequences fixated on certain practices and sites, including the sewers. Today, the recurring motif of "open sewers" in contemporary Western journalism on Third World cities still viscerally evokes the dangerous disorder of things out of place (in distinction to the Western city where the "closed" sewer does not pollute the urban landscape[5]).

Yet Douglas's analysis also suggests that simple binary oppositions like closed/open and clean/dirty cannot always contain the multiple meanings channeled into the sewer.[6] In a stimulating literary and historical survey of the complexities of "the high/low opposition" in literature and culture, Peter Stallybrass and Allon White explore "the gradient and direction of flow of metaphor and symbolic substitution from one domain to another."[7] Let us follow these currents where they take us.

Receptacles of the excluded, sewers are equally underground passageways. Wendy Lesser and Rosalind Williams have recently uncovered the importance of the literal and literary construction of veritable down towns in Europe and the United States beginning in the nineteenth century.[8] Public interest in sewers was only one manifestation of a general fascination in France with the underground (and especially bodies of water underground) in this period, from the opening of the famous underground lakes of Padirac for boat trips to the success of novels like Emile Zola's *Germinal* and Gaston Leroux's *The Phantom of the Opera*.

Placing sewers in this culture of the subterranean elucidates the mental topography of class relations. As the etymology of "bourgeois" suggests, the bourgeoisie was characterized as much by its relationship to the city as to capital. In his classic *Laboring Classes and Dangerous Classes*, Louis Chevalier suggestively linked the Parisian bourgeoisie's concerns about the security of the social order during the first half of the nineteenth century to a charged urban landscape of *barrières* and barricades.[9] The sewer occupied a crucial place in this world. In times of civil strife, the sewer could surge to the surface. Of the barricades erected during the uprising of June 1832, Victor Hugo wrote, "There was something of the cloaca in that redoubt and something olympian in that tangle."[10] For many bourgeois of the period, the sewer called to mind the diverse threats—1832 was a year of cholera as well as insurrection—social disorder presented to civilization.

Concerns about a disruptive world below helped give impetus to the unprecedented efforts taken to control and transform the subterranean in nineteenth-century Paris. How in particular was society to prevent its unattended underground waste from breeding very real epidemics which could strike back unexpectedly at the society which had secreted that waste? The answer came in the form of the Second Empire sewer system which, as David Pinkney has shown so well, was one of the engineering triumphs of the last century; it contributed decisively to the decline in severity of water-born epidemic diseases in Paris.[11]

However, in recognizing this, we must beware the danger of fixating on the hygienic and the technological in this history to the exclusion of imbricated representations of the aesthetic and the moral, of barbarism and civilization. What we may be tempted to filter out and retain as scientific was inextricably blended into representations of the ways a civilized society should look and smell and its citizens act. Only with this in mind can we understand, for instance, how the great public health expert Alexandre-Jean-Baptiste Parent-Duchâtelet could bring together explanations of why sites of filth throughout Paris were less dangerous than many thought with sometimes impassioned calls for their reform or dissolution. And even when we suspect that references to the recognizably nonscientific were secondary to their authors, we must remember that technical discourses often have their greatest success in the public sphere when suitably clothed and shod in categories like the aesthetic, the moral, and the civilized in which citizens can recognize themselves and their social aspirations.

In formulating strategies to evacuate wastes, public health experts and engineers condemned fear and disgust as irrational, uncivilized responses.

They preached a fundamentally romantic reconciliation of people and their refuse. Unlike Freud's death instinct, the detritus of society was made by humans, and therefore could be mastered by them. The danger to civilization came from unthinking repression of waste; only by processing this refuse could society conquer its anxieties and turn to profit the hidden worth of what it rejected.

The sewer, antithesis of the sublime, became also the seat of sublimation. In the first decades of the nineteenth century the sewer was a locus of social confusion, a site where, as Marx and Engels said of capitalist society, "all that is solid melts into air." [12] Rotting refuse releasing mortal miasmas offered one form of sublimation—the mysterious, seemingly unnatural passage from solid to gas without an intervening liquid phase. Conversion of sewage to fertilizer presented a different sublimation: a deep threat society presented to itself was made to support (agri)culture. The hidden flow of the city thus led not to tragedy, but to comedy: a sewage-irrigated plot in which city and countryside were reconciled.

Sewers are, by definition, "wastelands," but they are not devoid of people. Analysis of how sewermen have been represented and have represented themselves invites reflection upon the material and cultural foundations of everyday life. The "otherness" of sewermen (and cesspool cleaners) has both removed them from normative public discourse on the working class and made them the occasional recipient of an almost obsessive concern. Such groups, to paraphrase Robert Darnton (evoking Claude Lévi-Strauss), have proved good to think. Parent-Duchâtelet saw in the community of sewermen a world secure from the corruption of nineteenth-century society. For the sanitation engineers who tamed the sewers, cesspool cleaners embodied an argument for a unitary sewer system, while sewermen formed a model army of labor in an era of social upheaval. Socialists and their critics found themselves pondering society after the revolution in terms of who would clean the cesspools and sewers. For the dramatist Jean Giraudoux, the very marginality of the sewerman gave him the force necessary to cleanse the city of the enemies that would destroy it.

At the turn of the century, the Paris sewermen's union itself entered into the debate on who sewermen were and how they were to be represented. As organized workers in the public sector, sewermen were among the early beneficiaries of Third Republic social reforms. The union responded by fostering a language and culture of corporate, quasi-familial solidarity among sewermen, and creatively applying it to the problems which work in a dangerous occupation entailed.

My model in writing this book has been the tours of the sewers (both those offered by the administration and the union): an illuminating spectacle which does not interfere with—and in fact, takes advantage of—the flow of the text. Like a body of water, this study shimmers for some reader-visitors and has depth for others. Their reflections on what they perceive to be matter out of place are revealing: one may see in these pages labor history polluted by a slick of literary theory; the next can discern the troubling outlines of social theory mired in urban history. This work's effort to look at social practices and representations in light of one another seeks to open up traditional urban and labor history by bringing together study of the infrastructure and the subaltern, whether done for their own sake or as the material foundations of upper-class society, with the construction of the cultural supports and scaffolding of that society (and, as such, it understands itself to be part of that process of construction). This book is surely another instance of Gertrude Himmelfarb's new history gone "bottom-up."[13]

The basic premise of this study is that social, economic, and cultural institutions, actors, and actions cannot be extricated from the signifying systems that inscribe and describe them. Rather than going down some deconstructive drain, the realities of health and illness, low wages and raucous behavior, are flushed out in the plurality of representations through which they are known and interpreted. The nature of these particular representations allows for incorporation of the sights, sounds, and smells of everyday existence into sensually charged gestalts, which order and explain the world, and in turn open up new possibilities for, and endow with new meaning, the practices of social life.[14]

In contemplating subjects as fundamental as the delineation of waste and its disposal, engineers, public hygienists, bourgeois urbanites, and sewermen developed means of naming, parrying, and acting on concerns born of city life and social inequality and of evaluating manual labor in terms of the presence or absence of moral virtue. As we appreciate better how such representations are produced and given sense, our understanding of all forms of social experience will be enhanced.

· I ·

The Sewers

1

The Old Regime

Civilization and fermentation are synonymous . . . Tell me, intelligentsia, where the rot is, and I will tell you what you are thinking.
—Régis Debray, *Teachers, Writers, Celebrities*

Paris can be considered a huge melting pot, in which meats, fruits,
oils, pepper, cinnamon, sugar, coffee, the most distant products come
to mix; stomachs are the furnaces which decompose these ingredients
. . . Isn't it likely that all the essences concentrated in the liqueurs
which flow in great torrents in every house, which fill whole streets
(like la rue des Lombards), form those refined elements which pass
into the atmosphere and pinch the nerves [in Paris] and not other
places? Maybe this is the origin of the light and lively feeling which
distinguishes Parisians . . . that *fleur d'esprit* particular to them.
—Louis-Sébastien Mercier, *Tableau de Paris*

OLD REGIME authors were acutely aware of the urban paradox. Cities
were centers of culture and civilization, yet their concentrations of people
also made them progenitors of a pervasive social corruption visible not
only in the inhabitants but in the environment itself. City life embodied
the seemingly timeless dichotomies of mind and body, of high and low,
which structured social thought and social practices. Yet urban ecology was
not without a history. Although *philosophes* measured Paris by the standard
of ancient Rome, the medieval town offered a greater contrast to the cities
of their own day.

The Medieval Town

The waterways which traversed the typical twelfth-century northern
French town (or, in the case of Paris, the river) and the moat which surrounded it helped cleanse the city. Tanners and dyers generally worked
along different canals; the chemicals they dumped in the water acted as
purifying agents, but were too dilute to kill fish. Skinners, glove-makers,
and curriers often located downstream from dyers, to take advantage of the
alum they flushed in the river. Human feces provided fertilizer for backyard

gardens. *Tout à la rue* governed the disposal of household garbage; pigs consumed much of it.[1]

Beginning in the fourteenth century, a long period of war and disruption of trade undermined this apparent golden age of urban ecology by imposing autarky on the city. The area around cities turned into deserted no-man's-lands; moats became stagnant marshlands. In Paris, each *quartier* created dumps outside the city walls. Some achieved such heights that in the reign of Louis XIII they had to be incorporated within the city fortifications for fear that enemies would use them for gun emplacements during a siege.[2] Artisans collected urine and canine excrement for industrial purposes, while municipal authorities gathered human and animal feces and stored them for use in making saltpeter. The unavailability of chemicals like alum led to the development of new biological techniques for dyeing and paper-making which depended on humidity, putrefaction, and fermentation. The more a city stank, André Guillerme reports, the richer it was said to be. The "Little Ice Age" accentuated the effects of what he refers to as "the fungal economy" to create "an extremely cloudy micro-climate" in urban areas which lasted right into the eighteenth century.[3] Commentators portrayed Paris as an enclosed universe, breeding and trapping its own horrific odors. The narrator of the sixteenth-century *Satyre Ménippée* lamented, "We are packed, pressed, invaded, buckled from all sides, and we take no air but the stinking air between our walls, of our mud, and of our sewers."[4]

Urban Refuse

During the Old Regime state and municipal authorities intermittently addressed the problem of disposing of human and other wastes in Paris.[5] Every plague elicited a flurry of ordinances. Three years after the plague of 1530, a royal decree summoned property owners to construct cesspools in each new dwelling; a further decree in 1539 threatened the property owner who failed to comply with confiscation of the house and use of the rent to pay for installation of the cesspool.[6] The new cesspools often leaked—they needed to be emptied less often that way. Only in the early nineteenth century did municipal authorities dictate that cesspools had to be water-tight and built according to certain specifications.

However, cesspools were not the main recipients of the city's organic waste. Paris produced enormous quantities of mud impregnated with rotting organic material, especially horse manure. It made excellent fertilizer, but gave off a pungent odor and was reputed to burn whatever it touched.[7] Lutetia, the Roman name for Paris, was said to mean "city of mud," and contemporaries attributed to Jean-Jacques Rousseau the parting words, "Adieu ville de boue," as he left Paris.[8] In 1780 street cleaners under contract to the city removed about 270,000 cubic meters of mud annually (ten times what cesspool cleaners collected).[9] Until the second half of the eighteenth century, street sweepers and cesspool cleaners brought their refuse to dumps scattered throughout the city. Only in 1674 had an ordinance required that fecal matter be kept separate from other types of wastes at these sites.[10]

In the decades before the Revolution, a new concern with the dangerous effects of miasmas arising from decaying refuse spurred a series of regulations governing the collection and disposal of garbage. With sieges no longer the concern they had been in the past, the crown attempted to break with the waste-retentive world of the early modern metropolis. A royal ordinance of 1758 required that future dumps be located outside of the city. Three years later, municipal authorities designated Montfaucon, northeast of Paris, as the city's primary dump. To mollify inhabitants of the neighborhood, it moved the existing Montfaucon dump three hundred meters to the foot of the Buttes-Chaumont. In 1781 the city closed other refuse heaps, leaving Montfaucon as the city's sole dump.[11]

Montfaucon had an enduring reputation. From the thirteenth to the seventeenth century thousands of criminals had been hanged there; the bodies of those who had died during torture were strung up on the gallows. The corpses were left dangling until their bones fell to the ground. The remains were thrown into the pit used as a dump for household garbage and fecal matter. This practice had two aims. Denial of Christian burial was a final punishment for those who had broken the law; the odors which wafted to Paris recalled to inhabitants the fate which awaited lawbreakers. Although executions took place elsewhere during the seventeenth and eighteenth centuries, the authorities continued to bring criminals' bodies to the garbage pits. Deep cultural associations of execrated criminals and society's excretions merged in Montfaucon.[12]

The Revolution ended the practice of denying cemetery burial to criminals, but the association of flesh and waste at Montfaucon continued into the nineteenth century with the operation of a vast slaughter house. Another major business at Montfaucon was the production of human guano—poudrette—through open-air fermentation of fecal matter. After selling produce in the city, farmers loaded their carts with poudrette which had been aged for a couple of years in the city dump.[13]

As one effort to distance offal from the city confines, Montfaucon was a mixed success. The odor of rotting carcasses from the slaughterhouse was confined to a radius of a few hundred meters; the smell of poudrette in the making could be discerned many kilometers away. The potent combination made Montfaucon "the epicenter of stench in Paris."[14] If the winds which transported the smell of criminals' corpses had once performed the laudatory service of reminding Parisians of their duties to civil authority, they continued long after to carry disgusting and, many scientists came to believe, insalubrious odors to the city.

Sewers

Late-nineteenth-century engineers and public health officials would come to see the sewer system as the antithesis of dumps like Montfaucon. No such claims could be made for the twenty-six kilometers of sewers in Paris at the outbreak of the Revolution. The first sewers were often little more than gullies running down the center of the street. A heavy downpour could turn them into torrents easily overflowing their banks, especially on streets that did not go directly downhill. Well into the nineteenth century, *pontonniers volants* appeared during rainstorms with planks and charged pedestrians a small fee to accompany them across open sewers on their boards. Since little effort was made to take into account the ultimate destination of individual sewers, they often reached a depression where they formed a stagnant marsh filled with mud, garbage, and putrid organic matter. These pits smelled horribly and constantly threatened to flood surrounding neighborhoods. A report prepared at the end of Louis XIII's reign revealed that Paris had twenty-four sewers in 1636: most were in serious disrepair or clogged with rotting debris.[15]

Although individual city fathers (*prévôts de marchands*) made efforts to provide Paris with an adequate sewer system, they received lukewarm support from the crown (except when royal noses were offended). In 1370 *prévôt* Hugues Aubriot built the first covered sewer at the rue Montmartre. It flowed into the Ménilmontant brook and became known as the beltway sewer (*égout de ceinture*). As this sewer emptied into the Seine, it served as a "collector" for sewers on the right bank. Louis XII complained to the *prévôt* repeatedly of the smell of the *égout de ceinture* as it ran past his Tournelles palace between the Place Royale and the Louvre; his successor François I could not abide the sewer smell and, to escape it, bought the Tuileries a quarter of a mile down the Seine for his mother. Henri II continued to live in Tournelles palace, but was unable to do anything about the foul smells; it was torn down after his death in 1564. Things were not much better at the Tuileries, however, where odors from the sewer at the Porte Sainte-Honoré were difficult to endure. Yet the crown did little to improve the sewer system. Parent-Duchâtelet commented that the condition of the capital's sewers reached a nadir when Louis XIII appropriated the proceeds of the wine tax which had been set aside for sewer upkeep.[16]

More damaging to the establishment of a rational sewer system during the Old Regime than royal indifference was the fact that responsibility for the construction, maintenance, and upkeep of sewers was not a clearly delineated public function. Inhabitants paid for the construction of sewers in the late Middle Ages with no more far-reaching concern than directing stormwater out of their neighborhood and into the next. Some sewers were private: both the Palais de Justice and the Archévêché had their own sewers which drained into the Seine. In 1605 the *prévôt* François Miron had the particularly foul sewer of Ponceau covered at his own expense. Taking a different tack, residents of certain parts of the city became so disgruntled with the overflow from the *égout de ceinture* that they offered to pay for its destruction in their neighborhood.[17]

The city did not regularly maintain the sewers, but instead hired contractors to clean and repair them when it deemed necessary. While the city paid for the upkeep of aboveground sewers and those below streets, a 1721 *arrêt* of the Parlement of Paris required property owners to reimburse the city for the cost of cleaning sewers which ran under dwellings. Assessed individuals naturally felt justified in using the sewers to dispose of refuse. In 1736 the *prévôt* was forced to issue an ordinance which set a fine of 100 *livres* for householders and corporal punishment for their servants—even first-time offenders—found dumping garbage in the covered sewers. The Parlement had to reiterate this prohibition in an *arrêt* in 1755.[18]

Municipal authorities continued to cover Paris sewers during the Old Regime. By 1663, almost one-quarter of the city's more than ten kilometers of sewers were enclosed. Covered sewers hid their contents, but were hard to clean since their galleries were of widely varying sizes and built with little incline. The lack of uniform height made it difficult for air to circulate, and with the exception of a few sewers near fountains, water flowed through them only when it rained.[19] Because records were poorly kept, the location of underground sewers was often forgotten. They were put out of mind until a sudden downpour flooded a neighborhood and residents raised a ruckus with the *prévôt*.[20] Nicolas Edmé Restif de la Bretonne was not alone in suggesting that Paris was not ready for the responsibilities covered sewers brought.[21]

The problems of leaving the maintenance of unseen sewers to private individuals contributed to the downfall of the one great sewer project of the Old Regime. Not surprisingly, the location of the royal domicile inspired this operation. When the regent and the young Louis XV decided to settle in Paris in the 1720s, the decision was made to build a new quarter between the Grange Batelière and the Ville-l'Evêque to house courtiers. The stench rising from the *égout de ceinture* threatened to nix this plan. Since correcting the offending sewer was out of the question, the authorities sold it and the surrounding property and used the proceeds to purchase land for a new sewer.

The *prévôt* Michel-Etienne Turgot, father of the future minister, launched the affair in 1737. He constructed a large reservoir at the head of the sewer to provide water for cleansing and established sluice gates to retain water for flushing (and for putting out fires). Turgot had five-foot-high walls built along the sewer with occasional footbridges over it. Men walking on the walls could easily clean the sewer. In a rare display of royal interest in sewers, Louis XV and his entourage attended the initial release of water from the reservoir in 1740; the king remained a good half-hour, chattering on about the "beauty" of the project.[22]

The city granted rights to build or garden on top of most of the "Turgot sewer," as it came to be known, on the condition that owners would vault the sewer with hewn stone and pay a contractor appointed by the city to clean it. This was one origin of the Chaussée-d'Antin quarter. Despite a strict prohibition of the practice, many new property owners installed illegal hookups to the sewer and vented wastes from their kitchens and privies into it: no parliamentary *arrêt* could stop them. They balked at paying to cleanse the sewer and before long, horrific smells emanated from it. For the disgusted Louis-Sébastien Mercier, the sordid story was more evidence of the selfishness of his age: "the interest of a few individuals has imprisoned the plague in a healthy neighborhood." He lamented that it was too late to think of flushing out the sewer. No worker would leave it alive; the odors released would decimate the area.[23] Victor Hugo would recall Mercier to the effect that the cloaca "was left to itself and became what it could."[24]

After Turgot's death, the municipality largely abandoned his sewer. In 1779 the city sold the land on which the reservoir had been built and destroyed it the following year.[25] That very year a report confirmed that Paris was losing the battle of the sewers: seventy sewers were chronically clogged with mud.[26] The 1789 *cahiers de doléances* of the Third Estate of Paris pleaded for better sewer maintenance.[27] Parisians increasingly saw disease as airborne and wanted functioning sewers to flush away waste before it rotted and gave off dangerous miasmas.[28] Writing several generations later, Hugo interpreted the condition of the sewers of Paris on the eve of the Revolution as a reflection of the breakdown of a society which was "no more capable of sweeping away the trash than the abuses." "They were no better able to find their way in the trash heap than to come to an understanding in the city; above, the unintelligible; below, the inextricable." "As to cleaning [the sewers], they confided that job to the storm, which blocked up more than it cleansed."[29]

If construction of an adequate sewer system would eventually require a broad range of modern engineering knowledge, such a project had classical inspiration. In his description of Rome, had not Pliny made the city's sewers, "the most noteworthy achievement of all"?[30] As the quintessential utilitarian public works project, the sewers of Rome attracted the attention of *philosophes,* who saw them as an example of enlightened state action. The occupational health pioneer Bernardini Ramazzini cited approvingly the Emperor Theodoric's praise of "the magnificent sewers of the city of Rome which astounded strangers who came to see them, so that they easily surpassed the marvellous sights of all other cities."[31]

Invidious comparisons between the sewers of Paris and those of Rome gave social critics an opportunity to denounce the egotism of their society. Mercier contrasted the strictness with which the Roman aediles enforced ordinances against individuals who interfered with the smooth operation of the sewers to the neglectful demise of the Turgot sewer. The Chevalier de Jaucourt, author of the article "Cloaque" in the *Encyclopédie,* celebrated the Roman sewers as the embodiment of the spirit of civic patriotism sorely lacking in late eighteenth-century France. He reported that laborers working in the sewers of Rome had come across a female statue. Struck by this find, the Romans made of her the goddess of the sewer, Cluacina. This goddess had appeared as a figure of ridicule in Saint Augustine's *The City of God*. De Jaucourt neatly transformed her into an emblem of the civic religious spirit he so admired in ancient Rome.[32]

Cemeteries

The project of building a sewer system which would differentiate the wastes of urban life, concentrate them, and render them anodyne reenacted archetypal events of modern urban development: separation of the self-sufficient and the poor, the sane and the insane, the living and the dead. Given the nature of the Old Regime city, it is not surprising that, as historians from Johan Huizinga to Philippe Ariès have noted, early modern society was fascinated with decay and death.[33] Eighteenth-century Parisians lived in close proximity to the deceased. Cemeteries grew up in and around churches: it was popularly believed that bodies buried there would have a better chance in the afterlife. The largest cemeteries became widely used public spaces. Thousands of persons of all social ranks were buried annually in the common grave at the Cimetière des Saints-Innocents. The *charniers* above the arcades on top of the walls around the cemetery were said to hold the bones of a million individuals. There lovers held their trysts, preachers preached, and merchants hawked their wares.[34]

In the eighteenth century the educated upper classes repudiated the "fungous economy"; their fears centered on the disease-inducing "miasmas" thought to arise from putrefying organic matter. In the 1780s, this phobia focused on the odors emanating from rotting corpses in cemeteries like Saints-Innocents. Numerous tales circulated of gravediggers succumbing to the vapors from the graves.[35] Was their fate a premonition for others? Such concerns led authorities to order the deconsecration of Saints-Innocents cemetery, the removal of the bones, and the establishment of new cemeteries on the outskirts of the city.[36] The *philosophe* Voltaire had long proclaimed the utilitarian virtues of the rural graveyard. In his 1738 *Préface de Catherine Vade,* he had Guillaume Vade condemn the custom of church burial (and lament that he would probably end up at Saints-Innocents). Voltaire's Vade commends the Greeks and Romans for establishing cemeteries outside cities. "What a pleasure it would be for a good citizen to go enrich, for example, the sterile Sablons plain, and to help make abundant harvests grow there!"[37]

Removal of the contents of Saints-Innocents offered authorities an opportunity to emulate the ancients. Beginning in December 1785, laborers worked winter nights for close to two years, carting the bones to abandoned quarries underneath Paris, long known to be populated by thieves. These were called the Catacombes, in imitation of the catacombs of Rome. Unlike the disorder of medieval ossuaries, bones in the new catacombs of Paris were carefully stacked by type as had been done in the Imperial City.[38] The transfer of the contents of whole cemeteries continued through the first two-thirds of the nineteenth century. The Catacombes are now estimated to hold the remains of six million Parisians.

The nobility of the Old Regime loved novelty. In 1787 the Comte d'Artois and ladies of the Court picnicked in the Catacombes and the next year Mme. de Polignac organized another subterranean *repas*. In 1811–12 Napoleonic officials opened the catacombs to select visitors, including Francis I of Austria. In so doing, imperial authorities transformed human remains—a feared source of disease (as well as a reminder of man's own decay)—and the underground quarries—a place held to be the haunt of criminals—into a source of wonder and amusement. Public tours of the Catacombes began in 1874.[39] Visitors could marvel at both the "rational" (and sometimes humorous) organization of the ossuary and at the way in which the authorities had triumphed over a public health menace and the forces of reaction which had sustained it.

Sanitation and sovereignty were never far apart in Old Regime Paris: the conflation of excretions, executions, shame, and punishment at Montfaucon; the *mélange* of royal and private interests in the sewer system; and the contemporary perception of a triumph of reason over obscurantism in the displacement of the dead. The same can be said of the politics of urban sanitation which evolved in the nineteenth century: intermingled threats from below posed and processed; articulation of a pre-eminent public interest; and transformation of the conquests of modern urbanism into spectacles for the bourgeois voyeur.

2

Sewers and Social Order

The history of men is reflected in the history of sewers . . . The sewer
of Paris had been a formidable old thing. It had been a sepulchre; it
had been an asylum. Crime, intelligence, social protest, freedom of
conscience, thought, theft, all that human laws prosecuted or have
prosecuted, was hidden in this pit . . .

—Victor Hugo, *Les Misérables*

We are the sewers of history.
—Daniel Cohn-Bendit, quoted in H. Hamon
and P. Rotman, *Génération*

PARIS grew rapidly in the first half of the nineteenth century. A city ap-
proaching one-half million under Louis XIV and still only a little over that
in 1800, it surpassed one million by 1850. The "laboring classes and dangerous classes" swelled in size. The July Monarchy bourgeoisie viewed this
underclass living in squalor with suspicion and fear. The revolutions of
1789 and 1830 had revealed the ability of the populace to overturn the
political and social order. The outbreak of cholera in 1832 gave new ur-
gency to these concerns. Seeming to emanate from sites of poverty and
urban decay, the epidemic scaled the barriers separating poor from rich.
Louis Chevalier points to contemporaries' concern with a "Paris malade":
an urban society literally sick of itself and ripe for revolution and epidemic.[1] For Victor Hugo, the sewers presented a rich culture media in
which to raise to consciousness fears of hidden threats to society. Contemporary sanitary engineers and public hygienists saw themselves as explorers
of the uncharted material analogue to Hugo's (sub) *terra incognita*. From
their experiences came the vision of a society renovated by renovation of
the urban infrastructure, below ground and above.

Political Upheaval

The Paris sewers served as one of the myriad sites of possible seditious
activity during the French Revolution. Fears of mysterious goings on in

the sewers fed the culture of suspicion which infused the period. On 24 June 1790 a citizen demanded that the authorities search the sewer under the Ecole Militaire for "matières suspectes"—gunpowder—which might be used to disrupt the upcoming Fête de la Fédération. Several months later, 130 prisoners attempted to escape through the sewer at the Pont au Change; almost all of them were shot down by the Garde de l'Hôtel de Ville.[2]

A more complicated association of sewers and politics spawned by the Revolution centered about the scurrilous and scrofulous journalist and "friend of the people," Jean-Paul Marat. While Marat spent extended periods hiding from the authorities in basements, some believed that he had lived in the Paris sewers.[3] Certainly his repulsive body odor and disfiguring prurigo, characterized by open, sometimes running sores, seemed like the kind of affliction which a sewer dweller would contract.

Marat's connection to the sewers did not end with his assassination in 1793. Post mortem, he was summoned to play the well-known role of Saint Sebastian, whose corpse had been thrown into the Cloaca Maxima in the time of Diocletian. Early in 1795, only five and one-half months after Marat had been given a place of honor in the Pantheon, his remains were removed. The *jeunesse dorée* led the populace in repudiation of his memory. To the applause of the crowd, youths threw busts and effigies of him into the "Mont-Marat" (Montmartre) sewer, chanting "Marat!, voilà ton Panthéon." Popular tradition, repeated through the nineteenth century, had it that Marat's very remains were cast into the Montmartre sewer. (Later research revealed that he had been reburied in a cemetery near the Pantheon).[4]

In the first half of the nineteenth century, the dual relationship of the sewers to revolution persisted. The sewers remained a dangerous, because unsupervised, locale from which to undermine the state. Thus during the Restoration Monarchy the sewer which ran from the Tuileries Palace was cleaned only once a year—when the king was gone—for fear of a French Gunpowder Plot.[5] Alongside this tactical appreciation, however, one continues to find the sewer depicted as the suitable symbolic culture for sustaining the physical essence of social revolutionaries. In his memoirs of the Revolution of 1848, Alexis de Tocqueville described the archrevolutionary Auguste Blanqui with a metaphor of sewer life:

> It was at that moment that I saw a man go up onto the rostrum, and although I have never seen him again, the memory of him has filled me with disgust and horror ever since. He had sunken, withered cheeks, white lips, and a sickly, malign, dirty look like a pallid, mouldy corpse; he was wearing

no visible linen; an old black frockcoat covered his lean emaciated limbs tightly; he looked as if he had lived in a sewer and only just come out. I was told that this was Blanqui.[6]

Into the Intestine of Leviathan

No French author refers more often to sewers than Victor Hugo[7]: a psychobiographer has linked Hugo's interest in sewers to his fascination with his own birth.[8] However, in his portrayal of the Paris of the post-Napoleonic era in *Les Misérables* (published in 1862, but begun during the July Monarchy), and in other writings, Hugo developed a sense of the sewer as both illicit pathway and seat of social pathology which transcended the personal. His widely read works affixed a content to the intuitive, but inchoate, ideas about sewers circulating below the surface of the Parisian *mentalité*.

As a geographic locale, Hugo's sewer was home to an underworld of crime that spread throughout the city. Hugo made literal the metaphoric association of sewer to the sites of low life (and lower forms of life) which novelists of the day located in rough neighborhoods. Thus, Eugène Sue launched *Les Mystères de Paris* with this description of a disreputable bar: "If a crime has been committed, the police cast their net . . . in this mire; almost always they find the guilty parties. The reader will penetrate into horrible, unknown regions; hideous, frightening sorts swarm in these impure cloacas like reptiles in the swamp."[9] In *Les Misérables,* the thief Gueulemer has his lair in the sewers.[10] Both wily street urchins and hardened criminals make regular use of the sewers to escape the police.[11] The criminal Thénardier possessed a master key to the locks on the grills at major sewer entrances. "The sewer was evidently in league with some mysterious gang. This taciturn grill was a fence."[12] And, of course, the escapees from the law and political repression respectively, Jean Valjean and Marius, take to the sewers after the abortive revolt of 5 June 1832.

However, for Hugo, the sewers of early nineteenth-century Paris served more importantly as a potent cultural symbol of moral disintegration and political disorder. He presented them as the true reflection of the civilization above. "The sewer is the conscience of the city. All things converge and confront one another there. In this ghastly place there are shadows, but there are no more secrets. Everything takes on its true shape, or at least its definitive shape. One can say this for the refuse heap—it is not a liar . . . All the filthiness of civilization, once out of commission, falls into this pit of truth where the immense social slippage ends up."[13] In this portrayal, the sewer is no longer simply an extension of the city's poor and criminal classes. It is equally the resting place for the relics of the misdeeds of the city's well-to-do. The sewer is a locus for repression—both within and without the bourgeoisie—of all that challenges its moral code and social order. This explains why political revolutionaries like Blanqui, who embodied the threat that the workings of society presented to itself, took on the physical characteristics of a sewer dweller.

Hugo would have agreed with the English social investigator Henry Mayhew: the contents of sewers show how "close is the connection between physical filthiness in public matters and moral wickedness."[14] Under the rubric of "The sewer is a cynic. It tells all," Hugo breathlessly enumerated the objects found in the confusion of the sewer, not excluding "a livid fetus wrapped in the spangles which danced the last Mardi Gras at the Opera."[15] Hugo's description captures the indiscriminate mixing in which all the fine distinctions of society vanish. It is precisely this breakdown of the categories that order the world aboveground which, following Mary Douglas in *Purity and Danger,* makes Hugo's sewer potentially so threatening.

Not only all the antisocial elements of contemporary society, but also all challenges to the social order throughout history are encapsulated in the sewer. In this, Hugo's sewer resembles Dante's *Inferno:* "In the eye of the dreamer, all the murders of history are there, in the hideous penumbra."[16] Hugo perpetuates the association of Marat and the sewers of Paris. Citing as his source—presumably apocryphal—a sewerman who accompanied the engineer Pierre-Emmanuel Bruneseau on his exploration of the city's sewers during the First Empire, Hugo reports that Bruneseau found something he thought it was better to leave out of his official report: the (anti-Christ) Marat's shroud.[17] (The shroud was made out of a garment of Marat's noble lover, a further example of the social confusion entombed in the sewer.) Physical evidence is thus adduced for Hugo's earlier evocation of the Paris underground as the final resting place of Marat's subversive ideas.[18]

Explorers of the Urban Underground

Hugo recognized only one figure that stood above the filth and moral confusion of the sewer: the engineer Bruneseau. In *Les Misérables* Hugo proclaimed that during the nineteenth century there had been not just progress in sewer construction but a "revolution"—and that Bruneseau had made that revolution possible.[19] In a nation where the recurrence of political revolutions and counter-revolutions had strengthened the state without ushering in political stability or social justice, many began to look to

the engineer as a figure who could penetrate the labyrinth left by past regimes and cleanse the Augean stables of inherited social antagonisms.

The sewers were a new land for nineteenth-century engineers. Hugo
captured the idea of the engineer as explorer in the memorable passage in
which he introduced Bruneseau, appointed Inspecteur Général de la Salubrité for Paris in 1805. Thieves knew their way around the sewers of *Les
Misérables:* what of the upright? "Even the police did not have the idea of
exploring these leprous regions . . . Yet someone presented himself. The
cloaca had its Christopher Columbus." "One day, in 1805, during one of
the Emperor's rare appearances in Paris, the Minister of the Interior went
to the *petit lever* of the master . . . 'Sire [he said to Napoleon], yesterday I
saw the bravest man in your empire.' 'Who is this man?' the Emperor said
brusquely, 'and what has he done?' 'He wants to do one thing, Sire.'
'What's that?' 'To visit the sewers of Paris.' "[20] Well after Bruneseau's seven-
year exploration, the leader of each new expedition to the sewers found
them an uncharted world. The team sent to clean the Amelot sewer in
1826 discovered that there was no accurate diagram of it.[21] Seven years
later, the sewer engineer H. C. Emmery—Hugo's primary source on the
sewers of Paris—lamented the absence of a map of the city's sewers and
described them as "the portion of the city which has remained unexplored
up until now"[22]; in 1838, this project was still incomplete.[23]

In his reports to the Emperor (not Hugo's imagined ones), Bruneseau
developed the relationship between the condition of the sewers and political order. He emphasized the disastrous effects of political upheaval on the
sewer system: "Such is the inevitable effect of the convulsive movements
of great revolutions that a certain time is required to return to an equilibrium, and the equilibrium is never better appreciated than by those who
participated in the movements." Years of revolutionary turmoil had left the
sewers at an impasse. "Because the sewers are under an immense city where
the government sits and which is the site of that which is most important
and most remarkable in the Empire, the cleaning of these subterranean
passages should not be neglected in the least. Yet they are now at the point
where they are so plugged up that they cannot be entered."[24]

By cleansing the sewers, the Empire could demonstrate its superiority to
the monarchy and the revolutionary governments which had preceded it.
"Cleanliness of the body is the image of the cleanliness of the soul; the
cleanliness of a house is the image of the order which reigns there. So I
think I am justified in saying that the cleanliness of the city is the image of
the purity of the morals of its inhabitants, one more attraction, something
foreigners truly admire and respect, and that insalubrity is among the major causes of depopulation."[25] "Cleanliness," he concluded, "should be

more sought after than adornment. It embellishes any state."[26] Yet because of the repugnance of the task, "Only strongly felt love or passion for the commonweal could lead a government leader or a private citizen to take care of it efficaciously."[27] Bruneseau died in 1819 with his mission of reforming the Paris sewers far from completion.

Public Health

In the decades after Bruneseau's death, however, it was not engineers but the new community of public health experts which emerged as the leading champions of urban sanitation in France. These individuals undertook careful studies of diverse aspects of the urban environment. Louis-René Villermé, for instance, established correlations between poverty and mortality, and examined working conditions in the emerging textile industry.[28]

The sewers did not escape the attention of public health experts. One of the most pre-eminent, Alexandre-Jean-Baptiste Parent-Duchâtelet, studied both Montfaucon and the Paris sewers before researching his famous book on prostitution in Paris. Parent-Duchâtelet saw his time in the sewers as a prelude to his work in brothels: "If I was able to enter the sewers, handle putrid matter, spend part of my time in refuse heaps, and live in some sense in the midst of what society closets off as most abject and disgusting, without scandalizing anyone, why should I be embarrassed to take on a cloaca of another sort (a cloaca more filthy, I admit, than all the others), in the justified hope of doing some good, by examining it from all sides?"[29] Memories of the dangers he had faced in the sewers gave Parent-Duchâtelet courage to persevere in his study of prostitution.[30]

No psychoanalyst is required to see the connection which Parent-Duchâtelet made between sewers and female anatomy. In the social economy of purgation, prostitutes' vaginas, like sewers, performed a necessary function. It was the responsibility of the state to monitor and contain ignoble and illicit excretory practices within cesspools, sewers and brothels in order to prevent them from becoming sources of infection. Citing Saint Augustine, Parent-Duchâtelet defined the unity of his œuvre: "Prostitutes are just as inevitable in an urban district as are sewers, dumps, and refuse heaps. The authorities should take the same approach to each."[31] Such faith that the state could impose rational order in these disorderly realms set off the view which Parent-Duchâtelet and his fellow public hygienists took to the urban underworld from the fevered visions found in *Les Misérables*.

Two years after the July Revolution, the horrific cholera epidemic of 1832 killed some twenty thousand in Paris and its suburbs and touched off

riots against municipal authorities, doctors, and the rich.[32] To ensuing out-
breaks of bourgeois hysteria which saw in cholera signs of seemingly uncontrollable biological and social uprisings, public health experts responded with sober, technical prescriptions. Although the water-borne
nature of cholera was not recognized until after mid-century, the public
hygienists' anti-contagionist belief that miasmas given off by putrefying
matter transmitted such diseases led them to include in their recommendations the cleansing and expansion of the Paris sewer system.[33]

The public hygienists were joined in this effort by youthful Saint-
Simonians like Stéphane Mony who, under the pseudonym, Stéphane Flachat, penned a four-page pamphlet *Religion saint-simonienne. Le Choléra—
Assainissment de Paris* in 1832. Before cholera reached France, pundits had
expected that French "civilization" would preserve the country from the
Asiatic plague. The devastation wrought by the disease confirmed for
Saint-Simonians the failings of that very civilization. Mony/Flachat—
member of the Collège de la Religion Saint-Simonienne, Chef de fonction
du degré des Industriels (and later a leading industrialist during the Second Empire)—called for the dissemination of running water in Paris and
for a sewer system which would whisk waste water "away from the immediately disorganizing influence of the heat and the atmosphere."[34] Inno-
cent of the impurities of egotistic interests, sanitation projects like sewer
construction appeared to offer solutions to social ills which partisan politics only exacerbated.

Saint-Simonians were not alone in framing their proposals in terms of a
certain conception of civilization and its potential. During the eighteenth
and early nineteenth centuries, public health experts disputed as to
whether civilization increased the incidence of disease, as Jean-Noël Hallé
believed, or whether civilization was on the whole an agent for the improvement of public health, the position taken by his successors like Villermé.[35] The sewer could be interpreted as emblematic of one element of
this debate. As J.-B. Monfalcon and A.-P. I. de Polinière recognized, well
built and maintained sewers rendered immense services to a city, but the
inverse presented a greater health hazard than no sewers at all.[36] Could
men civilize the sewer or would the cloaca remain untamed?

3

Engineering and Empire

So many Parisians solely occupied with their pleasures, or concerned
with their affairs, cross the city every which way without ever thinking
that they cannot take a single step without trampling underfoot the
most useful monuments, since these monuments contribute to the
preservation of health, and that if they were for a single instant to
cease to exist, or even to be regularly maintained, the city would be
rendered uninhabitable.

—A.-J.-B. Parent-Duchâtelet, "Essai sur la cloaque"

A THREE-DAY revolution in February 1848 toppled the July Monarchy
of Louis Philippe and ushered in the short-lived Second Republic. The
revolution and later workers' uprising in June 1848 embodied the political
irruptions from below many Parisian bourgeois had so feared. The cholera
epidemic in 1849 presented the biological complement to these events.
The pattern of revolution followed by cholera which had characterized
1830–1832 returned. President Louis Napoleon overthrew the Second
Republic in a coup d'état in 1851 and replaced it the following year with
the Second Empire. In pursuing the urban renewal of Paris, the Emperor
Napoleon III transformed Paris under ground as well as above. Not only
did this improve public hygiene in the city, it also disrupted the metonym-
ical relationship of the sewers to the social threat from below.

Sewers before the Second Empire

Napoleon I had built a few enormous sewer lines, but Parent-Duchâtelet
was not alone in seeing them as misguided efforts to match the magnificence of the city's Imperial monuments and asking "What good is such
luxury underground?"[1] In the decades after the First Empire, engineers
introduced important innovations in the construction and maintenance of
sewers. Until the 1820s, sewers had been built with hewn stone. They had
rectangular bases and silted up quickly. During the Restoration Monarchy,
engineers substituted millstone and cement mortar for hewn stone. This
new procedure allowed the introduction of curved sewer floors, which
made flushing easier. Use of millstone also reduced the cost and duration

of construction, an important factor given the disruption created above ground by the laying of sewers.[2] The shock of cholera and the recommendations of public hygienists gave new impetus to sewer construction in Paris: in 1832–33, 14 kms. of sewer line were laid—more than one-third the length of the existing system. The system reached 96 kms. in 1840. When the last open sewer was covered in 1853, Paris had 143 kms. of sewers.[3]

Engineers also made efforts to improve the cleaning of sewers. H. C. Emmery, head of the Paris sewer system from 1832 to 1839, placed fountains at the heads of streets in northeastern Paris and redid these streets so that water no longer flowed down a channel in the middle but went into gutters under sidewalks, which emptied periodically into a sewer.[4] The sewers he constructed had a regular incline and, like all sewers built later, were large enough to allow a man to move about standing up. The sewers flowed into central collectors, which did not drain into the older clogged sewers, but directly into the Seine.

Each of these developments marked an improvement over the sewer system Paris had inherited from the Old Regime. Serious problems remained, however. Construction of new buildings on open land during the Restoration Monarchy increased rainwater runoff, putting further strain on the city's sewer system.[5] The sewers continued to overflow into the streets with every downpour.[6] Twice daily, after the street-fountains had been opened and the sewers emptied into the Seine, the river darkened and the two pumps which took water from the river for Parisians' use "sucked up nothing but a fetid and disgusting liquid."[7]

Sewer grates, a legacy of construction techniques before Emmery, were a constant menace. Mercier was far from the last Parisian to complain of the danger to pedestrians and horses of slippery metal grates flush with the street.[8] More frightening, however, were the vertical grates found on sloping streets. Two meters or more in height, three meters wide and covered with a grill often clogged with garbage, they could be unsightly and smelly, as well as an impediment to traffic. It was feared that children would crawl under the grates that errant carriages had dented. (In 1855 the poet Gérard de Nerval hanged himself on the enormous sewer gate on the Rue de la Vieille-Lanterne.[9])

The sewers could not function without the strenuous labor of a small corps of sewermen (24 in 1826). In galleries where the muck had hardened, sewermen broke it up with spades. Where maintenance had been abandoned (as in the infamous Amelot sewer in 1826) this material could reach the ceiling of the sewer. In such cases, the sewermen's job resembled that of coal miners. They had to be careful not to undercut the mass of solid rotting matter for fear of roof falls. Fortunately, the new design of the sewers, the attention given their incline, and the increased amount of water supplied by Emmery's fountains reduced the occasions on which sewermen had to extract hardened sewage.

The sewerman's primary tool was the *rabot*, a two-meter pole with a paddle attached at a right angle. When sufficient water from rain or fountains was available, sewermen used their *rabots* or small wooden barriers to set up dams with sluice gates. When released, the water flushed the muck along. Parent-Duchâtelet credited sewermen with discovery of this technique, the basis of all future methods of cleansing the Paris sewers.[10] With the aid of this water, sewermen employed their *rabots* to loosen the muck and push it along. When three or four sewermen put their rabots side by side, they referred to the method as a *trainée*. To prevent the boards from sliding along the top of the muck, some men pushed directly on them.

In addition to rotting animal and vegetable matter, sand from construction sites and the street (where it was spread to prevent horses from slipping) clogged the sewers. The weight of the sand caused it to settle at the bottom of the gallery and sewermen pushed it to the side when propelling the organic matter along with their *rabots*. Periodically, sewermen had to shovel the wet sand into buckets which could be hoisted by pulley to the street. When sewermen were working near manholes, they passed the eighteen-to-twenty kilogram buckets of sand from one to the other like a fire brigade. However, the distance from one manhole to the next could be as much as one hundred meters. Parent-Duchâtelet reported that when the distance was too great to permit the handing of buckets down a line, the sewerman had to perform the backbreaking labor of lugging each heavy bucket to his fellow worker.[11] Because of the difficulties removal of sand presented, the police authorities in charge of maintaining the sewers allowed large piles of sand to accumulate, removing them sporadically only after organic matter had begun to ferment.[12]

The Second Empire

A Belgian commented in 1852 on the "water mania" sweeping across Europe. Spurred by the example of the British public health movement, it was successor to the "railway mania" of the 1840s.[13] By the end of the century virtually all major cities in northern Europe had built or were building new systems to distribute water and to evacuate liquid waste which far surpassed the modest system the Second Empire inherited from previous regimes in Paris.

Edwin Chadwick, the leading British public health advocate, argued

1. A sewerman with his *rabot* over the shoulder (1842).

that urban social pathology was largely attributable to environmental conditions, particularly poor housing and inadequate sanitation. Translated to the Parisian context, an extensive sewer system would help cleanse the city not only of its sewage, but also of underlying causes of the social tensions which had culminated in the revolutions of 1830 and 1848. While Chadwick's ideas recalled those of French public health pioneers like Parent-Duchâtelet and Villermé, their British pedigree gave them added weight in Second Empire France. Chadwick, ever the skilled propagandist, saw Napoleon III on several occasions and was said to have replied to the Emperor's query as to what he thought of Paris, "Fair above, Sire, foul below." According to Chadwick's biographer, the Englishman made a more direct appeal to Napoleon III's imperial aspirations: "Sire, they say that Augustus found Rome a city of brick, and left it a city of marble. If your Majesty, finding Paris fair above, will leave it sweet below, you will more than rival the first Emperor of Rome."[14]

Napoleon III's enterprising Prefect of the Seine, Baron Georges Haussmann, made frequent reference to the Roman precedent evoked earlier by Enlightenment writers to promote sanitary reform for Paris. He saw modernization of the water and sewage system as fundamental to the transformation of Paris into "the Imperial Rome of our time."[15] His engineers even incorporated portions of the original Roman aqueducts in the extensive system which brought water to Paris from the Dhuys, the Vanne, and the Marne.

paradox!

In 1854 Haussmann wrote that the increased supply of water entering Paris would require renovation and expansion of the system to expel it. The excavations occasioned by street building offered an unparalleled opportunity to construct an urban circulatory system free of blocked arteries and foul orifices—to correct the sluggish intestine left by the old *régime:* "The underground galleries, organs of the large city, would function like those of the human body, without revealing themselves to the light of day. Pure and fresh water, light, and heat would circulate there like the diverse fluids whose movement and maintenance support life. Secretions would take place there mysteriously and would maintain public health without troubling the good order of the city and without spoiling its exterior beauty."[16]

fluids

The project was very much in line with the diffuse Saint-Simonianism which pervaded Second Empire social thought. (The original Saint-Simonians had favored an even more elaborate corporeal metaphor of renovated Paris as woman complete with fountain-breasts and the works.) Haussmann put together a team of talented engineers under the direction of Eugène Belgrand, whom he had plucked out of provincial obscurity.[17] These engineers, full of *grandes écoles* technocratic aspirations, took charge of sewer construction from local authorities.[18] Haussmann got the municipal council to separate the Service des Eaux et des Egouts from the Service de la Voie Publique. Direct supervision of sewer cleansing passed from the Prefecture of Police to the engineers of Haussmann's Prefecture of the Seine in 1859.

Even before Haussmann became prefect in 1853, a new approach to Paris sanitation practices began to take shape. The streets of mid-nineteenth-century Paris were muddy and malodorous because Parisians dumped their household and kitchen waste water into the gutters.[19] Regulations dating from the Old Regime which expressly forbade the direct linkage of houses to the sewer system remained in force. In 1852 the prefecture reversed this policy and ordered that direct sewer hookups for waste water (other than from cesspools) be installed in all new buildings and buildings undergoing major renovation on streets with sewers. For the practice to be truly effective, however, Haussmann saw that all Paris streets would have to be equipped with sewers. While the length of city streets doubled during the Second Empire (from 424 kms. to 850 kms.), the sewer system grew more than five-fold (from 143 kms. to 773 kms.). Old sewers were rebuilt to meet new standards. Each street was given one (or for large thoroughfares, sometimes two or more) small sewers (*petites lignes*); this accounted for most of the increase in the size of the system. Haussmann's engineers continued the earlier practice of placing water mains in the sewers and making the sewers large enough to permit workmen to repair water mains as well as cleanse the sewers.

Belgrand designed the new sewer system to take advantage of the natural incline of the Seine river basin from the southeast to the northwest. Sewers were given a slope of three centimeters per meter—enough to permit sewermen to walk without slipping, while allowing sand to be swept along. In the plan developed by Belgrand, the *petites lignes* and medium-sized sewers flowed into three main collectors (five by the turn of the century) which served as the large intestine of the system. To take advantage of the force of gravity, the collectors were built in natural valleys in the city's topography.

Belgrand and his engineers realized that a constant flow of water would be a far less effective means of cleansing sewers than periodic concentrated purgings. Water for this purpose was trapped in small reservoirs fed with river water throughout the system; there were more than four thousand such reservoirs at the turn of the century. The sides of the sewers were given an ovoid shape to facilitate flushing. Solid material moved through the system at different rates. Perhaps with Hugo in mind, engineers determined that the body of an animal might take eighteen days to pass from one end to the other, while confetti could make the trip in six hours.[20]

Sewermen continued to wield their *rabots* in the *petites lignes,* forming *trainées* when necessary, just as they had done in Parent-Duchâtelet's day. The wider galleries were built with a channel or *cunette* in the middle and side paths for sewermen to walk along. Sewermen manipulated their *rabots* and hand-held barriers to dam up water in the *cunettes* and then released it through a sluice gate for flushing. The real innovation came with the adaptation of this principle to *wagons-vannes* (sluice-carts) in larger galleries and to *bateaux-vannes* or sluice-boats in the collectors.

2. Two sewermen in a *petite ligne* (early twentieth century).
All Paris sewers are tall enough for workers to walk upright.

Carts with hanging metal plates are used. The plates are lowered by the screw rod on the cart until the sewage begins to back up behind, which causes a strong current to pass under the plates and wash away the sediment. The cart is moved along to a great extent by the pressure of the sewage.[21]

Flushing is accomplished by . . . boats or carts, at the front of each of which is fixed a shield having the exact dimensions and shape of that portion of the sewer through which the water flows. The shields or flood-gates are pierced with holes large enough to permit water to force itself through, but small enough to check more solid matter, and as the boats go downstream in the canals all solid accumulations are pushed along in front of the sluice gate. . . . Boats are used in the main collectors; in the smaller ones the work is done by carts running on rails set on each side [of] the canal, and which of course are also supplied with sluice-gates. . . . The flood-gates in the front part of the boats or carts are lowered into the current, and the body of water which forms before them makes an energetic wash when the vehicles move quickly.[22]

"A moving dune," to use the engineer Georges Bechmann's phrase,[23] up to several hundred cubic meters in size, was pushed along in front of the sluice-boats. "The work of a single boat equals the work of a squadron of one hundred men," another nineteenth-century observer marvelled.[24]

When the cart or boat had reached the end of the sewer, workers lifted the sluice gate and pulled it back against the current to its point of departure. Returning the large boats to their starting place was the most physically demanding operation in the sewers. It remains so to this day, since motors cannot be used in the sewers for fear of an explosion. Anywhere from ten to forty men line up on either side of the boat, holding ropes tied to it over their shoulders and pulling in unison.

A siphon placed under the Pont d'Alma sucked water from the Left Bank collector to the Right Bank. From there it passed to the Clichy collector, where it emptied into the Seine downstream from Paris. Engineers developed an ingenious way to clean this siphon in only a few minutes:

The [siphon] is 170 yards long by 3 feet in diameter, and constructed with a very smooth interior. A wooden ball, almost exactly the same size as the tube, is inserted at an opening on the left bank of the Seine, by the pressure of the stream it is carried down and underneath, and then, by reason of its lighter specific gravity, it rushes up to the surface at the other side, chasing before it the sand, stones, or other obstacles which may have settled in the pipe.[25]

Haussmann expanded street-cleaning during the Second Empire. Visitors remarked how much cleaner the streets of Paris were than those of London and Berlin. This operation naturally increased the amount of sand and silt which flowed into the sewers.[26] The new sewers were equipped with depressions in the galleries known as *bassins de dessablement* which allowed for more regular removal of accumulated sand than had been possible in the past. When these basins filled, water was diverted into bypasses and sewermen shovelled the wet sand into wagons for removal from the sewer. Because of the putrid odors given off by rotting material in the sand, it was hoisted out only at night.

Although elements of sewer cleaning like pulling the boats against the current and excavating wet sand still depended on the brute expenditure of

3. Sewermen operating a sluice-cart in a collector sewer. The pipes on the ceiling carry drinking and nonpotable river water.

4. Sewermen lift the lid of the ball used to clean the syphon.

energy by sewermen, the engineers who built and operated the new sewer system celebrated its mechanical elegance. Mains in the sewers piped water throughout the city; the force of gravity flushed waste water out. At a time when other sources of energy were displacing water power in industry, it enjoyed its final triumph in the sewers. The early nineteenth-century sewer evoked by Hugo had been a stationary resting place in which traces of the distant past could supposedly be found. In the Second Empire sewer system, systematic flushing provided the means to cleanse the sewers. "The cloaca no longer has any of its primitive ferocity," Hugo wrote in *Les Misérables* in 1862. "The rain, which sullied the sewer before, now washes it."[27]

The network of sewers continued to expand during the Third Republic along the lines laid out by Belgrand, reaching 1,214 kms. in 1911. Between 1788 and 1907, the length of sewer per inhabitant increased eighty-four-fold, from five millimeters to 42 centimeters.[28] Extension of the sewer system contributed significantly to the decline of water-borne epidemic disease in Paris; cholera epidemics in the city fell off in frequency and intensity after 1854.

Yet the sewer system was not without occasional detractors, who described it as an expensive plaything of the engineering corps.[29] These critics complained of the cost of building and maintaining a sewer system in which every gallery was large enough for a man to move about erect. Defenders responded by pointing to the multiple functions the sewers performed and the ease with which these operations could be monitored and repaired in a fully visitable system. The sewer tunnels housed two sets of watermains—one for drinking water and one for water from the Seine used to clean streets and to water city parks. Telegraph and telephone wires, pneumatic tubes for the postal service, tubes carrying compressed air, and later the electrical system governing traffic lights stretched across the roof of sewer galleries. The Second Empire sewers thus largely fulfilled Haussmann's dream of a multipurpose subterranean urban circulatory system which would disencumber the boulevards above.[30]

The terms "sewer" (*égout*) and "cloaca" (*cloaque*) had been used interchangeably during the Old Regime and the first decades of the nineteenth century (and in accounts of this period like *Les Misérables*). Only gradually was a clear distinction drawn between a sewer, defined as a place where "the water and the refuse have an outflow," and a cloaca, defined as a site where "the water is stagnant and putrid."[31] Use of the word cloaca carried with it the zoological connotation of a common intestinal, urinary, and generative canal (as in Parent-Duchâtelet's deployment of the term when comparing his visits to sewers and brothels). By the Second Empire, the fact that the term sewer denoted a social construction, not an anatomical borrowing, had taken on significance. Even when described in corporeal terms, as by Haussmann, the Second Empire sewer was less a natural organ than a natural form subordinated to man's use: designed by man, the sewer clearly operated under his supervision and in his interests. References to the Second Empire sewers as cloacae were increasingly reserved for comparisons to the Cloaca Maxima of ancient Rome.

Thus for the sanitary engineer A. Mille, the new sewer system was the Cloaca Maxima enhanced by modern science.[32] The earliest sewer engineers were explorers; their successors employed the analogy to Rome to portray the sewer as a civilizing agent. This was the role assigned the sewer in the symbolic restructuring which accompanied the Haussmannization of Paris. As rebuilding of the city forced the lower classes to the suburbs, the sewers removed detritus from the center of Paris. New construction destroyed many historical edifices aboveground; the extended sewer system below washed away Hugo's vision of the sewer as the receptacle of a sordid historical past. Haussmannization transformed the Paris sewers from a potential site of disease and sedition to a locus of health and public order. As one contemporary wrote, in remaking Paris above and below ground, Napoleon III "worked at the same time against the plague and against revolutions."[33]

• 4 •

The Visit

The charm of a boat excursion in well-diluted sewage does not lend itself to being recreated in the tale one can tell of it.

—J. Bertrand, *Eloge historique d'Eugène Belgrand*

A reformer is a guy who rides through a sewer in a glass-bottomed boat.

—Jimmy Walker, mayor of New York, in 1928 speech

"How towns love to hide under clean busy streets and elegant promenades, the subterranean canals of the filthy sewers where the sexual life of the young is supposed to take place invisibly," remarked Arthur Schnitzler to Freud as they walked across the Schönbrunn Gardens one somber Viennese day.

There was a pregnant silence.

"Did you just make that up?," asked Freud somewhat at a disadvantage . . . "By the way," he countered, grandiloquently, "did I tell you? My daughter Sophie's getting married!"

—Ralph Steadman, *Sigmund Freud*

From the mainstream of rationality the pollutants, the sewage of emotionality, are filtered off and locked away hygienically in a storage basin—an imposing mass of subjective value qualities.

—Jürgen Habermas, *Theory and Practice*

WRITING in the 1830s, Frances Trollope explained that the English were more refined in their speech and manners than the French because of differences in national character, national wealth, and its use.[1] As the English have become richer, they have been better able to keep "out of sight every thing that can in any way annoy the senses." She continued: "When we cease to hear, see, and smell things which are disagreeable, it is natural that we should cease to speak of them; and it is, I believe, quite certain, that the English take more pains than any other people in the world that the senses—those conductors of sensation from the body to the soul—shall convey to the spirit as little disagreeable intelligence of what befalls the case in which it dwells, as possible."

Things were not the same in France. Because decorative items for the house were inexpensive there, the middle-class French home had far more of these than its English counterpart. "Mirrors, silk hangings, or-molu in all forms; china vases, alabaster lamps, and timepieces, in which the onward step that never returns is marked with a grace and prettiness that conceals the solemnity of its pace,—all these are in abundance." But if the French home far outstripped its English counterpart in vanities like mirrors and clocks which hid the march of time, it was, by comparison, sorely lacking in plumbing and running water. The money lavished on the Church of the Madeleine in Paris, Trollope commented, might have been better spent on sanitation. For it was the lack of sewers which did the most to contribute to the coarseness of the French people.

> But great and manifold as are the evils entailed by the scarcity of water in the bedrooms and kitchens of Paris, there is another deficiency greater still, and infinitely worse in its effects. The want of drains and sewers is the great defect of all the cities in France; and a tremendous defect it is.
>
> That people who, from their first breath of life, have been obliged to accustom their senses and submit without a struggle to the sufferings this evil entails upon them,—that people so circumstanced should have less refinement in their thoughts and words than ourselves, I hold to be natural and inevitable. . . . [T]he indelicacy which so often offends us in France does not arise from any natural coarseness of mind, but is the unavoidable result of circumstances, which may, and doubtless will change, as the wealth of the country and its familiarity with the manners of England increase.

Trollope concluded with a paean to technology as the ultimate agent of civilization: "This withdrawing from the perception of the senses everything that can annoy them—this lulling of the spirit by the absence of whatever might awaken it to a sensation of pain—is probably the last point to which the ingenuity of man can reach in its efforts to embellish existence."

For Trollope, when the French chose to live in a more refined environment, their character would become more refined. While such a way of thinking pervaded interpretations of the sewer as an agent of civilization, it was joined by other conceptions of people's relation to their waste. Could technology, instead of simply banishing what was disagreeable and a threat to public health and the social order, make waste a source of interest and value? And might the sewer system be interpreted not just as contributing to a purification of public discourse, but as serving as a symbolic receptacle for what this purified discourse left unarticulated? While the public visit to the sewers embodied the first line of thought, debates over naturalist novels and the emergence of psychoanalysis incorporated the second.

The Visit

Haussmann did not leave contemplation of the wonders of the new sewer system to engineers and sewermen alone. Even before the Second Empire, the occasional wit had suggested introducing the public to the subterranean labyrinth. Back in 1842 Emile de La Bédollière had asked if there was any architectural work to compare with the sewers and encouraged foreign visitors to take a stroll through them. He claimed in mock seriousness that the few who had—Englishmen, of course—had found the experience well worth while.[2]

A humorous aside during the July Monarchy became a regular practice a quarter-century later. The sewer administration began offering public tours of what the engineers fondly referred to as "un second Paris souterrain"[3] during the Exposition of 1867, and the practice continues today. Frenchmen and tourists alike were invited to experience an otherworldly environment devoted to mastery of a former locus of fear and disgust. The King of Portugal was the first dignitary to ask to visit the sewers; many followed.[4] The *Larousse* reported in 1870 that "everyone knows that no foreigner of distinction wants to leave the city without making this singular trip."[5] At the turn of the century, the administration offered tours every two weeks during the summer; six hundred curious visitors took the voyage each time.[6] Parisian journalists and foreign visitors delighted in describing their time in the sewers; their dramatic accounts and the fanciful drawings which accompanied them brought word of the new world below ground to a mass audience.

The tour originally began at Châtelet. (The itinerary changed over the years.) The public descended into the sewers by means of "an elegant iron stairway." Visitors traveled through the sewers in deluxe versions of the vehicles used to cleanse them.[7] They accomplished one leg of the journey in a *wagon-vanne*, whose metal plates had been removed and in which seats for passengers had been installed ("a chariot with cushioned seats, its corners illuminated with oil lamps"[8]). Visitors made the other part of the visit in a sixteen-person *"bateau-vanne"* ("a veritable gondola with carpeted floor and cushioned seats; lit up by large lamps, less picturesque perhaps than a Venetian, but much more luminous"[9]). In the early years of the tour, only women rode the sluice-boats; their male companions walked alongside. Both men and women rode the carts.[10] The blade on the boat was lifted to allow it to move by water power; the cart was "towed against

5. The line to visit the sewers (c. 1910).

the slow current by [sewermen] wearing white canvas blouses and overalls."[11] "Signal is given by sound of trumpet of the rails being clear, and off the carriages start, propelled forward by four men running at the sides of them, at the rate of something like six miles an hour. . . . [E]very now and then the cars shoot past some rushing cascade of dirty water tumbling into the sewer with a roaring sound."[12]

The tidiness and order of the new sewer system impressed visitors. Only the water was unclean: "everything else, walls, flooring, roofing, the cars, the boats, the clothing of the workmen, are all the perfection of neatness."[13] Wide side paths above the waterways allowed "for the passage of the workmen, and so perfectly are they kept that a lady might walk along them from the Louvre to the Place de la Concorde without fear of bespotting her dainty skirts," gushed one admiring visitor.[14] Even thieves could no longer feel safe in the sewers; during his visit, Maxime du Camp spotted a police agent on the lookout for pickpockets.[15]

Guidebooks offered assurance that the visit of forty-five minutes to an hour was one "in which ladies need have no hesitation in taking part"[16] and that it could be made "without fatigue or fear of anything not clean."[17] Ladies wore their finery on the tour: "the women, in stylish costumes, light bonnets, and high heels, hardly suggested an exploration of the sewers."[18] One American tourist mused, "The presence of lovely women can add a charm to the sewer."[19]

In early nineteenth-century accounts of the Paris sewer, it had been a wild, untamed world. For Parent-Duchâtelet, conflation of prostitutes' orifices, brothels, and sewers encouraged a more specific conception of the sewer as gendered, a feminine site controlled by nature and not reason. Excretion and ejaculation were unavoidable natural functions; the (male) state would have to intervene vigorously to regulate both. In contrast to the sewers Parent-Duchâtelet visited, those of the Second Empire exuded signs of a "male," technical rationality, where nature was controlled rather than in control. Only men explored Parent-Duchâtelet's and Hugo's sewers. In the male-coded sewers of the Second Empire, however, women's display of their feminine finery reinforced rather than threatened the social order.

The sewers were literally a spectacle of enlightenment. They were illuminated "with some thousands of moderator lamps, each provided with its silvered reflector. . . . Rows of lamps that grow fainter and fainter in the distance, light up the vaulted gallery and cast their reflections in the black turgid waters at our feet."[20] The play of light and shadow gave the sewers an enchanting, otherworldly aspect in which the "white-robed" sewermen looked like "so many ghosts"[21]:

6. Sewermen walk *wagons* of visitors through the sewers (1870).

7. The boat trip through the sewers (1896).

This underground excursion is made more delightful by the luminous effects of a *coup d'oeil féerique,* set up at certain points along the way.[22]

Now imagine the lights of the car plunging ahead into the immense underground tunnel, throwing their reflections on the travellers, and sketching on the walls the reflection of the sewermen, and you will grasp the picturesque aspect of the trip.[23]

One visitor wondered, only half in jest: "Couldn't one also decorate the big and small collectors with painted pictures? What a vast space open to the imagination and talent of young artists who dream of big composition."[24]

In 1865, after patenting a device to photograph with artificial light, Nadar spent three months photographing the catacombs and sewers of Paris. His sewer photographs, Walter Benjamin commented, mark "the first time that the lens is given the task of making discoveries."[25] Nadar's stark photographs spread images of the sewer's austerity and mystery to those who had not visited them. He photographed mannequins dressed as sewermen because a pose of up to eighteen minutes was required in the artificial light; this gave an eerily antiseptic aura to the sewer.[26]

The sense of smell was as important as that of sight to those who visited the sewers. In the 1820s, Parent-Duchâtelet had identified six types of odor in the sewers. An 1841 guide for English visitors reported that the contents of the sewers gave off "a nauseous sickly undefinable vapour, which is said to be quite peculiar to these sewers."[27] In the renovated sewer system of the Second Empire, however, the rapid evacuation of waste and the ventilation provided by the movement of water limited the formation of odors; the engineer Bechmann proudly claimed that only one of the smells identified by Parent-Duchâtelet remained, an innocuous *"odeur fade."*[28]

Visitors marveled that they could watch trash float by and yet encounter no "noxious nasal trials."[29] Bechmann saw the visits as the best way to prove to the public that the sewers could not be held responsible for any unsavory odors encountered in the city above.[30] In a society which Alain Corbin has reminded us, was obsessed with the danger and repugnance of foul smells, the odorlessness of the sewers provided evidence of the sanitary revolution which had taken place in them.

A Gloss on *Les Misérables*

As unique as a tour of the sewers may have seemed, most visitors "read" the event in light of an interpretive framework borrowed from literature. In turn, modern technology gave visitors the opportunity to experience familiar texts in a new way. Some thought of Charon ferrying the dead

8. The Paris sewers; photograph by Félix Nadar (1865). Note the *cunette* running down the middle of the gallery.

across the Acheron and others of Dante's description of Hell. "The muffled sounds of the horns and silent white figures of the crews carried the imagination into all kinds of strange similes. The Inferno and River Styx!"[31] Others, perhaps with Hugo's evocation of the Leviathan in mind, saw themselves like Jonah being swallowed by the whale.[32]

9. A mannequin dressed as a sewerman; photograph by Félix Nadar (1865).

But for most visitors, a tour of the sewers was an opportunity to relive a climactic moment in *Les Misérables*. Hugo's masterpiece was one of the best-loved and most widely read novels of the nineteenth century, not just in France, but in Great Britain and the United States as well. Hugo's evocation loomed larger than anything visitors heard on the tour. Told of four sewermen who had drowned after a storm dumped a flood of water into the sewers, one visitor admitted frankly, "But we think less of the real tragedies that have taken place here than of the scene drawn for us by the pen of the master of modern fiction—of 'Jean Valjean saving Marius'."[33] And visitors also could not help but compare their trip through the sewers to that described in *Les Misérables:* "We had been through the sewers of Paris and Victor Hugo, but in a more comfortable manner than the way poor Jean Valjean saw them."[34]

The evident change from the sewers which Jean Valjean braved in 1832 to those which members of the upper classes visited at the end of the nineteenth century underscored the reassuring nature of the experience. Ironically, Hugo—inveterate opponent of the Second Empire—helped secure Napoleon III's reputation through his vivid description of the preimperial sewers. It has become a commonplace of social history and literary criticism to see the carnival as a disruption of the outward manifestations of social hierarchy which reveals repressed threats to the social order. From this perspective, the visit to the sewers constituted the anti-carnivalesque, in which a "transgression" of the world of surface appearance did not expose subversive possibilities, but instead assured the bourgeois that their order reigned below.

The New Politics of the Sewers

Construction of large galleries that could be easily traversed by visitors made the sewers of Second Empire Paris the true successors of those of Rome. More than sewers in other European and American cities, the ones of Paris seemed to live up to Pliny's exaggerated claims for the great works which Tarquin is given credit for having built beneath Rome: "the tunnels [were] large enough to allow the passage of a wagon fully loaded with hay."[35] In the famous *Paris Guide* of 1867—the year sewer tours began—Alfred Mayer, an architect for the city of Paris, evoked the voyage through the Cloaca Maxima of the aedile Marcus Agrippa in 33 B.C.: "Almost two thousand years had to pass before such a trip could be taken in Paris."[36] Even ironic observers of Haussmannization couched their comments in terms of the Roman analogy.

"They still speak to us of the aqueduct of Ancus Martius and of Tarquin's cloaca! These are children's playthings, suitable for relegating to ancient history with the seven wonders of the world, and which would make the least of our municipal councillors smile with pity. The Romans are surpassed, this much is clear, and if any incorrigible Stoic dares to be insufficiently proud of his country and his era, the only thing left would be to send him to the big collector sewer." [37]

Everyone remarked on the spatial reorganization of Paris during the Second Empire. In similar fashion, Napoleon III's regime appropriated the city's underground, displacing the political and criminal underworld which had symbolically inhabited it. Hugo—bitter critic of "Napoleon the Little"—recognized this grudgingly (although his lavish praise of Bruneseau was a way of providing a Napoleonic counterpart to Haussmann's engineers and the work they were undertaking at the very time Hugo was completing *Les Misérables*). In the novel, Hugo described the sewers of 1862 in Trollope-like terms of English respectability; they evoked for him the elevation of an individual from the baseness of private commerce to the exalted reaches of public life: "Today, the sewer is clean, cold, upright, proper. It attains almost the ideal of what is understood in England by the word 'respectable.' It is dull and presentable; in a straight line; one might almost say dressed to the nines. It resembles a tradesman turned *conseiller d'Etat*. One can almost see clearly in it. The mire is well-behaved." [38]

Even the siege of Paris and the ensuing Commune could not dispel such representations of the new, visitable sewers. In his famous six-volume *Paris: Ses organes, ses fonctions et sa vie dans la seconde moitié du XIXᵉ siècle* (1869–1875), Maxime du Camp praised the sewer system as an engineering feat of the first order and a monument to the Second Empire. He explicitly associated construction and maintenance of the sewers with a politics of order. Echoing Bruneseau, du Camp wrote that during the Great Revolution, the sewers had been left to themselves: "these great questions of civic administration were put aside for deceptive discussions of *une politique à outrance*." [39] This had not happened in 1870–1871. Despite deep anxieties about the Paris Commune (chronicled at length in his four-volume *Les Convulsions de Paris* [40]), du Camp dissociated the sewer system from the upheaval. While his inclusion of an appendix listing all the weapons found in the sewers after the Commune could be seen as a comment on the violence of the Parisian masses, he implicitly turned the sewer into an agent of their social pacification, explaining that Communards dropped their weapons down manholes to avoid being captured armed by government troops. [41]

Sewers and the Culture of Filth

The long-standing metonymic use of sewer for filth persisted in the final decades of the nineteenth century, at precisely the time when open and overflowing underground sewers became things of the past. The sewer's improved capability to concentrate urban waste ironically enhanced its attraction as a signifier for all that was rotten and fetid in modern society. Reversing Trollope's argument, conservative Catholic critics of free-thinking and naturalism linked the amoral technologies of the modern world, embodied in the creation of a new sanitary order, to the generation of a new vulgarity in society.

In his 1867 *Les Odeurs de Paris,* the Ultramontane critic of the Second Empire, Louis Veuillot, combined the concepts of the sewer as an immoral repository and as an instrument of public order to suggest that corruption pervaded public authority itself. Veuillot interpreted Haussmann's opening up of Paris above and below ground in terms of the regime's wanton destruction of the traditional moral and religious barriers to the dissemination of immoral and vulgar ideas. Veuillot's Second Empire Paris was a world turned upside down. Haussmann's grand boulevards resembled his sewers: "To see these streets from atop a house, it is like an overflowing river carrying along a society's debris."[42] In fact, the sewers were the true boulevards of the new Paris: "The sewers of Paris merit having something illustrious happen in them. People who have seen everything say that the sewers are perhaps the most beautiful thing in the world. Light explodes in them and the mire maintains a mild temperature. People take boat rides and hunt rats. Meetings are set up and already more than one dowry has been settled upon there."[43]

The boulevards and sewers which provided free circulation of intellectual and material trash also allowed for a new technology of public order. If the authorities were to find the streets blocked off, their men could pass through the sewers. This would give the troops the upper hand. "For today's ideas are not made to stand up to regiments, especially when they encounter them where they were not expecting them." Yet, since perverted ideas pervade the sewers (pulled in by gravity), Veuillot would not be surprised if a battle took place and *victoire toute infecte* came out of a manhole.[44] The Second Empire, in letting immoral ideas circulate, had been tainted itself: a corrupt police state was the best one could expect.

> Truly Paris is an inundation which has submerged French civilization, and is sweeping away the debris. Where has it brought the remains? For my part, I think it is bringing it to the police prefecture, whatever victory arises from the sewers. If the prefecture will be able to make another civilization from all

what does it mean to author a text!"

this debris, I cannot say. Those who want to know what this civilization will be like need only read Tacitus and Petronious.[45]

The sewers of Paris lead Veuillot not to the glories of Rome, but to imperial dissoluteness.

Veuillot's metaphor of modern society creating not simply better sewers, but sewers which facilitated the concentration and transmission of previously inexpressible filth, was a *leitmotif* of discussions of naturalism and especially the work of Emile Zola. "I heard my work treated as a puddle of mud and blood, as a sewer, as filth," Zola complained.[46] Certainly the Catholic critic Léon Bloy seemed unable to discuss Zola's œuvre without reference to outhouses and sewers.[47]

The Paris sewers had connoted revolution, crime, and contagion to many July Monarchy bourgeois. Transformation of the sewers challenged such associations. For the engineers who authored it, the new sewer system was an expurgated (and expurgating) text in which all could read evidence of a society able to reveal and restrain its once rebellious refuse. Parisian bourgeois familiar with Hugo's imaginative evocation of the horrors of the July Monarchy sewer could experience the fruits of technological progress in a promenade through its successor.

Yet the sewers remained a metaphorical locus for the baser elements of life. The late nineteenth-century interest in the unconscious encouraged such mapping of a psychological underground. Freud recognized that society required its members to repress and sublimate those elements of their psyche which threatened their existence and that of civilization. Yet this process was rife with conflict and troubled revelations on the analyst's couch. If the sewers were a structure for concentrating and disposing of refuse far more efficiently than in the past, public visits to them (and to the catacombs) were something like a sanitary group therapy, a means of reintroducing men and women to that which society had taught them to fear and despise.

However, the differences between Freud's understanding of the social unconscious and the late nineteenth-century engineers' view of the sewers are more significant than any similarities. For Freud, entry into the unconscious was a difficult and dangerous journey. There were no iron stairways or obliging sewermen in this world, only dreams and psychoanalysts. More important, instincts could never be traced back to human actions (as could deposited refuse), nor could they be so easily channeled in a healthy direction. The greater the efforts to control them, the more likely were they to rebound to destroy individuals and society. In contrast, the engineers' model of the sewers offered the technocrats' optimistic view of the social order. Given free rein, engineers could devise technical solutions to social problems. That which civilization required people to reject—waste—was not a threat in itself. The public visits to the sewers showed this. Only repression or avoidance of the unknown and the resulting fear created the conditions for refuse to become a danger.

A Postscript

Until the Second Empire, the sewers of Paris participated in two ways in the political imagination. They were obviously a place where seditious activities could be performed away from the public eye. But in the first half of the nineteenth century, the untamed muck of the sewer was also conceived as the natural home not only of cholera, but of the most fearsome criminals and revolutionaries as well. This second element was flushed out with the construction of a large, easily traversible sewer system made familiar through public tours. After Haussmann, the sewers no longer figured as a place which nurtured political radicals with characteristics associated with mire. The political underground became sanitized; it was cultural radicals like Zola who were most frequently described in terms of sewers.

However, the earlier understanding of the sewer as site of real and fantastical tactical maneuvers was encouraged by the expansion of the new sewers: after all, such a well-laid out underground thoroughfare was of potentially far greater use to subversives. A turn-of-the-century foreign visitor had little trouble imagining that fear of explosion did not explain why gas mains were not in the sewers: "The real reason . . . lies in the fear of Communism. In case of a 'Revolution' or uprising, the Communists would in all probability be in possession of some locality, and so have access to the sewers. It would not be difficult for them to descend into the sewers and blow up the gas mains." [48] Such thoughts were not always idle speculations. In 1917 Trotsky studied the various passageways under St. Petersburg and had two workers explore the sewers which went below the residence of the general staff. Curzio Malaparte reported this information in his *Technique du coup d'état,* the bible of Eugène Deloncle, leader of the clandestine right-wing Cagoule in the 1930s. [49] The Cagoule obtained detailed maps of the sewer system and other underground passageways in Paris, constructed underground headquarters, storehouses, and prisons, and equipped their commando units with arms and various tools necessary to launch an assault on the Republic (and the private homes of prominent republicans) from below ground. [50]

During the Occupation, the Germans used the sewers as air-raid shelters; to protect themselves from surprise attacks in their hideouts they set up almost three hundred barriers composed of several meters of barbed wire. The Resistance looked to the sewers for shelter as well. At the end of the Occupation the leadership of the Forces Françaises de l'Intérieur (F.F.I.) in Paris worked out a plan to make use of the sewers in cooperation with Taves, head of the Bureau du Service des Eaux et Egouts. Colonel Rol-Tanguy, leader of the F.F.I., temporarily made the sewer facilities at the rue Schœlcher his headquarters before moving to the nearby Catacombes under the Place Denfert-Rochereau. According to Raymond Massiet (commandant Dufresne), *chef d'état-major* of the F.F.I. for the department of the Seine, the F.F.I. planned to use the independent telephone system in the sewers in the event that the Germans declared a state of siege and communication by the regular telephone network became impossible. If these underground lines had been cut, the F.F.I. could count on a team of 250 sewermen to carry messages to various parts of the city. Other plans were made to use the manholes in the streets to hide armed Resistance fighters. The rapid retreat of the Germans from Paris made this unnecessary. However, during the street fighting which accompanied the Liberation, the *Résistants* set up their first-aid station in the sewer at the rue Gay-Lussac.[51]

In the early 1960s, the right-wing terrorist Organisation Armée Secrète (O.A.S.), like the Cagoule twenty-five years earlier, studied the sewer system and pondered how it could use the labyrinth under Paris to further its plans. The Prefect of Police remarked that the Paris underground was like Gruyère cheese and at the height of the O.A.S. terrorism in 1961, the Minister of the Interior ordered that special precautions be taken to prevent the sewers and other underground passageways in Paris from being used to launch an attack on the Senate in the Palais du Luxembourg.[52]

In the early nineteenth century, the sewers were thought by some to house thieves. Like the relation of sewers to sedition, that of sewers to crime has now become purely tactical. In recent years, bank robbers have used the sewers to gain entry to banks and to escape. One guide book even explains that this is why the cart and boat rides are no longer a part of the public tour.[53] But is this the reason? More likely, municipal administrators recognized that the very success of the visit over the years had diminished both its primary goal of providing novel entertainment and its secondary pedagogical *raison d'être* of encouraging the public to shed its misgivings about what went on in sewers (and to place faith in future debates over urban sanitation in the hands of those who operated the sewers). The city can now no longer justify the expense of deploying personnel simply to satisfy the public's lingering curiosity. The sewer has become just another mechanism of urban life. Post-modern Paris has its pyramid; who remembers its Cloaca Maxima?

♦ 5 ♦

The Irrigation Fields

We must ask . . . how dirt, which is normally destructive, sometimes becomes creative.

—Mary Douglas, *Purity and Danger*

ENGINEERS are often castigated for having contributed to the creation of a society of wasteful consumption threatened by its own dangerous by-products. Yet there is a long tradition among engineers of seeking "elegant" and economical solutions to the disposal of waste generated by modern technology: it is the engineers' version of the physicists' search for the perpetual motion machine. In the nineteenth century, for example, engineers devoted themselves to capturing energy lost in steam engines and blast furnaces. Nowhere is this engineering tradition stronger than in France, where technocrats now push forward the development of breeder reactors which, whatever their drawbacks, have the advantage of using their by-products in the making of fuel.

This engineering ethos partakes of the artisanal ingenuity which characterized urban existence until the end of the nineteenth century. The ragpicker who recycled discarded materials back into the economy embodied this way of life. This tradition was adapted to the renovated sewer system of the final third of the nineteenth century. The sewer administration dredged salvageable goods out of the sewers, cleaned them, and sold them to junk dealers. Every visitor to the sewers commented on the multitude of corks which floated by (probably because this was the one thing which they could identify in the sewage). The administration directed sewermen to skim these corks off the top of the water. It then sold them to perfumers, who cut them down for use as stoppers in perfume bottles.[1] Thus did the foul meet the fragrant.

The city even collected the sewermen's old hip boots and offered them to the highest bidder. The soles were made into galoshes for workers in the peat bogs at Méru in the Oise. Bootmakers bought the uppers. They prized them for precisely the quality which had rendered the boots unusable for sewermen. Over time, the leather became rock-stiff from the interaction of fats and acids in the sewage. This trait made the boot uppers perfect for women's high-heeled ankle boots which otherwise required a metal arch to preserve their shape. As the metal arch weighed down the shoe, bootmakers preferred to use the leather from old sewermen's boots.[2] Du Camp reported that it made "the most supple, the finest, most beautiful leather imaginable; more than one elegant lady quite unknowingly wears it in the form of half-boots."[3] As did public tours of the sewers, such projects of recuperation questioned the boundaries delineating the lower depths and high society, the fetid and the feminine.

The "Circulus" and the Ouroboros

Social thinkers had long seen agricultural use of urban waste (as with the *poudrette* of Montfaucon) as offering advantage to both city and countryside. In 1786 Mathieu Géraud proposed that all of the organic waste of Paris be converted, through *fermentation putride,* into fuel to heat the city; the ashes could be used as fertilizer.[4] In *Les Nuits de Paris,* Géraud's contemporary Restif de la Bretonne described a group of Parisian street sweepers negotiating with sometimes reluctant householders to sweep in front of their dwellings. When the sweepers had collected a large pile of refuse, they dumped it into the Seine. If the city were to sell the refuse as fertilizer, Restif de la Bretonne explained, the proceeds could be used to support a municipal street-sweeping service free of the whims of individual householders. "The inhabitant of Paris, who has no idea how precious fertilizer is, seeks only to dispose of it. The authorities could remedy this by requiring landowners to buy so many cart-loads of fertilizer from the refuse dumps, at one *écu* a cart-load and in proportion to their acreage, and the income would be used partly to pay for public street-cleaning, partly to increase the number of sweepers."[5]

Such utilitarian schemes pale beside the nineteenth-century socialist Pierre Leroux's development of the "circulus" to refute Malthus's pessimistic vision of a population perpetually outstripping its food supply. Leroux argued that everyone is both a producer and a consumer; the "waste" an individual produces can be used to raise the food necessary to keep that individual alive. Therefore, social practices, not nature, are to blame for so-called Malthusian crises. Leroux named his discovery the "circulus" as an ironic commentary on the cycle of impoverishment in economists' conception of the "circulation" of wealth.[6]

Leroux first come up with his theory in 1834 to explain why a Fourierist phalanstery had failed.[7] For decades he expounded what he considered "the peaceful solution to the problem of the Proletariat" in the face of widespread ridicule. Living in exile on the island of Jersey after the fall of the Second Republic, Leroux used his own excrement as fertilizer and tried to convince authorities there to adopt this system as public policy. In *Aux Etats de Jersey: Sur le moyen de quintupler, pour ne pas dire plus, la production agricole du pays* (1853) he explained: "If men were believers, learned, religious, then, instead of laughing, as they do, at socialism, they would profess with respect and veneration the doctrine of the *circulus*. Each would religiously gather his dung to give it to the State, that is to say the tax-collector, in place of a tax or personal levy. Agricultural production would double immediately and poverty would disappear from the face of the earth."[8] Leroux believed that the destitution of modern society derived from the fundamental social error of designating as refuse to be discarded a substance which was potentially a great source of wealth. Leroux's organic vision suggested that society need not be disdainful of its waste and that if turned to productive use, this waste could be an agent of social regeneration. *early modern organic farmer*

Hugo visited his friend and fellow exile Leroux in Jersey and there became a proponent of the circulus.[9] He devoted an admiring chapter to an aquatic adaptation of the theory in *Les Misérables*. Part Five, Book Two begins, "Paris throws twenty-five million francs a year into the water." In contrast to his other descriptions of the sewer, Hugo continued, "And this is no metaphor."[10] "We believe we are purging the city; we are weakening the population."[11] "A sewer is a misunderstanding,"[12] the locus of a social theft of far greater proportions than that of the sewer's criminal denizens. Hugo reworked Trollope's vision of Paris. The wealth Paris lost in its sewers, "if used for welfare and for pleasures, would double the splendor of Paris. The city spends it cloacas. Such that one can say that the great prodigality of Paris, its marvellous *fête* . . . its orgy, its gold flowing from full hands, its splendor, its luxury, its magnificence, is its sewer."[13] The sewer was the fruit of "the blindness of a bad political economy."[14]

If the sewers of ancient Rome provided an inspiration for those of Paris, he implored his contemporaries not to repeat the Romans' error. " 'The sewers of Rome,' Liebig says, 'absorbed all the well-being of the Roman peasant.' When the Roman countryside had been ruined by the Roman sewer, Rome drained Italy, and when it had put Italy into its cloaca, it threw in Sicily, then Sardinia, then Africa. The sewer of Rome swallowed the world."[15] Paul Claudel poked fun at Hugo for offering no other solution to society's ills than the better utilization of sewage,[16] but for many looking to redeem the city and civilization in the nineteenth century, Leroux's ideas, transferred by Hugo from the individual fecal levy to the collector sewer, offered a welcome panacea.

In all probability, the inspiration for Hugo's sewer-circulus was Leroux's contemporary, the influential British public health expert Edwin Chadwick. He viewed the countryside as suffering from too much water and too little manure, while the city lacked the water to cleanse itself of its wastes. Chadwick and his followers argued that social harmony could be achieved if the organic balance between town and country were restored by the pumping of clean water from the countryside into the city and the evacuation of waste to the countryside where it could be used as fertilizer to raise food for the cities. In so doing, Chadwick wrote in 1845, "we complete the circle and realize the Egyptian type of eternity by bringing as it were the serpent's tail into the serpent's mouth." [17]

Chadwick conceived his hydrological ouroboros while doing research for the famous Sanitary Commission report of 1842. Authorities in Edinburgh, eager to rally Chadwick's support for their campaign against insalubrity in their city, showed him where the sewers containing wastes from the city's streets and privies emptied into a stream known as the Foul Burn. What caught Chadwick's attention were the farmers who diverted the Foul Burn to irrigate their fields. While this produced horrible odors which wafted back to the city, the farmers, pointing to the astonishing fertility of the irrigated fields, refused to abandon the practice. [18] Instead of condemning such *fertilisation sauvage* as his guides had expected, Chadwick saw in it a solution to the problem of urban waste disposal. All that would be necessary to control the smell would be to transport the sewage in enclosed pipes to the agricultural fields.

Chadwick became an ardent proselytizer for spreading the wealth via liquified human sewage (versus Leroux's *auto(di)gestion*). Like Hugo, Chadwick found confirmation for his faith in the findings of the German chemist Justus Liebig: liquified sewage preserved the valuable nitrogen lost when human excrement was dried for use as fertilizer. "All smell is disease," Chadwick wrote in 1846, but "All smell of decomposing matter may be said to indicate loss of money." [19] Above all, what appealed to Chadwick was the idea that the use of liquified human sewage for agriculture would finance operation of the sewer system. This, Chadwick thought, would do more than anything else to hasten the introduction of running water and flush toilets in cities.

Chadwick went on to argue that the resulting improvement in sanitation would provide the demographic foundations for a conservative social order. Youths, not mature workers, supported strikes and demonstrations. Better sanitation would assure that more workers lived to maturity.

[Chadwick] wrote that by reducing life expectancy, insanitary conditions "check the growth of productive skill, and abridge the amount of social experience and steady moral habits in the community: that they substitute, for a population that accumulates and preserves instruction and is steadily progressive, a population that is young, inexperienced, ignorant, credulous, irritable, passionate, and dangerous, having a perpetual tendency to moral as well as physical deterioration."[20]

In one form or another, Chadwick's ideas spread far and wide. In Volume III of *Das Kapital,* one even finds Karl Marx identifying the waste of human sewage as characteristic of capitalism: "Excretions of consumption are of the greatest importance for agriculture. So far as their utilization is concerned, there is an enormous waste of them in the capitalist economy. In London, for instance, they find no better use for the excretion of four and one-half million human beings than to contaminate the Thames with it at heavy expense."[21] The engineers who built and operated the Paris sewer system during the Second Empire also looked with interest on Chadwick's ideas, although the well-entrenched system of cesspools and excrement dumps in Paris initially forced them to exclude irrigation with human sewage—the only kind of sewage Chadwick thought appropriate since the contents of storm sewers would arrive in the fields when needed least.[22] Leroux feared an imperial appropriation of the circulus for which he had suffered such scorn: he wrote his address to the authorities in Jersey, in part to claim the honor of having come up with the concept rather than let the Second Empire take credit for it[23] (much as Hugo gave Bruneseau, not the engineers of the despised Napoleon III, the leading role in taming the sewers of Paris).

The Circulus at Work

The contents of the expanded sewer system of the Second Empire continued to flow into the Seine. While this sewage no longer entered the river within city limits, 450,000 kilograms of it poured in downstream daily at Clichy and Saint-Denis in 1874. The Seine lacked the volume of water and rapidity of flow to absorb this waste. According to a German engineer at the end of the century, multiplication of the speed of the current and the quantity of water which passed daily through Paris produced the lowest rate of the twenty-two European cities with rivers flowing by them which he had surveyed.[24] From Clichy and Saint-Denis, the sewage moved along in a stinking mass which hugged the right bank of the Seine without mixing into the river: "The water is entirely black. For close to a kilometer, it leaves mud shoals which renew themselves continually, despite constant dredging. Immense bubbles of gas [up to one meter in diameter during the summer] escape from this rotting matter and break through the water's surface."[25] The sewage obstructed navigation. And, unlike the river, it did not freeze in the winter.[26] One had to go 75 kilometers downstream to Meulan before the Seine resumed its normal appearance.[27] Dredging presented further problems since farmers refused to take the sewage, claiming that its fertilizing power had been leached out. Used as fill to raise the banks of the Seine at Asnières and the Ile Saint-Denis, the sewage rotted and gave off a foul odor.[28]

Was there a better way for Paris to dispose of its nonhuman sewage? One group of experts—whom Belgrand initially favored—argued for treating the sewage chemically. Others, led by A. Mille, supported filtration through the soil. If Bruneseau had been an explorer of the wilds of the unknown underground, Mille was the engineer as agent of civilization. In 1848 the young engineer had believed that his transfer from railways to taking charge of the Parisian human sewage dumps at La Villette and Bondy (successors to Montfaucon) was a "disgrace." Over the course of his career, Mille complained that sanitation was not considered true engineering by some and that this specialization slowed down his advancement.[29] In the case of Mille and many engineers and scientists who worked in urban hygiene (including Parent-Duchâtelet), the feeling that neither society nor their peers appreciated their work turned them into crusaders. By the end of his career, Mille had come to see progress in hygiene during the nineteenth century as "a revolution perhaps as great as that of the railways."[30] He envisaged his work as a purveyor of civilization in mythic terms: "I remembered that Telemachus, exiled in the deserts of Libya, got back on his feet by civilizing the uncouth shepherds who surrounded him and I tried to improve men and things."[31]

As a child, Mille had seen human excrement used as fertilizer: "The application of fertilizer to the ground came of itself as a remembrance of my native country, Flanders."[32] During the Second Empire, Mille visited cities in Italy, Spain, and Great Britain to study sewage treatment by filtration and irrigation (with the organic residue serving as fertilizer) and returned to France a convert.[33] He carried out a series of tests using human waste at La Villette and Bondy, and 200,000 cubic meters of nonhuman sewage spread over a one-and-one-half hectare tract at Clichy in 1867–68. At the town offices in Clichy, Mille set up a little demonstration. He put soil and sand from nearby Gennevilliers in a two-meter deep cistern. Each day for a month, ten liters of sewage-laden water was poured in it and clear water came out the bottom.[34] Although the Clichy plot was located near factories and dwellings, Mille proudly reported that he received no complaints from the inhabitants about his operations. Even better, filtration proved an effective means of purifying sewage-laden water. When Mille compared his results with those obtained by engineers using chemicals to treat the water, he was able to show that the water which had leached through the soil was purer.

Mille also took advantage of these experiments to demonstrate the fertility of land irrigated with water from the sewers. He raised twenty-seven types of vegetables whose market value was six times that of the grain which had been cultivated on the land before irrigation.[35] Vegetables from the model garden garnered compliments at the 1867 Universal Exposition.[36] Chadwick lent his support to these projects. Years later he recalled:

> At Paris I prevailed upon the late Emperor to order some trial works to be made with sewage manure, when the first produce, though the sewage was not of the best sort, was an enormous amount of grass. An Academician pronounced it to be gross, and unfit for the food of cattle. I appealed from the judgment of the Academician to the judgment of a cow on the point. A cow was selected, and sewaged and unsewaged grass was placed before it for its choice. It preferred the sewaged grass with avidity, and it yielded its final judgment in superior milk and butter of increased quantity.[37]

Throughout these operations, Mille was ably seconded by the gifted young engineer Alfred Durand-Claye. The social and technological benefits of treating sewage by using it to irrigate farm land became the focal point of Durand-Claye's professional life. In 1861, as a twenty-year-old student at the Ecole Polytechnique, he had an epiphany. He and his friends were in the habit of distributing alms on Sundays to poor families who lived near the school. After frequenting these filthy dwellings, Durand-Claye decided he wanted to devote his life to cleaning up Paris.[38] He graduated first in his class in 1866. So taken was he with Mille's work that he passed up the more prestigious posts for which his class rank qualified him and went to work with Mille.[39] (This pitted him against his brother Léon, a proponent of the use of chemicals to process sewage.)[40] As Mille's assistant and successor, Alfred played a crucial role in convincing Belgrand of the merits of sewage farming as an adjunct to sewage treatment.[41]

Leroux and Hugo had envisaged the agricultural use of sewage primarily in terms of social economy. For the sanitary engineers of the Second Empire and Third Republic, however, the agricultural value of sewage was secondary to the technical advantages of filtration. Using sewage for agricultural irrigation complicated the process of water purification.[42] No one, Belgrand wrote in 1875, would spend as much money as had been put into the Paris sewer system simply to render a few thousand hectares more fertile.[43] Yet, since filtration proved the best method of purification, he encouraged his engineers to pursue sewage farming.

Gennevilliers

Mille and Durand-Claye were unable to obtain land to expand their operations in the growing industrial community of Clichy. In 1869–1870 they
crossed the Seine and established a model garden fertilized by nonhuman
sewage on six hectares of city-owned property in the sparsely inhabited
presqu'île of Gennevilliers. The sandy soil there was very porous and had
never been much good for agriculture. The combination of infertile terrain
and rural isolation made it ideally suited for Mille's and Durand-Claye's
purposes. Francisque Sarcey, an ardent supporter of the project, described
Gennevilliers as "a sort of oasis of barbarism in the heart of civilization":

> a perfectly isolated place, and which until these last years had remained, one
> could say, outside of all civilization. The inhabitants, I was going to say the
> natives, had something of the savage about them.
>   Many had never left their *presqu'île* and only knew Paris through hear-
> say. . . . They had kept the savage ways [*moeurs farouches*] which one does not
> find any more except in certain lost villages, deep in mountainous, hard-to-
> reach provinces.[44]

The sewage of Paris, far from devastating the community of Gennevilliers,
would serve as its entrée to commerce and civilization.
     Not surprisingly, the inhabitants of Gennevilliers were less certain of this
than Sarcey. Initially they strongly opposed the scheme, seeing it as another effort by Paris to ruin the countryside. An infuriated Durand-Claye
ridiculed the charge that sewage treatment caused fevers in the town. He
got particular pleasure recounting the case of a twenty-three year old
woman who, feeling a fever come on, drank a glass of her husband's urine
each morning and evening. Only when that failed did she go to a doctor
to complain of the ill effects of the sewage.[45] In order to win converts in
Gennevilliers, Mille and Durand-Claye irrigated their small plot regularly
and allowed some forty volunteers from the town to raise crops on it for
free. The results astonished villagers and visitors alike. In July 1870, 165
of the community's farmers petitioned Paris for an extension of the free
distribution of sewage water.[46] Perhaps a little skeptical, Napoleon III went
"incognito" to Gennevilliers, but left with an abundance of beautiful vegetables for his table.[47]
     The Franco-Prussian War disrupted operations, but also clinched the
support of city officials for the project. After peace was restored, they approved the irrigation proposal not only as a means of cleaning up the
Seine, but, with memories of the siege of 1870–71 still fresh in mind, as
an important nearby food supply.[48] Given a tour of the facilities at Gennevilliers and treated to a round of the purified water, the municipal council

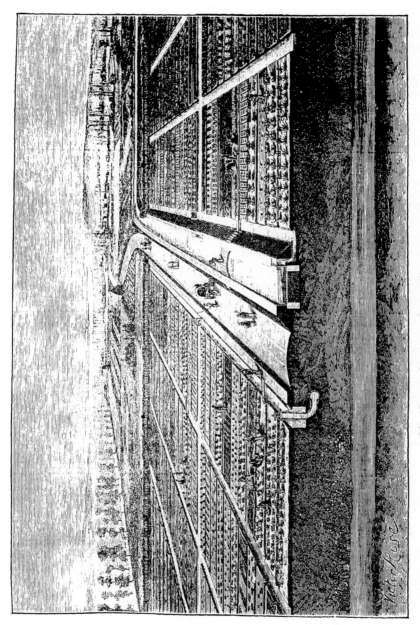

10. Sewage farming at Gennevilliers in the 1870s.

readily accepted the idea of treating the city's sewage through filtration.[49] And a basketful of vegetables grown at Gennevilliers was apparently sufficient to win over President Adolphe Thiers of the new Third Republic and his wife.[50]

Yet many deputies and senators remained dubious. Durand-Claye frequently took one or two skeptical parliamentarians on a tour of the sewage farm and patiently explained to them its merits.[51] "I drank sewer water," the deputy Martin Nadaud announced to his laughing colleagues in the Chamber in 1888.[52] Durand-Claye's efforts paid off, but too late for him to see the fruits. In 1889, the year after his death, sanitation engineers led by Belgrand's successor, Georges Bechmann, triumphed with the passage of a bill providing funding for construction of an aqueduct and pumping stations to carry sewage for irrigation projects beyond Gennevilliers and for purchase of land to be irrigated at Achères.

This victory was clouded only by the adamant refusal of suburban communities like Argenteuil (favorite of Parisian bourgeois on holiday[53]), to accept the extension of sewage farming into their communities. This opposition forced the city's engineers to select less suitable irrigation sites and prevented them from achieving their goal of disposing of all of Paris' sewage through filtration. By the turn of the century, however, the city was irrigating some five thousand hectares of land; each hectare received close to forty thousand cubic meters of sewage daily.[54]

With passage of the 1889 bill, municipal engineers completed a system to remove mud, sand, and debris from the sewage at the Clichy collector before pumping it to Gennevilliers and beyond in pipes underneath bridges spanning the Seine. Sewage arrived at Gennevilliers at an elevation of three and one-half meters, flowing at a rate of eight hundred liters per second. The height allowed gravity to distribute the sewage through an extensive system of ducts. The delivery of water was not continuous throughout the field; each portion was irrigated every four or five days. The sewage soaked the roots, never the stems or leaves of plants. Below ground, at a depth of four meters, engineers set up a system of drain pipes which directed the filtered water into the Seine so that it did not back up and impede continued irrigation.[55] Microbe counts in the purified water were not significantly higher than in the source waters which flowed into Paris.[56] Inhabitants of Gennevilliers had no qualms about digging wells to tap the filtered water for domestic use.[57]

After irrigation, the formerly barren land at Gennevilliers was capable of producing 40,000 heads of cabbage, 60,000 artichokes, or 200,000 pounds of sugar beets per hectare. Farmers also had success with spinach, green beans, peas, celery, onions, asparagus, turnips, lettuce, chicory, and strawberries.[58] A prominent Parisian perfumer even raised aromatic plants, including peppermint, which had been imported in the past.[59] Everyone marveled at the produce. "The sugar-beets seem borrowed from the gardens of *One Thousand and One Nights* and the oranges are as big as melons."[60] "Vegetables grow with an inexpressible vigor."[61] Contrary to expectations, the produce was not water-logged. The best hotels in Paris clamored for vegetables from Gennevilliers.[62] While vegetables remained the mainstay of sewage farming, successors to Chadwick's cows thrived on sewage farm forage. Some eight hundred milk-cows fed on the Gennevilliers plot in 1885[63]; between 1889 and 1901, eight cow-barns, a pig farm, and a sheep farm were built there.[64]

As Sarcey had predicted, the introduction of sewage farming transformed Gennevilliers. The irrigated land there expanded from 128 acres in 1872 to 1,940 acres in 1893; the average rent on these plots increased from 40 francs to 180 francs per acre during this period.[65] The population of Gennevilliers kept pace, rising from 2,100 in 1870 to 7,400 in 1896.[66]

Sewage farming in suburban Paris created opportunities for small-scale family truck farms and spawned large tenant farms where agriculture had struggled before. A little over two-thirds of the irrigated land, including the Gennevilliers plot, belonged to small farmers who received sewage water free of charge. The city owned the rest of the irrigated land. The individual farmers had their own faucets which they could turn on and off at will.[67] They took much more water in the summer than in the winter and did not irrigate at night. Municipal engineers generally left these farmers to work the land on their own, but tried to get them to adopt techniques which would permit purification of the maximum quantity of sewage.[68] The municipal farms had to compensate for the irregular demand of the private farmers by absorbing large quantities of water in the winter and at night, while taking significantly less in the summer. The city leased its farms to a few wealthy tenant farmers who employed wage laborers to cultivate crops like sugar beets which, although less profitable than those raised by individual truck farmers, were unaffected by the irregular irrigation practices. The city constructed a distillery next to Achères to convert the sugar beets and grains raised there into alcohol.[69]

Enthusiastic partisans wrote that the Gennevilliers plain was destined to become "the big factory of vegetables for Paris."[70] (And the leading opponent of the project argued, among other things, that the system would produce more vegetables than Paris could consume.[71]) Unlimited quantities of water were available to individual farmers, even during the hottest

11. Work in the Paris municipal sewage farm at Haute-Bourne.

months of the summer; in the winter, the sewage water did not freeze and kept the ground from freezing. This made the irrigation fields an especially valuable source of produce outside the normal growing season. Well into the twentieth century the sewage farms acted as a regulating agent to control fluctuations in the prices of a number of common vegetables, including peas, carrots, spinach, and cabbage.[72] The amount of land at Gennevilliers devoted to truck gardening began to decline in the years before World War I as more industry moved into the town, but new irrigation fields in Achères, Triel, and Méry-Pierrelaye—seven times as large as those of Gennevilliers in 1921—continued to filter the bulk of Parisian sewage after the war.[73]

Sewage Farms and Social Thought

For Second Empire engineers and their successors, sewage farming was one instance of a broad vision of urban waste disposal as a means of bringing to city dwellers some of the pleasures and benefits associated with country life. Haussmann's renowned engineer Adolphe Alphand converted the closed Montfaucon dump into the idyllic Buttes-Chaumont park. And, Lewis Mumford contends, Haussmann's (unrealized) plan to establish a single large cemetery outside of the city limits of Paris, connected to the city by rail, was intended to allow for the expeditious disposal of the dead, while surrounding the city with a "green belt." A century before, the living had mingled with the bodies of the dead, breathing their potentially mortal odors. In Haussmann's vision, the dead were to be segregated away from the city and to perform the role of providing the citizens with life-giving air. Haussmann chose Méry-sur-Oise as the site for the proposed cemetery because its sandy soil assured rapid decomposition and would therefore allow for individual burials, even of those unable to afford a plot.[74] Not surprisingly, the same qualities later made nearby Méry-Pierrelaye the site of an extensive sewage irrigation field.

While farmers had long used urban refuse as fertilizer, much was made of the way in which sewage farming rectified the centuries-old urban rape of the countryside. For the *L'Avenir de Seine-et-Oise* (1888), it would, through "the reciprocity which is in the laws of nature," finally begin to reverse the cities' seemingly inexorable "impoverishment of the national soil."[75] The efficient removal of sewage improved the conditions of the lower classes in the cities and, along with better housing, reduced the likelihood of lower-class disorders. At the same time the use of sewage as fertilizer bettered the lot of the peasant, the backbone of France. Du Camp celebrated the introduction of sewage farming as a stroke of genius and the distribution of sewage to small farmers as "démocratique au premier chef"[76]—an example of the beneficial politics of the Second Empire so different from the destructive Paris Commune which followed.

If a promenade through the sewers allowed readers of *Les Misérables* to reenact Jean Valjean's flight, touring a sewage farm on a Sunday in the summer allowed them to contemplate the realization of the visionary aspect of Hugo's work.[77] For Sarcey, "there is nothing more curious and, I dare say, more amusing than this spectacle. The fields resemble striped fabric; the stripes are small ditches, which stretch the length of the fields."[78] Visitors to the previously dry and infertile Achères toured the luxurious, odorless grounds on the ten-kilometer small gauge railroad used the rest of the week to transport produce.[79] At the behest of the tour guide, visitors drank a glass of the limpid, filtrated water, and could compare its appearance with the sewage-laden liquid they had seen flowing into the fields.[80] "Numerous strollers come to see for themselves the effects of agricultural purification, stopping in the *jardins d'agrément* laid out next to the open drains, and not missing the tasting of the cool clear water which flows from them."[81] The Paris press brought the two elements of Hugo's tale together when they held a benefit tour of the sewers ("an excursion into the land of the rats") which culminated in a dinner of cooked carrots, potatoes, peas, and beans from Gennevilliers.[82]

The engineers who promoted sewage farming viewed it primarily as a side benefit to the primary objective: treatment of the city's liquid waste. However, many observers shared the vision of Leroux and Hugo, and saw the conversion of previously noxious waste to productive purposes as an exemplary instance of contemporary social management or even as an element in the transformation of modern urban capitalist society. Some described the sewage farms as "veritable Gardens of Eden,"[83] in which technology had recreated the world before the Fall by reintegrating man and his waste products. For others, sewage farming allowed the market to perform its civilizing function: "The sensational assassin has become a peaceful trader."[84]

Sewage farming was not limited to Paris or to France.[85] Durand-Claye felt a surge of patriotism in 1878 when the Berlin municipal authorities abandoned chemical purification of sewage and adapted the system used at Gennevilliers.[86] By the turn of the century, Berlin had some seventeen thousand acres devoted to sewage farming. In 1905 an American professor described the Berlin farms as a little utopia in *Political Science Quarterly*. Three thousand men, women and children lived in rent-free cottages on the municipal farms. There they cultivated a wide variety of crops, including grains, vegetables, and roses. Their health was exceptional: "Probably no rural population in the world has more intelligent care expended upon the preservation of its health."[87]

> The perfect confidence of the municipality in the sanitary security of the sewage farms is shown by the fact that it has erected on four of the estates homes for the benefit of patients sent out from hospitals in the city. One of these is designed for convalescent women, particularly those recovering from maternity cases, another for convalescent men, and the remaining two for consumption cases. The city manages the homes directly, charging rates sufficient to pay expenses. In no sense, therefore, may the patients be classed as paupers remaining upon the farms because they have nowhere else to go. Over two thousand persons are cared for annually by the four homes, and there is always a large waiting list—facts which speak well for the public confidence in the sanitary condition of the sewage farms and in the management of the institutions for convalescents located upon them.[88]

The use of workhouse labor on the Berlin farms harkened back to Old Regime ideas of *marginaux* in service to the commonweal.

> In addition to the free laborers employed on the Berlin farms, there are always from seven to eleven hundred workhouse prisoners, mostly beggars, vagrants and tramps arrested in the city, who are forced to work out their sentences in the fields. The sewage farms thus provided simple, open-air employment to an almost unlimited extent for a class of persons whose maintenance in institutions would not only be less satisfactory from a sanitary point of view, but would also cost the city more than under the present arrangement. Worked in gangs, housed in cheerless barracks, clothed in uniforms of rough brown cloth and sparingly fed, these *Arbeitshaüsler* of the sewage farms nevertheless seldom attempt to escape, partly because it is practically impossible to avoid being caught within a few days, and partly because they prefer working outdoors for Berlin to imprisonment in other places. Although short-term prisoners exclusively, there are not a few among them who contrive to be sent back time and time again until they become almost as permanent as the regular employees. Thus by a sardonic but truly poetic justice the sewage of a great city and its human riff-raff are forced to work out their salvation together.[89]

Even without such an explicit realization in mind, the French author of an 1886 article in the conservative *Réforme sociale* drew the analogy of prisons and workhouses to sewage farming: "One does not correct [the inmates], it's true, but isn't it something to have an outlet, a sewer collector where the mire of the big cities gathers? In the cities, it would dirty the streets;

[in institutions] it undoubtedly remains mire, but it fertilizes the land, which is certainly something."[90]

Social visionaries with wider aspirations projected sewage farming into a better tomorrow: as a bulwark of the urban utopia; as the basis of a society of independent communities of peasant farmers living in a symbiotic relationship with the city; and, with the municipal farms in mind, as the future first sites of collectivized agriculture in France.

Jules Verne incorporated filtration and agricultural irrigation of sewage in his portrayal of the model city in *Les Cinq Cents Millions de la Bégum* (1879). In this novel a Dr. Sarrasin inherits an enormous fortune and uses it to build a metropolis in the American West along the lines of hygienic science: "Individual and collective cleanliness is the great idea of the founders of Frankville. To clean, clean unceasingly, so as to destroy the miasmas constantly emanating from a large community, such is the principle work of the central government. For this purpose, all the contents of the drains are led out of the town, condensed, and daily transferred to the fields."[91]

Other social commentators turned their attention to sewage farmers. In *The Conquest of Bread* (1892), the Russian anarchist Prince Peter Kropotkin envisaged truck farming—and the sewage farming at Gennevilliers in particular—as the basis of a new cooperation between the peasant and the worker in the city. This link would be embodied in an anarchist commune composed of the existing departments of the Seine-et-Oise and the Seine. The ingenious workers of Paris would apply their technical expertise to the problems of intensive agriculture; the farmers of the Seine-et-Oise would feed the population of Paris.[92] "The combination of agriculture and industry, the husbandman and the mechanic in the same individual—this is what anarchist communism will inevitably lead us to."[93] Past revolutions had foundered on the opposition of town and country; this new commune, unlike that of 1871, would survive.[94]

The French left gave a third gloss to sewage farming in the early twentieth century. The city leased its sewage farms to large tenant farmers who employed hundreds of agricultural laborers and housed them, company-town style, in nearby settlements. Labor relations were always difficult on the municipal farms; they resembled those of a factory more than those usually associated with agriculture. The Confédération Générale du Travail (C.G.T.) organized municipal agricultural workers and in the summer of 1909 led them in a successful strike that contemporary observers feared would be a prototype for future strikes of agricultural laborers on large farms elsewhere in France.[95] Later, the Communists projected these municipal operations as the first in France to be turned into Soviet-style collective farms after they took power.[96]

Sewage farming incorporated the duality which characterized the sewers themselves: at once a technical response to a problem of urban waste disposal and a stimulant to the social imagination.[97] Both the free market and electoral democracy had failed in mid-nineteenth-century France to deliver on their promises to channel the disorder of human passions into a new social order. The sewer, once a locus of concern about political and biological disorder, became through sewage farming a means of contemplating a new political and biological order. Social change would involve a redistribution not only of the fruits of labor, but of its detritus as well.

The phenomenal growth of the Parisian suburbs since the last decades of the nineteenth century revealed the final stage of the Haussmannization of Paris. Rising land values in suburban Paris eventually made the widespread use of filtration fields uneconomical. Projects to pump sewage further from Paris were not feasible because it would begin to rot and give off odors intolerable to farmers and inhabitants.[98] In the early twentieth century the city started to supplement filtration with the use of biological agents to purify the water. This technique retained certain of the ecological principles of irrigation. The treatment facility was fueled by the methane gas given off during the purification process; the dried debris was used as fertilizer or landfill.[99] In the mid-twentieth century, one expert explained that while biological purification was perhaps less costly than irrigation, it would never replace sewage farming completely, both because the farmers in the area depended on it and because the fields had become an invaluable source of vegetables, especially for the lower classes.[100] Although the sewage farms had declined to 4,487 hectares by 1948, they still produced more than one-tenth of the vegetables sold at the central market of Les Halles.[101] By the 1980s, however, only 2,000 hectares remained irrigated by sewage. (Of this land, 1,150 hectares belonged to the city.)[102] These fields received only about 5 percent of the sewage which went to the Achères sewage treatment plant, only one of several sewage plants processing the sewage generated by Paris and its suburbs.[103]

There is a coda to the decline of the sewage fields of Paris and other cities. If sewage was the archetypal hazardous waste of the mid-nineteenth century, its place has now been taken by radioactive refuse. Perhaps it is not surprising therefore that the American Kerr-McGee Corporation has developed a process for turning raffinate, the by-product from production of fuel for nuclear power plants, into a liquid fertilizer which it spreads extensively over its own fields on which it raises hay for livestock. Despite concerns over the presence of hazardous materials in the fertilizer, Kerr-McGee is currently seeking permission to market it.[104] The example of the nuclear industry reminds us that technology can produce as well as alleviate social concerns—it renews the social and symbolic processes that appeared so clearly in nineteenth-century interpretations of sewage. Technology is not of a piece. It offers both dreams of mastery and nightmares of contamination.

6

Montfaucon Liquidated

> How many times has it happened to you that in the night, while
> you are sleeping the sleep of the just, you feel yourself awakened,
> about half past midnight, by the monotonous tick-tock of a kind of
> hammer pounding with dull regular strokes? . . . What is it? What
> could it be? Take a whiff, my friend . . . The air which envelops you is
> filled with foul emanations. Nothing can protect you. They filter in
> through door joints and cracks in the windows. You are bathed, like
> the whole house, in a stale, nauseating stench . . . It is the knights of
> the night who are performing at your place, unless it is next door or
> down the street. Their barrels are under your windows, waiting in
> perfect order. And when they are full, horses will drag them through
> the neighborhood, leaving behind a long trail of abominable odors.
>   And it is in Paris, capital of the world, that these things happen! Yet
> we suffer through it without saying a word!
>   —Francisque Sarcey, *Les Odeurs de Paris*

> Since Vespasian, there has never been so much speculation on hu-
> man excrement as there has been in Paris the last couple of years.
>   There has been no question which has provoked more inventions,
> presented more saviours of pestilential humanity, solicited more stock-
> holders, promised more profits.
>   —E. Deligny, *Observations du Président de la
>   Commission des eaux et égouts*

THE LAYING of new sewers and establishment of sewage farms encountered only episodic, localized resistance during the Second Empire and first
decades of the Third Republic. However, the sanitary engineers' plans for
the collection and utilization of human sewage were not so easily realized.
It was widely recognized that maintenance of individual cesspools and
their periodic purging presented a public nuisance and a potential health
risk; the question of what do do with the contents of the cesspools after
removal obsessed public health experts, engineers, and the citizens of Paris
throughout the nineteenth century. A variety of corporate and financial
interests entered the fray; they found expression in a true cacophony of
moral, aesthetic and scientific discourses. Ultimately, implementation of a
single solution to both cesspool cleaning and the treatment of human

waste marked the crowning expression of the engineers' vision of urban sanitation in nineteenth-century Paris.

Montfaucon

Until the middle of the nineteenth century, Parisian cesspool cleaners continued to bring their nightly haul to Montfaucon. There they dumped it into large settling basins which covered a surface area of ten hectares. The liquid on the surface poured into a second tier of settling basins below. Each set of basins filled for a period of months or years until the sediment attained the consistency of thick mud. This deposit reached a height of four to five meters in the upper basin. The first step in converting the contents of the basins to fertilizer was to dry it out. To hasten this process, workers dug deep channels to allow fluids to run off. They then spread out the fecal matter and tilled it two or three times daily to allow for the evaporation of remaining liquids. When the deposit had dried, it was collected into large heaps—eight to ten meters deep, sixty to eighty meters long, and twenty-five to thirty meters wide, and left for one to three years (a process later abridged by the addition of burnt peat). The resulting *poudrette* was warm and subject to combustion: "The *poudrette* then appears like a mould of a grey-black colour, light, greasy to the touch, finely grained, and giving out a particular faint and nauseous odour."[1] Entrepreneurs supplemented sales to local farmers by shipping it down the Seine and various canals the length of the Loire to the Norman and Breton coasts and beyond.[2] Parent-Duchâtelet began his career with a study of the ship "Arthur" loaded with *poudrette* from Montfaucon, which arrived in Guadeloupe with half its crew dead and the other half near death because of the effects of decomposition of the cargo.[3]

Henri Joseph Gisquet, prefect of police in the 1830s, has left us with a graphic account of his visits to Montfaucon:

> I saw totally nude men spending whole days in the middle of basins, searching there, in the mass of fecal matter, objects of value which it might contain. I saw others, fishing out rotten fish, which the market inspectors had ordered thrown in there as having reached a state of putrefaction. Spoiled and stinking mackerels which had filled two carts had just been thrown into the biggest of the basins. Two hours later, all the fish had disappeared.[4]

But what really disgusted Gisquet were the slaughterhouses. After leaving them and returning to the pools of fermenting fecal matter, he "breathed, with pleasure, with happiness, as if the atmosphere was redolent of all the perfumes of Arabia."[5]

Montfaucon took on the traits of an immoral world, as threatening to the public order of the July Monarchy as anything germinating underground in the sewers.[6] In 1844 the doctor Louis Roux reported that not only was Montfaucon the potential source of contagions which could devastate Paris at any time, but it was also the place where most crimes in the city were plotted. Montfaucon encouraged and facilitated barbaric behavior among the underclass. Equally appalling, Roux's Montfaucon, like Hugo's sewers, ignored class boundaries: it offered licence for profanity and immorality in all social classes. Paris, Roux concluded, "will not be able to merit the title civilized city until Montfaucon no longer exists."[7]

Reforming Montfaucon

Almost from its designation as slaughterhouse and sole dump site for the human sewage of Paris, Montfaucon was the object of projects of transformation or suppression.[8] While most Parisians looked upon Montfaucon and what went on there as unfortunate facts of urban life, individual reformers proposed that new types of sociability or social symmetry could emerge from the displacement or redesigning of Montfaucon; others said that its destruction would require a prior moral revolution.

In the final years of the eighteenth century, the Paris municipal administration commissioned the architect Pierre Giraud to suggest a reform of Montfaucon. Like so many of his successors, Giraud conceived the project as a form of social redemption. He took as his epigraph a line from Terence: "I am human; I count nothing human as foreign." Giraud proposed replacing the dump and slaughterhouse at Montfaucon with enclosed, well-ventilated installations at Grenelle and the Plaine de Saint-Denis where fertilizer, tiles, oil varnish, and glue would be manufactured. The fire these processes required would burn off noxious gases while ventilating the area.

Giraud's goal in putting forward this proposal was to civilize the savage world of the waste dump and to make it a center of social intercourse in the city. "I would like the dumps, which one does not approach now except with fear and repugnance, to become a meeting place for the curious and for innumerable workers."[9] The building in which the various industrial processes took place would be surrounded by a park planted with elms or linden trees "under which workers of all kinds will come breath the fresh air." Little pavillions would be built in each corner for vendors selling food and drink. Giraud hoped that these amenities "would render the park interesting for all those who will come to instruct themselves in the Arts which we cultivate in the heart of these establishments."[10]

Although Giraud's plan was never realized, his vision of a single tamed and disciplined multipurpose dump continued to find occasional advocates in the nineteenth century. As late as 1844 Jules Garnier, professor at the Ecole Néopédique, argued that such an industrial model could be achieved at Montfaucon itself with the introduction of new methods of deodorization. A decisive element would be the imposition of regularity: "All will be calculated in such a way that the manufacture will never be encumbered with matter; each part of the establishment will furnish to the other an invariable proportion of work"[11]: "Montfaucon would become a manufacturing village, a veritable *ammoniapolis*. Montfaucon would then be worthy of Paris, great like all connected with Paris. For foreigners, it would become an object of curiosity and envy; each capital then, desirious to use the debris and the garbage which harms its salubrity, would also want its Montfaucon."[12]

Few of Garnier's contemporaries shared his optimism. Conditions worsened at Montfaucon as the volume of material brought there increased with the city's rising population and with the greater use of water for hygienic purposes (a portion of which ended up in the cesspools). In the absence of a truly effective means of deodorizing dumpsites, miasmatic theories of disease heightened concerns. Early in the July Monarchy, the shocked Gisquet named a committee to assess Montfaucon and its future.

Alexandre-Jean-Baptiste Parent-Duchâtelet

The public health expert Parent-Duchâtelet was an obvious choice to head up the study. He had been born into a well-to-do Jansenist family in 1790. His father was *correcteur de la chambre des comptes,* an office that had been in the family for three hundred years. This position, enjoyment of some seigneurial rights, and a few well-placed investments assured the family an annual revenue of 35,000 livres before the Revolution. Then, in 1792, the revolutionary government terminated the position of *correcteur* and the Parent-Duchâtelet family was forced to leave Paris for the family home at Châtelet, near Montargis.

The young Parent-Duchâtelet followed his parents' wishes and became a doctor in 1814, but felt deceived when he discovered that textbook medicine lacked the veracity he demanded: "many of the assertions made to him as incontestable truths revealed themselves to be false in patients' beds."[13] Parent-Duchâtelet forsook private practice, although he continued to treat the poor. The renowned Jean-Noël Hallé (himself once member of a commission charged with studying Montfaucon before the Revolution[14]) convinced Parent-Duchâtelet to take up public health and launched him on his way with the study of the ill-fated "Arthur." [15] Over his career, Parent-Duchâtelet researched all manner of urban hygiene problems, culminating in his two-volume posthumously published opus on prostitution in Paris.

Although renowned for these studies, Parent-Duchâtelet was a poor teacher. Appointed to the Ecole de Médecine, his great "timidity" prevented him from giving lectures. When it was his turn to pose questions during oral examinations, "he was scared, he trembled. Instead of intimidating the candidate, it was he who was intimidated." [16] (Or, perhaps, disillusioned with book-learned medicine, he felt uncomfortable at being a party to its inculcation.) Parent-Duchâtelet fared no better at the Ecole Centrale, where the directors found his lectures so disorganized that they dropped his course after two years. [17]

Indefatigable researcher and crusader, Parent-Duchâtelet was more at home exploring Montfaucon than expounding in the classroom. When he first visited the site for his report on the "Arthur," he drew a different impression than Gisquet: "this place, unknown or little known to the luxury-loving inhabitants of the capital, offers more than one kind of interest to the true philanthropist, and especially to the attentive observer, who sees the results of things which, at first glance, often seem worthy only of disgust." [18]

Yet interest did not lead to affection. Montfaucon would have no more passionate opponent than Parent-Duchâtelet. "Has not each generation of Parisians for two hundred years," he asked, with reference to the slaughterhouse and fertilizer operations at Montfaucon, "been raised with the idea that nothing equals the horror of these places and these operations, and that one cannot approach them even at a great distance?" [19] However, Parent-Duchâtelet's disgust was not that of the man on the street. For him, this "hideous and repulsive spectacle" [20] was an affront to his fervent conviction that the treatment of refuse need not be revolting and dangerous: whatever health risks might exist came from the conditions at Montfaucon and were not inherent in processing carcasses or nightsoil.

In the Jansenist Parent-Duchâtelet there was a bit of Rousseau and a dash of the revolutionary. Like the Federalist Lyon in the Year II, Montfaucon would have to be razed. Condemnation of Montfaucon should embody the general will of the community. That end seemed near as an exulting Parent-Duchâtelet described a public demonstration held at Montfaucon of a new technique for the "immediate and complete cleansing of fecal matter"—a "veritable revolution" in the drying and disinfecting of excrement. [21] "Everyone was convinced. In a memorable session held by the municipal council on the very grounds of Montfaucon, a meeting

attended by the two prefects of the Seine and the police, and which I had
the honor of attending, it was resolved unanimously that the current order
of things could no longer be tolerated and *that Montfaucon would be destroyed.*"[22]

Parent-Duchâtelet denounced creation of another Montfaucon on
marshy land purchased for the purpose at Bondy.[23] Instead, he advocated
taking advantage of new hygienic techniques for the deodorization of cesspools and the preparation of fertilizer (fortuitously employing ashes from
the incineration of bones from slaughterhouses) and the use of pressurized
steam to remove flesh from bones to allow the decentralization of operations currently performed at Montfaucon. Parent-Duchâtelet's great leap
forward would spread fifteen or twenty small waste treatment facilities and
slaughterhouses in the countryside around Paris.[24] An enthusiastic Jules
Janin read Parent-Duchâtelet's study and proclaimed that making *poudrette*
would now be "as easy and the demand as certain as for champagne."[25]

What stood in the way of implementing this program for eradication of
the public disgrace of Montfaucon? That *sans-culotte* of public hygiene
Parent-Duchâtelet pointed his finger at the egotistical self-interest of bourgeois and especially the doctors among them:

> It is a fact that the complaints never come from inhabitants of the country-
> side, but instead from the bourgeois of Paris who go to pass the summer
> months there, and as a natural consequence, the owners of houses who rent
> them as long as they are pleasant. But if these bourgeois could be given the
> choice of having this filth in their houses in Paris or in the fields around their
> country-houses, if they themselves had to clean their streets and privies,
> would not they do what the administration plans? And if they would not do
> things differently than the administration, what are they complaining
> about?[26]

Parent-Duchâtelet—a disillusioned doctor himself—was especially hard
on physicians who placed their class interests as members of the bourgeoisie above their commitment to the commonweal. He claimed that doctors
purposely misled the populace into thinking that all kinds of diseases
would result from the spread of operations into the countryside: "How do
we characterize the behavior [of the doctor], when personal interest leads
him to exaggerate evils in which he does not believe, and when, in his own
interest, he arouses whole populations?"[27] Parent-Duchâtelet's denuncia-
tion of doctors was so vitriolic in the report he originally wrote for Gisquet's commission, that the prefect rejected it and another member of the
commission had to put together a tamer one.[28]

In his bitterness, Parent-Duchâtelet took solace in the exemplary behavior his mentor Hallé had displayed in a comparable situation. A large sugar refinery had been built next to the street where Hallé, members of his family, and his best friends lived. The smells from the factory spread throughout the houses on Hallé's street. He drew up a petition demanding removal of the offending factory and presented it to the authorities. Since the city did not know if the fumes were unhealthy, it asked Hallé to study them. Hallé could find nothing deleterious in the odors and so the factory remained. His friends and their families severely criticized him, but Hallé remained steadfast. Truth, he answered, must prevail over private desires.[29]

Given the recalcitrance of the medical profession, how could Parent-Duchâtelet get the word out? His response was to go to the people. Launching a public debate in the press was important, but "to convince the multitude," Parent-Duchâtelet proposed going well beyond this in a campaign which anticipated marketing tables in an American shopping mall. At places where there were sure to be many passers-by, trained individuals would prepare fertilizer from excrement, using the most up-to-date methods. "We would give this preparation all the publicity possible. During the work we would distribute not only information to anyone who stops out of curiosity where we are carrying out the preparation, but also samples of the completed product."[30] This plan to make and distribute *poudrette* to pedestrians was one more effort to show that people's waste products were not inherently deleterious; only the methods of disposal made them so.

While Parent-Duchâtelet himself was exceedingly serious, some of his comrades in the public health movement displayed a child-like pleasure in breaking social taboos about human waste. The public hygienist Jean-Pierre D'Arcet was so thrilled with the discovery that the carbonized contents of a cesspool could serve as a deodorant that one evening he put some on a china saucer and, telling the numerous guests at his salon that it was a mineral, passed it among them. "Great was the surprise of his guests when he informed them afterwards what was the real nature of the pretended mineral."[31] (Unfortunately, this substance—like the ashes of slaughterhouse bones—proved impractical for widespread use.[32])

Bondy

Parent-Duchâtelet died in 1835, his excremental aspirations for Montfaucon unfulfilled. A few years later, the slaughterhouses were moved to a site near that suggested by Giraud, but, as Parent-Duchâtelet had predicted, closing Montfaucon in 1849 and moving the sewage dump to Bondy did not end the problems posed by human waste disposal. Because Bondy was so far from the city, cesspool cleaners brought their barrels to a remarkably clean, well-lit, well-ventilated installation at La Villette. From there the solid waste was shipped in closed containers down the Canal de l'Ourcq to Bondy; liquid waste was pumped to Bondy in a "long syringe of ten kilometers."[33] Despite this auspicious beginning, operations at Bondy itself left much to be desired. Bondy had been in service since the Restoration Monarchy; the techniques employed there during the Second Empire were simply a refinement of those used at Montfaucon earlier. To produce powdered fertilizer, workers laid the excrement out to dry; to make the more potent ammonium sulfate, they added sulfuric acid and then heated and distilled the mixture.

The contents of Paris cesspools continued to go to Bondy until 1870, when the firm under license to run the site refused the city's terms. In succeeding years several contractors went bankrupt trying to operate at Bondy. The drying basins filled to capacity—more than one hundred thousand cubic meters by 1877—and the wastes drained into the Seine near Saint-Denis.[34] Engineers estimated that at best only one-fifth of the human waste brought to Bondy was made into fertilizer; one-third decomposed and one-half washed into the Seine. The situation, engineers Belgrand and Alphand agreed, was "barbaric."[35]

Until mid-century, the leasees at municipal dumps had enjoyed a monopoly on the production and sale of human guano; in the years before Montfaucon closed, the city received more than one-half million francs annually for this right. After closing Montfaucon, the government began marketing this privilege to private operators of small dumps proliferating in the suburbs—although not under the conditions Parent-Duchâtelet had envisaged. The suburban dumpsites expanded rapidly during the 1870s to accommodate Parisian excrement. By 1880, there were twenty-four dumps in operation in addition to Bondy. Many manufactured ammonium sulfate; the process released ammonia fumes which could be carried by the wind to almost any part of Paris.[36] Engineers blamed this industry for the infamous odors which afflicted the city in the summer of 1880.[37]

As the situation worsened, discussions of human waste disposal in Paris became mired in the language of individual property rights and collective costs. Property owners found merit in Garnier's version of the "circulus": the collection of human wastes was an "indirect tax" on them since they had to pay cesspool cleaners while the city received hefty fees from contractors who ran waste dumps.[38] Critics of the profitable cesspool cleaning companies and dump operations posed another logic and another balance sheet. The problem, Aimé Girard of the Paris Commission d'Assainissement wrote in 1880, was that the treatment of human waste had always been considered a source of income, when, in fact, poorly done, its toll on society could be quite high.[39]

Cesspool Cleaning and the *Tout-à-l'égout*

In the early years of the July Monarchy Parent-Duchâtelet had both lauded the increased use of water for personal hygiene in Paris and forecast the crisis this would create as cesspools (and dump settling basins) filled more quickly. He favored separate fates for the solid and liquid contents of cesspools and complained that one consequence of the widespread introduction of Richer pumps to empty cesspools had been the unfortunate mixture of the two in a dilute fecal solution. Parent-Duchâtelet promoted the replacement of traditional fixed cesspools whose contents were periodically pumped in the dead of night with *fosses mobiles*—large barrels, removable during daylight hours, in which solid wastes would settle. As landlords were doubly loathe to pay for the installation of running water and the resulting more frequent cesspool cleanings, Parent-Duchâtelet proposed that permission be granted subscribers to the municipal water service to have the liquid contents of their barrels dumped into the sewers (it would cleanse them, he argued) or into the Seine.[40]

A minority of Paris property owners (15 percent of dwellings in 1871) introduced means of disposing separately of liquid and solid matter from cesspools (through *fosses mobiles* or, with payment of a special tax, screens allowing direct disposal of liquid waste into the sewers), but these proved unpopular and ineffective.[41] This did not overly concern late nineteenth-century sanitary engineers, who went further than Parent-Duchâtelet in seeing water as the great urban cleanser, beginning with the dream of flush toilets in each abode.[42] They envisaged a system in which Paris would follow the lead of other European cities, including London, Brussels, and Berlin: eliminate cesspools and use the existing network of sewers for the direct evacuation of all human wastes to the city's filtration fields.

Unlike Parent-Duchâtelet, the engineers were no longer willing to tolerate the disturbing, unsanitary presence of cesspool cleaners on the streets of the new Second Empire Paris. And while Parent-Duchâtelet had been an avid proponent of less noxious means of producing fecal fertilizer, late nineteenth-century engineers saw this very process as inefficient and outdated. Like Chadwick and Hugo, the engineers invoked the researches of Europe's leading chemists and agronomists, including Justus Liebig and J. B. Boussingault, who had condemned the production of *poudrette* at Montfaucon as squandering valuable nutrients.[43] More generally, the differentiation their opponents made between human and nonhuman, solid and liquid, wastes struck the engineers as a vestige of archaic, even atavistic, classificatory systems explicable now only in terms of base economic interests and social prejudice.

Mille and his lieutenant Durand-Claye led the battle for the *tout-à-l'égout* to rid the city of both cesspool cleaners and unsanitary dumps.[44] Haussmann referred to Mille's *apostolat* for the use of liquified human sewage as fertilizer and Mille's critics repeated the epithet; Durand-Claye too was known as *l'apôtre du tout-à-l'égout*.[45] The engineers argued that what property-owners paid as a sewer tax, they would save in cesspool-cleaning costs. This money could be used to purchase new land for treatment of the additional human sewage through filtration and irrigation.

The *tout-à-l'égout* encountered strong opposition from many quarters, beginning with Haussmann. Although he considered the current system of cesspool cleaning "a regime which civilization disavows," he expressed *répugnances invincibles* for the *tout-à-l'égout*. Haussmann cherished the idea that the sewers would in the future provide a solution to the inconveniences of cesspool cleaning through a variant of the existing system. Liquid wastes would flow directly into the sewers where workers would circulate freely, collecting and removing containers of solid waste by means of a specially constructed rail system; these containers would be taken to fertilizer factories in the suburbs. No longer would Parisians have to see and smell cesspool cleaners.[46] Like his engineers, therefore, Haussmann envisaged the sewer as a means of ridding Paris of human waste, but he could not bring himself to see his prize construction sullied with human feces. Nor did Haussmann find Mille's advocacy of the use of liquified human sewage as fertilizer appealing, even after Mille had roses grown with it in an experimental plot at La Villette sent to Mme. la Préfète.[47]

Well after the demise of Haussmann and the Second Empire, sanitation engineers and the city council (which could not forego such a valuable enterprise as the *tout-à-l'égout*—and its promised fees) faced stiff resistance from large cesspool cleaning companies and an important segment of the medical community, as well as property owners' associations. In the 1870s, two large cesspool cleaning firms absorbed their competitors and formed a monopoly in the city. These enterprises had important connections in the financial and journalistic world. In league with property owners—who contested the sewer tax—they legitimated their opposition to imposition of the *tout-à-l'égout* as a defense of private property against government intervention.[48]

A number of doctors and scientists joined the fray, attacking the Paris sewers as incapable of removing human wastes safely. Unlike sewers in cities where the *tout-à-l'égout* functioned well, the galleries of the Paris system were too large and did not slope sufficiently to allow rapid evacuation of human wastes; these would stagnate in the sewers, infect the air and in this way, many continued to believe, transmit disease. The absence of disagreeable odors in the sewers should fool no one; these escaped from the sewers through the gutters to invade the city.[49] Such arguments made sense to the numerous Parisians who blamed the notorious odors of the summer of 1880 on the sewers. Doctor Paul Brouardel—a leading opponent of the *tout-à-l'égout*—let it be known that he had walked the streets of Paris for more than a week that summer stopping to sniff at every sewer opening to satisfy himself that the sewers were the source of these noxious smells.[50] Critics of the *tout-à-l'égout* reminded Parisians that the Romans had invoked Cluacina to protect themselves against emanations coming from the sewers; she should not be interpreted as a goddess of good government, as the *Encyclopédie* had suggested.[51]

Most medical experts who weighed in against the *tout-à-l'égout* opposed the existing system of cesspools, favoring instead creation of a separate, air-tight sewer system for evacuation of human waste. Spread of the germ theory of disease also raised concerns about the use of human sewage as fertilizer. Louis Pasteur himself argued that filtration methods like those used at Gennevilliers did not kill offending organisms. He showed, for instance, that anthrax microbes could live for years in the soil. Pasteur's solution was to do what Hugo claimed was already happening: he favored pumping Parisian sewage into the sea. One enthusiastic partisan of sending *la merde* to *la mer* embraced pisciculture, arguing that the nutrients would not be lost since fish could be raised in the offshore sewage just as vegetables were at Gennevilliers.[52]

Doctors and scientists who opposed the *tout-à-l'égout* in the final decades of the nineteenth century did so on the grounds that previous decisions to build oversized sewers with moderate incline and to treat their contents by filtration dictated the need for different means to isolate, transport, and dispose of human sewage. Yet it was precisely the conceptual, technical, and personal investments engineers had made in the sewer system which spread underneath Paris during and after the Second Empire which helped assure that the unitary *tout-à-l'égout*—rather than, for example, a distinct system of tubes and pumps inserted in the existing sewer network and culminating in separate treatment facilities—emerged as the most viable alternative to the extant system of cesspools and suburban dumps.

Like Parent-Duchâtelet's campaign against Montfaucon a half-century earlier, the struggle against cesspools and for the *tout-à-l'égout* was redolent of a transmogrified social revolution. Bechmann echoed Parent-Duchâtelet's attack on those who impeded his plans, calling critics of the sewer system *coteries parfois intéressées.*[53] Republican engineers, Corbin writes, "demanded equal treatment for the excrement of rich and poor alike."[54] One supporter proclaimed: "Here is true socialism! Isn't there a set of problems here to resolve which are much more interesting than the mass of those which are the questions of the day? . . . The rich, in this instance, must have the same desires as the poor, for everyone breathes the air, drinks the water, and no one evades completely the miasmas which escape from [the cesspools] and the epidemics which they engender when they are tainted."[55]

"Yes," an exasperated wit wrote in 1892, "in the most civilized part of the world, it is impossible for two reasonable people to meet without inquiring first what they think of the *tout-à-l'égout.*"[56] The clash between supporters and opponents of the unitary sewer system continued until the appearance of cholera in 1892 rallied national political support for it. In 1894, Parliament passed legislation which authorized the city to compel property owners to hook up to the *tout-à-l'égout* and to pay for the privilege. The municipal council coupled passage of this legislation with a commitment to end the dumping of untreated sewage into the Seine within five years. The city was largely successful: it held an impressive ceremony—reminiscent of that described by Parent-Duchâtelet at Montfaucon—to mark the closing of the Clichy *cloaca maxima* on 8 July 1899, two days before the deadline.[57]

A year earlier Bechmann had evoked the play of professional identities and corporate ideologies in the struggle over the *tout-à-l'égout:* "Few subjects were so able to impassion to such a high degree engineers, doctors, scientists, hygienists, administrators; the discussions were lively, fiery, prolonged."[58] Sanitary engineers looked with evident satisfaction upon the result. They prided themselves on wresting human sewage disposal from private hands and placing it, in what they defined as the public interest, under their unitary control.[59] They were pleased to see their macro-oriented approach to sanitation triumph over fears of Methuselahian microbes. If cesspool cleaners and dump operators were ushered not so gently into that good night, *tant pis;*[60] as for real estate owners, the hookup costs and the sewer tax proved hardly onerous enough to precipitate a social revolution.[61]

In the nineteenth century, public hygienists and civil engineers set out to transform the resignation, repression, and repulsion with which the typical Parisian bourgeois seemed to approach the problems of urban refuse. These experts saw the triumph of egotism and the threat urban life posed to civilization just beneath the surface of the unquestioned dangers which untended sewers and city dumps presented to the health of the citizenry. But there was a way out of this cloaca. The widespread dissemination of water led to significant improvements in public health. These were accompanied by new collective strategies for enclosure of the unclean and in some cases its profitable exploitation. Such developments had social dimensions which extended beyond the purely technical: under the therapeutic guidance of a Parent-Duchâtelet or a Durand-Claye, people could be led to confront and even take pleasure in what they had ignored or reviled. Parisians had long waded through urban mire and drunk polluted water. Boat rides through the sewer, vegetables from Gennevilliers, and the refreshing glass of filtrated sewage water at Achères dramatically reenacted these experiences as *représentations* of society's alchemical mastery of the urban environment.

Representations
of Labor

Cesspool Cleaners and Sewermen

When I was occupied with researching the sewers of Paris, everything appeared perfect to me as long as I was content to study them
aboveground; but after having gone through them, often up to my
knees in muck, it became easy to get a sense of what had been wrong
[*vicieux*] in the system followed until then.
— A.-J.-B. Parent-Duchâtelet, *De la Prostitution*

SYSTEMS of social classification, whether by gender, race, occupation, or
some other category always seek to legitimate themselves as inherent in
nature and society. Far from fixing meaning, however, social classifications
are the sites of perpetual conflicts, in which competing parties brandish
their own representations, said to encapsulate the primary or true ordering
system. These are not sterile arguments fought in drawing rooms while the
true embodiments of social groups construct factories and barricades. On
the contrary, men and women who seek to build the future in building
factories and barricades act with certain representations of themselves and
others in mind. These representations both suggest and limit the possibilities for action and for describing and analyzing that action.

There were few more important terms of social classification in
nineteenth-century thought than "labor." One way to get at this problematic concept is to examine representations of workers like cesspool cleaners
and sewermen who fitted the era's norm (however incomplete) for workers
as individuals—male and native in this case—but which threatened to
transgress its normalizing discourses on labor, the body, and the body social. The "base" labor of these workers made them at once marginal to
society and ateliers of social thought.

We all dispose of waste, individually and collectively. For the individual
in modern Western society, mastering this process is crucial to development of the self. The central element in this project is learning to differentiate waste and to distance oneself from it.[1] The separation between the
population as a whole and those charged with assuring the disposal of

wastes is in turn a fundamental step in the social division of labor. This division is easily reified. Those who remove waste become the "other," untouchables outside society whose integral place in the functioning and identity of society is frequently obscured. For this very reason, examination of representations of social groups like cesspool cleaners and sewermen helps reveal the workings of those discourses which seek through differentiation, classification, and stigmatization to fix the meaning of labor and the order of society.

Cesspool Cleaners

In early sixteenth-century Paris, most residents did not live in dwellings equipped with cesspools. They placed their chamber pots in front of the door and workers passed by at assigned hours in the morning and afternoon to empty them. Royal ordinances in the 1530s overturned this system by requiring the construction of cesspools. Cesspool cleaners (*vidangeurs* or *maîtres fi fi*[2]) periodically emptied the cesspools, but only at night. The change reflected new attitudes toward human waste in the city. Householders had less contact with their own offal; cesspool cleaners had to perform their work under the cover of darkness. Cesspool cleaners generally arranged with property owners to skim the liquefied waste off the top of their cesspools using a system of ladles, buckets, and pulleys, but periodically they had to dig out the encrusted solid matter with shovels (every three or four years in the case of large cesspools).[3] They naturally worked in irregular bursts since they could not stay long in the more fetid chambers. After filling barrels with offal, cesspool cleaners were supposed to haul them to designated dump sites, such as Montfaucon.

The structures which underlay interpretations of manual labor in eighteenth-century France—external/internal; vile/honorable; and disgust/sympathy—were dichotomous, like the relationship of the cesspool cleaners' work to that of other laborers (done in part below ground, not above; at night, not during the day). Over the course of the eighteenth century, discourses centered on the second conception in each twinned structure challenged the hegemony of the first.

External/Internal. During the Old Regime, cesspool cleaners were perceived to be "external"—even opposed—to the hierarchical social order. They were agents of disorder seemingly capable of turning the world upside down on whatever street they worked at night. Confrontations with civil authorities only clarified their marginal status as workers outside the pale. Through a metaphoric association with bowel movements, cesspool cleaners were figures of mirth and anger. Their raucous presence in the neighborhood was like a long-delayed fart—unrestrained and unpleasant. Cesspool cleaners were reputed to be hard drinkers: they "filled their bellies with *l'eau de vie* which gave them reckless courage." They were known to smear offal on the houses of people who refused to have their cesspools emptied or failed to tip them. Working under the cloak of darkness, cesspool cleaners were sorely tempted to dump the contents of their barrels into convenient open sewers or into the Seine rather than haul it to the outskirts of the city. Many used barrels with holes in them (*lanternes*), from which a portion of the contents trickled on to the street. As the night wore on, cesspool cleaners became more and more tempted to neglect sanitation. Restif de la Bretonne reported that "in the middle of the night, when no one sees them, [cesspool cleaners] prove that Jean-Jacques Rousseau does not know what he is talking about when he assures us men are born good."[4]

Two institutions existed to impose order among the cesspool cleaners: the guilds and the police. Much to Mercier's astonishment (*Qui l'eût cru?*), the cesspool cleaners of Paris constituted a guild (with thirty-six masters in 1776). Like any guild, it pronounced itself the guarantor of good work and defended itself against interlopers. New masters were admitted after producing a *chef d'oeuvre* (!) and paying one hundred francs (fifty francs for sons of masters).[5] In 1670, frustrated *compagnons* attempted to go into business on their own but were rebuffed the following year, when the Parlement of Paris backed the masters' monopoly: a *compagnon* who struck out on his own was to be sent to prison. In 1729 the Parlement reaffirmed the master cesspool cleaners' monopoly of the trade in Paris.[6] Not surprisingly, however, the occupation continued to attract penniless veterans and laborers who risked more than civil penalties. They "offered to do the job for less, [but] often paid for their inexperience with their lives."[7]

Cesspool cleaning was carried out in a liminal world where a congeries of illicit behaviors constituted the norm. The police played a cat-and-mouse game with cesspool cleaners in an effort to catch them at illegal dumping. Police regulations promulgated in 1726 and succeeding years which laid out how cesspool cleaners were to accomplish their task (including a strict prohibition on stopping "at any cabaret or *eau-de-vie* seller") only served to confirm the cesspool cleaners' suspect reputation.[8] Naturally, the guild claimed the right to enforce such rules and appointed paid *jurés* to assure that members obeyed them.[9] Yet Corbin is right to see in the detailed extra-corporate police regulations "the genesis of future systems of control for which the refuse workers were undoubtedly the testing-ground."[10]

The authorities made one sustained effort to bring cesspool cleaning within their sphere of control. This was a typical project of the late Enlightenment in which the interests of the cesspool cleaners' guild were characterized as external and opposed to those of society as a whole; a new technology of cesspool cleaning and social organization to administer it was to transform the fundamentally unhealthy and antisocial nature of both the work itself and those who performed it. In 1776, the year Turgot abolished the *corporations,* a Compagnie du Ventilateur was given the monopoly for cesspool cleaning in Paris. This enterprise had developed a ventilator to evacuate the unpleasant and insalubrious gases which emanated from cesspools during cleaning. (The firm had tested the apparatus for eight days in the king's quarters—throne of thrones—at Versailles.) The company formulated elaborate precautions to ensure the cleanliness of its operations. It hired former master cesspool cleaners, but fired those who reverted to their old ways. The short-lived enterprise was a casualty of the failure of Turgot's reform. In the corporate restoration which followed the Compagnie du Ventilateur lost its monopoly, and the *lieutenant de police* Lenoir returned control of cesspool cleaning to the guild.[11]

Despite the demise of the company, the justification of the venture in terms of preventing the spread of unwholesome odors was indicative of the medicalization of discussions of social order in eighteenth-century France. Cesspool cleaners who strewed offal across the streets or surreptitiously dumped the contents of their carts into the sewers were not just a nuisance or an affront to civil authority; their illicit actions risked generating miasmas which were a threat to the well-being of all.

This very concern with public health made medical doctors as interested in the individual bodies of cesspool cleaners as the police were in their corporate body. Doctors' focus on cesspool cleaners' health rather than their job practices encouraged a view of these workers which was internal to (and in some sense exemplary of) the functioning of society. The pioneering eighteenth-century occupational health investigator Bernardini Ramazzini got the idea to study the effects of work on health in all trades from a discussion with a man cleaning the sewer across the street from his house. Defending his point of departure, Ramazzini wrote that doctors who studied the urine and stools of their patients had no right to ignore the men who cleaned the cesspools and sewers of their cities.[12] The very nature of modern medicine demanded it: "In these days when the art of medicine has been converted into a *mechanismus,* it will not be indecorous for us to have dealings now and again with mechanics of the lowest class."[13]

In the late eighteenth century cesspool cleaners were of particular interest to scientists because their experience with accumulated human refuse provided a microcosm of the urban experience of living in a world of mephitic exhalations. Research on cesspools became *à la mode*.[14] Cesspools emerged as the new frontier for eager scientists. Some experimented upon themselves, running to the site of a cesspool disaster to see if their contraptions and chemicals would allow them to survive where mysterious odors had felled cesspool cleaners. Mercier, it will be remembered, was terrified by the dangerous gases trapped in the sewer Turgot had constructed. He fervently hoped they would not escape, but if they did, "let's at least have recourse to those modern chemists, who make light of all the deadly miasmas and who offer to descend into cesspools with the same confidence that a dancer at the fair walks a tightrope."[15]

In 1777 King Louis XVI appointed a royal commission, composed of Antoine Laurent Lavoisier and other prominent scientists, to study *méphitisme*. As part of its work the commission evaluated proposals to improve the cesspool cleaners' job.[16] When the Lyonnais ophthalmologist Janin had the unfortunate idea of using vinegar to protect cesspool cleaners from the effects of mephitic odors, the commission agreed to test his theory. A police official, the Commissaire du Châtelet, five members of the Académie Royale des Sciences, and five members of the Société Royale de Médecine looked on as vinegar was spread in a cesspool in anticipation of workmen entering it. As expected, the vinegar reduced the odors for the workers who entered the cesspool—only a marginal improvement for workers "accustomed to count as nothing what is most nauseating."[17] But by masking the smell which generally accompanied mephitism without affecting mephitism itself, it made the situation worse. One laborer died of asphyxiation; two companions who went to his aid "lost pulse, respiration and movement"; and a fourth "entirely suffocated." This was enough for all concerned; the Commissaire and academics drew up reports on the experiment which the government published.[18] If the experience and the attendant publicity sullied Janin's reputation, it enhanced those of the intrepid scientists. The biographer of commission member Jean-Noël Hallé wrote that in measuring the stench emanating from the cesspool, he had "given proof of the most rare of all forms of bravery, that which does not shrink from foreseen dangers."[19]

While the police long viewed cesspool cleaners primarily as an external threat to policing—in the military sense—of the city, some medical authorities suggested that cesspool cleaners were their own social analogues. Ramazzini said as much in drawing a parallel between doctors and cesspool cleaners, both of whom handled human waste in their trades: doctors who viewed the body as a mechanism could not ignore the mechanics of the social body. And those intrepid scientists who subjected themselves to the mortal miasmas of the cesspool did so in the belief that cesspool clean-ers' bodies and work encapsulated phenomena common to all city dwellers and to the internal workings of the city itself. The lot of urbanites would be improved more through techniques developed to better the working conditions of cesspool cleaners than through police repression of these un-fortunates. This way of thinking infused discussions in the last decades before the Revolution, tempering the responses of both the police and the public to the once universally reviled cesspool cleaners.

Vile/Honorable. Cesspool cleaning was traditionally perceived as vile la-bor done by those at the bottom of the social ladder. Ramazzini recalled that the Emperor Trajan had convicts clean the sewers of Rome.[20] In 1350, two years after the Black Death swept across Europe, a royal ordinance recognized the *low* status of those who emptied chamberpots and cesspools (*ouvriers des basses œuvres*) by opening up the occupation to workers of all trades.[21] Even after establishment of the cesspool cleaners' guild, corporate discourses of pride and honor did not embellish the trade. Cesspool clean-ers were scorned in the world of late eighteenth-century labor, in which "the worker was valued, not for his work or for the degree of intelligence it required, but in terms of the material on which he worked."[22] Cesspool cleaners, to paraphrase Marx, were defined by their relation to the means of excretion.

Money was considered the only reason why a man would take up cess-pool cleaning—a clear indication of the base status of the trade. Ramazzini advised workers with weak eyes to find another line of work so that they would not "for the sake of vile and filthy lucre lose their sight and be forced to beg."[23] Mercier doubted that any law could condemn men, even crimi-nals, to destroy their health on a daily basis by descending into cesspools. "Yet," he concluded, "what tyranny and coercion could not do, a little money does without violence or coercion."[24]

But there was another side to this view of the cesspool cleaner. He per-formed a very necessary labor in society and to the extent that his utilitar-ian value was respected, he might be endowed with a certain honor in so-ciety. The royal ordinance of 1350 had included an almost certainly unenforced provision that anyone who insulted cesspool cleaners would be fined.[25] Enlightenment thinkers were forced to engage this issue more seriously. After all, if cesspool cleaning was base labor, it was base in the sense of "basic," as well as "vile." The authors of the *Encyclopédie* were of two minds about manual labor. They honored its utilitarian nature, even as they devalued it with respect to mental labor free of the gross materiality of the physical world.[26]

The maverick writer Jean-Henri Marchand—remembered now for penning insults which infuriated Voltaire—made this debate the subject of his 1777 play, *Le Vuidanger sensible*. Marchand intended his work as a response to those who said that even people from the lowest stations of life were a suitable subject for the stage. *Le Vuidanger sensible* tells the story of a virtuous London cesspool cleaner, William Sentfort, who murders his libertine son for having dishonored the family. The play was never performed, even in the intimate private gathering for which it was intended, because no one would play the roles of a cesspool cleaner and his family, honorable or not. Some complained that their imagination would be afflicted by waves of disgust, others that playing such a role would have deleterious effects on their muscular and nervous systems.[27] They were unmoved by the claim of Sentfort's daughter that cesspool cleaners embodied the civic spirit:

> I agree that my father's profession is not seductive; but if one judges the merit of things by their utility, it must be agreed that there are few positions more necessary and which require more courage in society than his: few people have soul enough to support it. Isn't a Citizen noble when, for the common good, he does what others would not, could not do? But people are attracted to what shines and disdain what produces good without glamour.[28]

The virtuous cesspool cleaner was at once another of Marchand's many sallies against cultural authority and an ironic reminder that the Old Regime untouchable could also be conceived of as the locus of civic and individual honor.

Beyond this utilitarian contention, some medical authorities who studied the cesspool cleaners developed a positive conception of their morality. These physicians emphasized the virtues which cesspool cleaners exhibited in dealings within their closed community, instead of viewing them in terms of their conflictual relationship with the rest of society. Defending cesspool cleaners against the usual injurious comments, Géraud concluded in 1786 that "learned men have often praised the [cesspool cleaners'] reciprocal humanity—quite frequently taken to the loss of their own life—their zealousness and sometimes even their intelligence."[29] The inconvenienced city dweller Restif de la Bretonne presented these workers as a refutation of Rousseau; those who penetrated the cesspool cleaners' world, however, might just as easily endow them with Rousseauistic virtues.

Disgust/Sympathy. The drunken, rowdy, noisome cesspool cleaner disgusted most Parisians. But those who pondered the cesspool cleaners' existence at the end of the eighteenth century expressed compassion as well. The cesspool cleaners themselves had always known how hard their work was. Their call went,

A curer le puys!
C'est peu de practique,
La gaigne est petite.
Plus gaigner ne puis.[30]

What was new was sympathy from others. Ramazzini's account of his discussion with the man cleaning the sewer in front of his house is wrenching. He asked him "why he was working so strenuously and why he did not take it more quietly so as to avoid the fatigue that follows overexertion. The poor wretch lifted his eyes from the cavern, gazed at me, and said: 'No one who has not tried it can imagine what it costs to stay more than four hours in this place; it is the same thing as being struck blind.'"

When the worker had finished for the day, Ramazzini examined his eyes and found them to be "extremely bloodshot and dim." He asked the worker if men in his trade had any particular remedy for this condition. "'Only this,' he replied, 'they go back at once to their homes as I shall do presently, shut themselves in a dark room, stay there for a day and bathe their eyes now and then with lukewarm water.' . . . Thereupon he wished me good-day and went home, keeping his hands over his eyes."[31] Géraud commented on the premature aging, blindness, and paralysis he saw among cesspool cleaners, and wondered whether they did not wish they had died in a work accident like so many of their comrades.[32]

Observers reinterpreted cesspool cleaners' least agreeable habits in sympathetic terms. According to Mercier, these workers had to stupefy themselves with *eau-de-vie* to face the *miasmes pestilentiels* in the cesspools, but could never overcome the poverty which drove them to cesspool cleaning precisely because they had to spend their wages on liquor.[33] For Mercier, then, the heavy drinking popularly associated with cesspool cleaners was not the sign of a moral flaw characteristic of the type of worker attracted to cesspool cleaning, but rather a necessity enabling him to brave his work environment. The scientists Laborie, Cadet le Jeune, and Parmentier found themselves unable to distinguish among the seventeen kinds of leaden feeling (*plomb*) which cesspool cleaners claimed to experience, but their enumeration of the symptoms of the disease offered a medical explanation for some of the cesspool cleaners' more raucous behavior: "involuntary and sometimes modulated cries which cause the workers to say that *le plomb* makes them sing; a convulsive cough, a sardonic laugh, delirium, asphyxia and death."[34]

For this trio, "humanity could not look with indifference" upon cesspool cleaning accidents. "The most deplorable of conditions by its abasement is made all the more so by its dangers."[35] Hallé hoped that his report on the ill-fated vinegar test would improve "the life of a class of useful and unfortunate men."[36] Mercier and others praised academicians for not disdaining such objects of study.[37] Mercier also saluted the police commissioner Lenoir for going beyond repression of cesspool cleaners' abuses to provide for infirm members of the trade. When Lenoir reestablished the cesspool cleaners' corporation after the failure of the Turgot reform, he set up a fund, supported by a contribution of four sous from each cesspool cleaner for each day of work. Half the money went to endow hospital beds for cesspool cleaners and the other half to support ill cesspool cleaners and their families.[38] "This attention given to a class of men plunged in the most humiliating state and from whom the least citizens turn away with disdain, merits the greatest praise . . . for are we not glad to have men who devote themselves to such disgusting operations, all for a few coins? And don't we owe them some compensation in the realm of simple equity?[39] For Mercier, it was wrong to blame cesspool cleaners for their wretched state and not enough to pity them. In recognition of the valuable services they performed for the community, the authorities had a responsibility to devote special attention to them.

The decades before the Revolution witnessed the spread of new representations of labor among both intellectual elites and civil authorities. Nowhere was this clearer than in a debased occupation like cesspool cleaning. While cesspool cleaners retained their reputation as disorderly, dishonorable, and disgusting, new voices spoke of them in terms of public health, honest labor, and the sympathy owed fellow citizens. This division deepened after the Revolution and continued in the guise of conservative analyses of immoral and moral workers and radical discourses about egotistical and communitarian workers (or lumpenproletarians and proletarians). In nineteenth-century interpretations, cesspool cleaners came to embody the characteristics of immoral, egotistical lumpenproletarians; sewermen emerged as archetypal moral proletarians and model workers. Parent-Duchâtelet was the direct descendant of the social commentators who displayed an appreciation for the downtrodden sanitation workers and their job in the eighteenth century.

Parent-Duchâtelet and the Sewermen

Sewer cleaning was done irregularly in Paris before the eighteenth century. For one thing, it was not easy to find men to work in dark, humid, cramped, poorly ventilated tunnels where they faced the twin dangers of asphyxiation and drowning. Convicts were occasionally pressed into service. During the reign of Louis XIV, *galériens* assigned to clean the sewers found that the waste bleached their scarlet uniforms and that their stench kept the police at bay. One group of prisoners followed the sewers to the Seine where they escaped on a boat going to Le Havre. When the next group of convicts was sent to the sewers, the police were careful to place guards at all exits; not surprisingly, their charges died of asphyxiation.[40] Although Colbert organized a skeletal service to maintain the sewers under the aegis of the police,[41] the general practice through most of the Old Regime was for the city to wait until an emergency occurred and then to strike a deal with a contractor to clean up the mess.[42] Cleansing the sewers became routine only in the eighteenth century: the city of Paris employed sixteen sewermen in 1792; twenty in An III, and twenty-four in 1804, the number in service at the time Parent-Duchâtelet undertook his researches in the 1820s.

When Parent-Duchâtelet wrote of these experiences, there was no body of literature on sewermen comparable to that on cesspool cleaners. Everyone knew, he said, when cesspool cleaners were in the neighborhood; and "if the slightest accident happens to one, the zeal of the newspapers to give all of the details immediately makes it a subject of conversation throughout the city." Yet no one thought of the sewermen at work underground. "I cannot account for the kind of disdain which most learned men have for [sewermen]." "Important, superb studies have been done of cesspools and of those who work in them, and nothing on sewers and sewermen," although sewermen's work was as important as that of cesspool cleaners and the dangers they faced greater.[43] In two long essays, Parent-Duchâtelet set out to rectify this injustice. He announced his researches on sewermen to be "absolutely like those" of his mentor Hallé on cesspool cleaners.[44] In his initial report, published in 1824, Parent-Duchâtelet evoked the loss he felt at Hallé's recent death; it is not hard to see his work on the sewers as a sign of fealty to Hallé as well as a test to prove that he was a worthy disciple.

While Parent-Duchâtelet was known for his curiosity concerning all facets of public hygiene, his particular interest in sewers could not but strike even his intimates as odd. The psychiatrist François Leuret commented after Parent-Duchâtelet's death that he "did not have for sewers the repugnance which these places naturally inspire; I would almost say that he liked them."[45] His friends took him to a *fête* at the Hôtel de Ville one evening. "Seeing so much movement to do nothing, so much zeal to change places and to display oneself, [Parent-Duchâtelet] remembered his previous evenings, so well spent. 'I would a hundred times rather go down in the sewers than come to this gathering,' he said in a low voice to one of the friends who had brought him. 'You won't see me here again.' And, in fact, he kept his word."[46] The falsity of society life offended the Jansenist in Parent-

Duchâtelet. He longed to flee a world where people were "decked out in obligatory evening wear" for one where, as Hugo would write, appearances did not deceive.

Investigating the sewers of Paris, Parent-Duchâtelet could not escape the role of participant-observer. Nor did he want to. "I did everything a man jealous of discovering the truth could do." "*I wanted to see everything myself . . . I went everywhere I describe.*" Spurred by a desire to make himself useful to his fellow citizens and to the sewermen, he "overcame without hesitation the repugnance and the dangers inseparable from such research."[47] Whatever he learned above ground about the sewers, he questioned below ground plodding about in muck up to his knees. Like an initiation rite, the shared physical experience of time spent in the sewers gave Parent-Duchâtelet a special sense of kinship with the sewermen. He monitored the effects of the environment of the sewers on himself with remarkable assurance. Analyzing the headaches he experienced after visiting one set of sewers, he informed readers that he had made efforts to assure that "neither the odor of the sewers nor the repugnance they inspire" were the source of his malady; he concluded therefore that the headaches must have been due to the "air" in these particular sewers.[48]

Parent-Duchâtelet's belief that self-experimentation was an important research tool figures prominently in his work on sanitation (prostitution aside). In proposing changes in the cesspool cleaning system, he denied that the release of urine into the sewers would pose a hazard to sewermen and cited the good health of those working around institutions like the Invalides and Salpêtrière where the cesspools already emptied into the sewers. (Parent-Duchâtelet believed that dishwater and soapy bathwater were far greater dangers to sewermen's well-being.[49]) To make his point about the innocuousness of diluted urine, the ever resourceful Parent-Duchâtelet pointed to the hole where liquid from cesspool wastes was dumped at Bondy. What leached out combined with water in the soil to make an odorless brown-tinted liquid: "we will add that it is tasteless because despite the disgust inseparable from such tests, *we were not afraid to taste it.*"[50]

In his first report on the Paris sewers, Parent-Duchâtelet tells the reader that he has done extensive research on the subject to supplement his personal experiences. He notes with bitterness that individuals in the administration had refused to share materials in their possession on the sewers. Parent-Duchâtelet's desire to see everything himself and his admiration for the honest sewermen were responses to the "mistrust and ill will" of those who refused him access to needed documentation and who misled him with false information.[51] Deceived and disappointed by his own social world (as he had been by the misleading claims of medical science), and denied full access to the world of writing, Parent-Duchâtelet interrogated sewermen closely. Ever suspicious, he talked with them at work and at home, individually and in groups, using each conversation as a control on the others. (Was all this questioning the timid Parent-Duchâtelet's *real* bravery in the sewers? Or did the lack of artificiality he discerned in the lowly men questioned dispel his timidity?) However, in the final analysis, Parent-Duchâtelet gave priority to neither written documents nor oral testimony, but to the knowledge he found inscribed in the sewermen's habits and on their bodies.

Parent-Duchâtelet accepted the popular wisdom voiced by the sewermen that sewage (the fresher the better) was generally neutral or perhaps even beneficial to those exposed to it.[52] In this respect, his study of sewermen, like all of his studies of occupational health, participated in a broad contemporary movement to challenge the pessimistic work of Ramazzini and his successors. The sewermen's health could be considered normal; their lifespan "not shortened in the least."[53] Parent-Duchâtelet singled out the case of the sewerman Charpian: "I know that Charpian has been given as an example of the influence which sewers have on the production of *maladies putrides;* it is true that he carries a gnawing ulcer [*chancre rongeant*] which has destroyed the corner of the lips, the cheek, the lower eyelid, and the teguments of the nose." But, Parent-Duchâtelet warned, appearances could be deceiving. Charpian had suffered from this ulcer for thirty-six years. Its slow development was, if anything, a testament to the salutary effects of work in the sewers.[54] So intent was Parent-Duchâtelet on showing the general good health of sewermen that he dismissed their accounts of *le plomb* which afflicted veteran sewermen[55]: "One should not accept the first answers of these workers when one asks them for some details on the illnesses to which their profession exposes them."[56]

The danger in an environment like the sewers, all medical authorities agreed, came from the presence of potentially deadly mephitic gases. These, Parent-Duchâtelet argued, had their worst effects on workers whose moral infirmities had physical consequences which made them susceptible to their ill effects. Work in the sewers was not inherently dangerous, but it could have mortal consequences for the crapulous. This idea, characteristic of medical thought at the time, made the harsh conditions in the sewers a litmus test for individual conduct. It also explains why Parent-Duchâtelet, who generally placed complete confidence in the sewermen, had trouble accepting their accounts of an endemic illness, like *le plomb,* which could not be correlated to specific behavior.

Parent-Duchâtelet lauded the sewermen of Paris. Where others had cited the Romans' use of convicts to clean the sewers, Parent-Duchâtelet claimed that the authorities in ancient Rome had recognized the importance of sewer cleaners by establishing severe penalties against those who hindered them.[57] Parent-Duchâtelet recalled the stereotype of work in the sewers as a punishment, but rejected the idea that sewermen were criminal types. The sewermen of Paris, he explained, are a "class of workers" who "voluntarily condemn themselves" to spend their lives underground.[58] Yet he denied that "the most downtrodden and ignorant class" became sewermen; all the sewermen with whom he spoke could read and write.[59]

Men who led temperate lives suffered few ill consequences from work in the sewers; intemperate individuals died. Individual sewermen required the same inherent personal rectitude to preserve themselves from the dangerous emanations of the sewers as Parent-Duchâtelet would later have to display in exploring the underworld of Parisian prostitution. In an extraordinary five-page footnote, Parent-Duchâtelet developed the widespread notion that men with venereal disease who went to work in cesspools and sewers were immediately stricken very ill; those who stayed on the job died.[60] "The virulence of the illness transmitted by female sewers, by the vaginal filth of fallen women," Corbin writes, "is naturally linked to the mire and to excremental effluvia."[61] Drunken workers succumbed to accidents.[62] Work in the sewers did not attract the dregs of society; on the contrary, it mercilessly eliminated precisely these individuals. When sewermen recognized that one in their midst suffered from venereal disease or was intoxicated, they tried to prevent him from entering the sewers.[63]

Sewermen were not foolhardy. Parent-Duchâtelet praised them for refusing to expose themselves unnecessarily to dangers ("unlike the majority of workers"). The men balked at entering areas they thought particularly infected or dangerous; the city had to hire other men to do this work.[64] Nor were sewermen money-grubbing. They told Parent-Duchâtelet of a young worker "extrêmement avide de gain" who spent his rest periods searching the muck for scrap metal and other objects to sell. He came down with a bad colic which forced him to enter the hospital; on his return he resumed the practice and once again became very sick. Having learned his lesson, he thereafter devoted his breaks to rest and had been healthy since. The moral of the story was clear: a sewerman who ignored the customary work rhythms and sought individual gain on the job could become seriously ill.[65]

Syphilis, drunkenness, and avarice signified for Parent-Duchâtelet and his readers a range of immoral behaviors. These could be disguised or hidden above ground, but not below. The sewer revealed not the moral character of society as in *Les Misérables,* but the moral character of individuals. This element of Parent-Duchâtelet's account of Paris sewermen displays one aspect of an increasingly visible figure on the social landscape: the moral proletarian.

Cleaning the Amelot Sewer

The Amelot sewer periodically belched forth rotting refuse into the adjoining neighborhood. Sewermen sent to work in it asphyxiated and efforts to clean the sewer had had to be abandoned; it became the standard by which sewermen evaluated the danger of work in any of the city's sewers. Parent-Duchâtelet concluded his 1824 report with a proposal to purge this notorious cloaca. He offered to take the place of the officials charged with municipal sanitation and himself lead the team of workers assigned the task: "the workers will be so sheltered from all danger, that I would not hesitate an instant to remain in their midst as long as their work lasts. I even offer to supervise them if my project is accepted."[66] Two years after Parent-Duchâtelet made his offer, the prefect took him up on it. He appointed a commission, in which Parent-Duchâtelet played the leading role, to supervise clean-up of the Amelot sewer.[67] Parent-Duchâtelet's participation in this operation gave him the chance to put his ideas about labor into practice.

Parent-Duchâtelet worked with a crew composed of sixteen sewermen and sixteen other workers hired for the job. He took what he had learned from his earlier experience with career sewermen and applied it to members of this hybrid group in order to assure that they would be physically and morally capable of carrying out the work safely. "Is it not a maxim," Parent-Duchâtelet wrote "to render independent of the will and superintendence of men, and above all of workmen, everything which appertains in a notable manner to their preservation?"[68] With this belief in mind, he pioneered a new, medicalized form of labor management.

Parent-Duchâtelet kept a daily record of the workers' health so that he could evaluate the medical efficacy of the workplace order he established.[69] "They were subject to a thorough examination; their diet, their drink, their clothes, their cleanliness, the amount of time they worked were regulated. Furthermore, it was decided that they would all be examined individually in the morning, and that any who appeared sick, who were not completely cured of a previously-detected ailment or exhaustion, or who showed signs of intoxication would be dismissed and would not work that day."[70] "Work time and rest time were regulated during the whole period the workers were under our direction." Work began at five in the morning and ended at six in the evening. Workers were given two one-hour breaks each day (as well as shorter breaks when work conditions required it) during which they were invited to take shelter from the summer heat and the chilly autumn and winter rains under a large tent equipped with chairs, benches, straw (for napping), water for washing, and a fire when it was cold. A licorice *tisane* and a mixture of eau-de-vie and water (one part to thirty) were provided for workers in the morning and during breaks. (Parent-Duchâtelet rejected the commonly recommended vinegar solution; he believed that the sweating it provoked would make workers absorb noxious gases more readily.) Workers were amply provided with alcohol—it cost one-ninth as much as the total wage bill[71]—but those who dispensed it were able to gauge and regulate its effects. Workers appreciated the refreshments, and, Parent-Duchâtelet explained, the system of controlled rest periods allowed for constant supervision and prevented the workers from going to bars with potentially deadly consequences for them on the job.[72] Parent-Duchâtelet ordered foremen to watch over the health, morality, and prudence of their workers and made them responsible for any accidents attributable to lapses in supervision of these matters.[73]

On Parent-Duchâtelet's recommendation, the Paris Conseil de salubrité appointed a pharmacist to provide assistance to workers who were injured or took sick on the job.[74] Workers were given instruction in first-aid techniques and a large poster ("written in big letters") listing the twelve rules to follow in case of an accident accompanied them from work site to work site.[75] Workers were also taught to monitor the effects of deleterious gases upon themselves and to get out before they succumbed to them.[76] Parent-Duchâtelet paid particular attention to aeration (a defect he had noted in his previous report[77]) and to the use of a dilute solution of *chlorure de chaux* to counteract the effects of mephitic gases. He made special efforts to ensure cleanliness. Workers had to dip their arms up to the shoulders in a chlorine solution and to change from their work clothes to street clothes before returning home.[78]

To make sure workers got enough to eat, Parent-Duchâtelet arranged to have the sewerman's daily wage raised 25 percent from the customary two to 2.50 francs.[79] To prevent workers from hiding their maladies, he pursued the existing city policy of paying sewermen for days they could not work as a result of illnesses contracted working in the sewers. As a result, workers monitored their own health carefully and promptly reported signs of fatigue and work-related illness.[80] The six-month clean-up operation was an arduous affair—workers extracted 86,000 cubic feet of sand and pushed three times this amount of muck into the Seine.[81] That there were no fatalities Parent-Duchâtelet attributed largely to workers' being free to take time off when necessary to recuperate.[82] Sure of the workers' morality, he never seems to have worried that higher wages would contribute to debauchery or that workers who claimed they had headaches or felt woozy might have been malingering.

Parent-Duchâtelet analyzed the constituent elements of veteran sewermen's behavior and, as Frederick Winslow Taylor would later do with machinists, made them the basis of a new organization of work which claimed to benefit workers while assuring more efficient execution of work. In his report on the cleaning of the Amelot sewer, Parent-Duchâtelet codified his findings into forty-seven lessons for future sewer-cleaning expeditions.[83] Most bourgeois observers at the time argued that workers' low wages and poor living conditions could be attributed to their immorality; higher wages would likely worsen the situation. Having established the morality of sewermen, Parent-Duchâtelet felt free to ask for a significant increase in the number of workers and wages, not just for clean-up of the Amelot sewer but in the service as a whole.[84]

Moral Proletarians

Parent-Duchatelet's pioneering effort at the medicalization of the organization of work, like Taylorization later, focused on the individual sewerman. Yet Parent-Duchâtelet did not see sewermen solely as individuals. On the contrary, he celebrated their solidarity. Why, Parent-Duchâtelet asks at one point, would anyone voluntarily go to work in the sewers? The question certainly occurred to others. In *Les Misérables,* Hugo commented in reference to the early nineteenth century that "the job of sewerman was formerly almost as repugnant to the people as a job in the slaughterhouse. . . . Good wages had to be offered to convince a mason to disappear into that fetid sap. . . . it was said proverbially: " '*to descend into the sewer is to enter the grave.*' "[85] Yet the sewerman's wages were not high. Parent-Duchâtelet offered another explanation as to why some men chose to work in the sewers: there they found a community which money could not buy. It was not just the sewermen's individual rectitude, but this collective fraternity which made them true moral proletarians for Parent-Duchâtelet.

Parent-Duchâtelet waxed eloquent about the men he got to know under the streets of Paris:

> Whatever the immense extent of the sewers of Paris, the number of workers employed in their upkeep . . . has never surpassed twenty-four. . . . Therefore, they all know one another. They cannot work alone. They know what dangers surround them; their dependence on their comrades in dangerous situations, the things they have done for one another in a variety of circumstances. (There is probably not one who does not owe his life to his comrade.) And as they are all without goods and without wealth, the most perfect equality

reigns among them. They are perhaps the only individuals who know all the charms of true friendship and I would not be surprised if one has to go search the sewers of Paris for true happiness, if happiness consists in the certitude of having a true friend, as several ancient philosophers thought.[86]

Rousseau and the romantics located the antithesis to the corruption of urban (and especially Parisian) civilization in the countryside. The world-turned-upside-down of Parent-Duchâtelet has a different social geography. He situated the community of naturally good men free from the vices and shams of civilization below the city of Paris. The sewermen embodied the antithesis of the egotistic bourgeois and doctors who had blocked plans to destroy Montfaucon. In the darkness and filth of the sewers there was the "transparency" for which Rousseau (and Parent-Duchâtelet) strove.[87] Parent-Duchâtelet helped develop a tradition among bourgeois intellectuals of attaching to a "lower" laboring class qualities they saw absent in their own milieu. For the naturalist novelist Zola, coal miners possessed a sexual freedom which the bourgeoisie lacked; for Parent-Duchâtelet, the sewermen had a capacity for fraternity missing in the bourgeoisie.

Parent-Duchâtelet had institutionalized the sewermen's moderate individual habits in supervising the cleaning of the Amelot sewer. He harbored the same ambition to organize the sewermen's community in a mutual aid society which would provide assistance to ill and retired sewermen under the aegis of the bourgeois Société philanthropique (for which Parent-Duchâtelet continued to work as a doctor after otherwise abandoning medicine.) The fund would be open only to married men of good character.[88] It would provide the cornerstone of a project to "supervise the health of the workers with as much care as the construction of the sewers themselves,"[89] and reinforce the medico-moral screening inherent in work in the sewers by giving a panoptical twist to sewermen's solidarity: "Is there a better means to avoid vice and to practice virtue than to know that fifty or one-hundred people who have the right to reprimand you and to expel you ignominiously from their society are watching and supervising you?"[90]

Parent-Duchâtelet saw in the sewermen elements of his own temperate, upright character as well as a sense of community lacking in the bourgeois society to which he was bound. He was like these men: armed with good moral habits, he was able to confront and overcome the dangers of work in the most morally and physically corrupt parts of the city.[91] Yet these very traits alienated Parent-Duchâtelet from much of bourgeois society; he was moved therefore to discover among sewermen a kind of camaraderie foreign to bourgeois culture, even if it was closed to an outsider like him. For Parent-Duchâtelet and like-minded bourgeois, selected groups of workers embodied representations of "the other" not as repressed refuse, but as a natural fraternity which the bourgeoisie could attempt to circumscribe through organizations like the Société philanthropique, but could never attain itself.

Parent-Duchâtelet's Sewermen Reconsidered

Studying a group hidden from public view, Parent-Duchâtelet was able to inscribe with unusual clarity his understanding of labor on the sewermen of Paris. Yet his interpretation was, of course, only one of several possible. Two points in his reports suggest, for instance, that his belief in the relation of individual deportment to occupational health made him largely oblivious to the *usure* of labor: over time the bodies of working people incur debts which accrue interest that cannot be retired. First, Parent-Duchâtelet tells the reader that he rejected the testimony of veterans who complained of the general malaise of *le plomb*. Second, it did not occur to him to ask why there were so few long-term sewermen. Only three of the sixteen career sewermen who worked with him in cleaning the Amelot sewer had spent much time in the sewers: fifteen, seven, and six years respectively. Of the other thirteen, one had worked sixteen months, one fifteen months, and the other eleven men had been employed one year or less (including the six-month clean-up of the Amelot sewer).[92] For the same reason that Parent-Duchâtelet dismissed the cumulative effects of labor identifiable in *le plomb,* he seemed genuinely surprised that many of the new recruits suffered less from respiratory and ophthalmological problems than seasoned sewermen.[93] The long career of a Charpian seems not to have been an anomaly for Parent-Duchâtelet. On the contrary, it provided him evidence that if select individuals could work in an environment and suffer no apparent ill effects, this should be within reach of all men whose moral practices sealed their bodies to the dangers that lurked in what (to the uninitiated—and the immoderate) might appear the most forbidding of *milieux.*

Fragmentary evidence from contemporaneous sources raises other questions. Were sewermen as literate as Parent-Duchâtelet believed? A paysheet from 1812 indicates that only two of five sewermen could sign their names.[94] Another paysheet from 1839 suggests that the ability to write was limited to the upper echelons of the sewermen's hierarchy. The four *chefs* and *sous-chefs* among the sewermen could sign their names, but only three of the forty workers who picked up their pay could.[95]

More telling is a report by the Inspecteur général de la Salubrité entitled "Observations touchant la mort de plusieurs ouvriers égoutiers," and dated 18 June 1822, two years before Parent-Duchâtelet's first study of the sewers. Parent-Duchâtelet was probably familiar with its contents: "M. Parent" is pencilled on the cover of the copy of this report in the Archives départementales de la Seine.[96] The Inspecteur général argued that the sewermen's daily wages should be raised 25 percent to 2.50 francs, to allow them to eat better; and that the number of sewermen should be more than doubled to fifty-two.[97] In fact, Parent-Duchâtelet probably lifted these specific recommendations from the official report.

The similarity between the accounts ends here, however, and leads one to interpret Parent-Duchâtelet's essays as an extension of his battle with the administration over the accessibility and content of their documentation. Taken together, the reports of the Inspecteur général and Parent-Duchâtelet provide a variant on the dichotomous representations which developed around sanitary labor—and labor in general—during the eighteenth century. The government report blamed a series of cases of asphyxiation and drowning in the sewers between 1810 and 1820 on foolhardy sewermen, sometimes blinded by "cupidity," and "encouraged in this direction by the *chefs égoutiers*."[98] In each instance, the Inspecteur général laid final responsibility on the two inspectors in charge of monitoring operations in the sewers. The point was clear: sewermen were imprudent individuals who required sound guidance, the opposite of what they were receiving from their foremen, and close supervision from the inspectors, who almost never visited the sewers.

Parent-Duchâtelet's account is very different in tone and content. He singled out the years 1793–1820 as fairly safe, in contrast to a string of serious accidents between 1782 and 1793.[99] His sewermen were generally cautious individuals and explicitly exonerated of "cupidity." While the Inspecteur général wondered if he could trust what a *chef égoutier* told him, Parent-Duchâtelet generally placed his faith in the acts and testimony of head sewermen over the written word of those in authority: these individuals were promoted from the ranks and had therefore endured longer in the sewers than their coworkers, perhaps a sign of their moral character. (In fact, one suspects that Parent-Duchâtelet committed a common sin of anthropologists (and political *militants*): he relied on members of the native/working-class elite as his primary informants—*chefs égoutiers* like Charpian in this instance—and then projected on to the collective population—all sewermen—traits he discerned in this exceptional sample.) Finally, Parent-Duchâtelet went out of his way to praise the two inspectors who supervised the sewers between 1810 and 1820.[100] And while he did extend control over sewermen when supervising clean-up of the Amelot sewer, he viewed his role as furthering traits which the sewermen already displayed rather than clamping down on them. Dichotomized readings like these of the character of sanitary labor and of workers as a whole were not outmoded vestiges of the Old Regime; on the contrary, they grew in intensity during the nineteenth century as urbanization and industrialization brought the interpretive category of labor to the fore.

Parent-Duchâtelet's sewermen are among the earliest examples of workers represented as what can be termed "moral proletarians": laborers whose individual and collective moral practices allow them to triumph over potentially degrading labor and penury. The idea of the moral proletarian has roots in the eighteenth-century transformation of the representation of labor. Parent-Duchâtelet's integration of a corporeal reading of temperate practices and a corporate spirit free from the sinful pride of the guilds gave new substance to this figure. Variants of the moral proletarian went on to play a major role in nineteenth-century social thought, whether as disciplined stalwarts of brochures published by paternalist firms or the model workers of syndicalist propaganda.

The recovery of Parent-Duchâtelet's moral proletarian participates in an important current of historical literature rooted in the experiences of French *gauchistes* in the early 1970s. They rejected the Communist party and its monopolistic hold over the representation of the true proletarian, and sought to understand the ways such representations took shape. François Ewald, Bruno Mattéi, Lion Murard, and Patrick Zylberman, among others, analyzed how conceptions of morality, solidarity, and the organization of work became conjoined in the *images d'Epinal* of the coal miner.[101] Jacques Rancière recounted the creation by both bourgeois radicals and working-class elites of representations of the working class which assured that they would always be disappointed by the living workers whom they recruited.[102]

Efforts to understand workers and work in a historical context lead back continually to representations of labor in which the doubts and conflicts elicited by the act of interpretation are often elided. The apparent coherence of such representations, far from an indication of sloppy thinking, frequently reveals the working out of fundamental belief systems in the face of unsettling information and intuitions. That one laboratory for doing so was located below ground should shock no one.

8

Disorder Above and Order Below

> They emptied my privy last night and those gentlemen the cesspool
> cleaners made so much noise that I couldn't close my eyes. In the kind
> of nightmare they gave me I dreamed: the Emperor and my niece!
> *Toutes les sommités*!
>
> —Gustave Flaubert, *Correspondance* (1868)

INFLUENCED by new currents of humanitarian thought and scientific
practice, some members of the upper class began to challenge entrenched
pejorative notions of labor in the second half of the eighteenth century.
This confrontation informed the deep structure of nineteenth-century discourses about manual workers: ass kissers versus loyal hands, outside agi-
tators versus provident employees, lumpenproletarians versus proletarians.
The ambivalent representation of cesspool cleaners before the Revolution
gave way to an opposition of cesspool cleaners to sewermen in the second
half of the nineteenth century. The cesspool cleaner came to embody the
worker as locus of disruption; the sewerman was transformed from an ambiguous character into a symbol of man's mastery of nature in the renovated Second Empire sewer system. The sanitary engineers' message was
that labor, like filth, was not inherently defiling or dangerous. Depending
on how filth was managed, it could lead to disorder, as during a cholera
epidemic, or foster order, as in the Gennevilliers irrigation farm. The same
was true of sanitation workers. Just as refuse dumps and sewers emerged
as two poles of urban life, cesspool cleaners and sewermen increasingly
stood for two fundamentally different representations of labor in the last
decades of the nineteenth century.

Cesspool Cleaners

In the nineteenth century doctors rejected the notion that cesspool cleaning was a particularly unhealthy profession. And the introduction of new
machinery and the success of large firms changed the nature of the job
from Old Regime corporatism to a capitalist service industry. Yet these

developments did not diminish the reputation for rowdiness which made cesspool cleaners emblematic of a representation of labor as disorder.

Parent-Duchâtelet and his contemporaries discounted much of their eighteenth-century predecessors' pessimistic evaluation of the effects of work on health. An 1842 study in the *Annales d'hygiène publique et de médecine légale* by a team of public health researchers strongly disputed the idea that "the job of cesspool cleaner is one of the most dangerous."[1] It echoed earlier studies in reporting that cesspool cleaners were, in fact, less likely than workers in other trades to become ill (although men with syphilis could tolerate cesspool cleaning no better than work in the sewers).[2] The authors dismissed the cesspool cleaners' eye problems, which had so bothered Ramazzini, as no worse than those experienced by workers in textile factories. They recognized that the work could cause skin problems, but also reported that some individuals became cesspool cleaners to rid themselves of skin diseases. A man whose health had been ruined by work in a lead-laminating factory completely recovered after taking up cesspool cleaning (a cure explained by contact with the sulfur in the hydrogen sulfide given off by degenerating organic matter).

Certain improvements in cesspool cleaners' health could be attributed to mechanization of parts of the job. Parent-Duchâtelet wrote at the beginning of the July Monarchy that a year might pass without any deaths of cesspool cleaners, whereas sixty years earlier there had often been several fatal accidents each month.[3] This change was due in large part to use of steam-powered vacuum pumps—"Richer" pumps—which limited the time workers spent inside cesspools (and therefore the dangers of asphyxiation).

This technical innovation did not reduce the number of cesspool cleaners (which rose from 200–250 in 1842 to 306 at mid-century) or lower their comparably good wages (3.5 to 5 francs per day). However, the cost of the steam pumps, as well as of contraptions to control malodorous emissions at work sites, transformed the business. As for so many Parisian trades, the 1840s were a crucial decade for cesspool cleaning. The authors of the 1842 article in the *Annales d'hygiène publique* had obtained their information from a host of *maîtres vidangeurs*, who generally employed ten or twelve workers each and maintained a form of the apprentice system. By mid-century there were only six cesspool cleaning enterprises in all of Paris. In the *bâtiment* category of the *Statistique de l'industrie à Paris 1847–1848*, cesspool cleaning had both the most workers and the highest gross income per entrepreneur.[4] Concentration of the cesspool cleaning industry continued through the Second Empire and first decades of the Third Republic.

These changes did not affect the Old Regime characterization of cesspool cleaners as the dregs of society; however, the nineteenth century did witness the effacement of the competing late eighteenth-century description of cesspool cleaners in terms of inclusion, honor, and sympathy. The public harbored deep suspicions about cesspool cleaners' morality and ethics. After all, who would take up such work? A team of doctors had written in 1830: "The job of cesspool cleaner being among the most repulsive, and being done only at night, was left to unlettered men, those expelled from society, one could say, and all the more so because people fled their presence."[5] The authors of the 1842 article found it necessary to remark that cesspool cleaners were able to find wives.[6] The one-time manager of *L'Atelier*, Henri Leneveux, placed the job of cesspool cleaning at the bottom of the professional hierarchy in his *Manuel de l'apprentissage* (1855).[7] "In all fairness it has to be admitted that the intelligence of cesspool cleaners appears quite limited. This comes perhaps from the fact that since their salary is higher than for any other profession, they take advantage of this to drink prodigiously, which cannot help but have a fatal effect on their mental faculties."[8] When cesspool cleaners came to exchange *fosses mobiles* in the minority of dwellings with this system, it was a general practice to assign a servant to watch them. "It is all too clear that the Company which employs them was able to choose for such shady work neither M. Talleyrand nor Saint Vincent de Paul. One could not let them wander about alone in the house they were perfuming."[9]

Not surprisingly, projects for reform of cesspool cleaning were often expressed in terms of limiting the sensual affronts its practitioners offered the public. Thus Parent-Duchâtelet promoted *fosses mobiles* because they could be changed in a half hour "in full daylight by workers whose appearance is not at all repugnant."[10] The competing "Richer" pumps were put forward as a means of limiting yet other of the cesspool cleaners' attacks on the senses. While every innovation set out to reduce the odoriferous consequences of the job, Richer claimed to protect Parisians' ears as well. Many cesspool cleaners employed immense carts containing twenty-four or thirty-two *tinettes*. One disgruntled Parisian reported that the careless loading of these tubs sounded like musket volleys; the clanging carts created a noise like "the charge of the heavy cavalry or the passage of an artillery company" as they bumped along the cobblestone streets.[11] Richer touted his pump truck as a solution to this problem.[12]

Mechanical and financial developments like those which took place in cesspool cleaning in the nineteenth century are often associated with the implementation of new forms of labor discipline, but this was not the case in this business. Even the large companies, pressed to defend themselves against Second Empire sanitary reformers, could give their employees only mixed ratings. Cesspool cleaners considered themselves engaged for only one night at a time. Aware of their scarcity, they demanded high wages and did as they pleased on the job. The firms praised the cesspool cleaners' industriousness—only twenty-one cesspool cleaners were on public relief in Paris in 1867 compared to forty-three sewermen—but argued that the companies could not be held responsible for these workers' actions on the job. (The record of infractions was serious; in less than eleven months in 1867 the largest cesspool cleaning company in Paris, the Compagnie Richer, was slapped with 1,666 citations.[13])

Criticism of cesspool cleaners abounded in the literature devoted to urban sanitation in the final decades of the century. In 1880, for instance, Paul Brouardel reiterated the old charge that since cesspool cleaners were paid for the number of cesspools emptied in a night, rather than for the volume of material removed, they were strongly tempted to pour the sewage into a nearby sewer rather than to cart it off to an authorized dumpsite. The police lacked the manpower to supervise the 130 to 150 cleanings done each night. (This *tout-à-l'égout sauvage* particularly offended Brouardel, opponent of the unitary sewer.) In any case, he continued, the cesspool cleaners apparently had a secret mutual fund to pay the small fine of five francs which this offense entailed.[14] The point was clear. When cesspool cleaners pooled their resources to assist one another, it was against the public good.

No doctor or scientist stepped forward in the nineteenth century to sympathize with the cesspool cleaners or praise their virtues. In their place one finds only Gustave Flaubert, who explained his craft in terms of cesspool cleaning: "*The artist must raise everything to a higher level*: he is like a pump; inside him is a great pipe reaching down into the bowels of things, the deepest layers. He sucks up what was pooled beneath the surface and brings it forth into the sunlight in giant sprays."[15] Flaubert celebrated the marginal, subversive element of the cesspool cleaners' job. He lashed out at the repressive bourgeois order of the Second Empire in a sketch for an ode on a cesspool cleaners' strike. The poem begins with a "Choeur des m——" in which the contents of barrels in basements complain that they are "disinfected": "We cannot smell ourselves any more. They torture us, they cover us like pralines." The ode concludes with a jibe at the classical pretensions of Second Empire Paris: an eruption of the cesspools covers the city "like Herculaneum under the lava."[16] Like the psychological novelist, cesspool cleaners perform often unappreciated, but necessary, revelatory and purgative functions in society. Flaubert's cesspool cleaners were not moral proletarians, but then Flaubert was no Parent-Duchâtelet.

Sewermen in the Public Eye before the Public Tour

Until the last third of the nineteenth century, a discourse of revulsion and fascination contested Parent-Duchâtelet's praises of the sewermen's virtues. Parisians felt they knew cesspool cleaners all too well. But the urbanites' ignorance of sewermen and their mysterious work underground generated slightly more ambivalent expressions of the disgust and suspicion shown cesspool cleaners. Only transformation of the sewers during the Second Empire firmly implanted new representations of sewermen in the public mind.

During the first half of the nineteenth century, the city of Paris contracted out municipal sanitation services, including sewer cleaning. Contractors supplied sewermen with tools and supervised them on the job, but the Prefecture of Police retained ultimate responsibility for work and working conditions.[17] After a jump in the numbers of sewermen in the years following Parent-Duchâtelet's reports, their total grew slowly from 72 in 1830–31 to 84 in 1842 and 90 in 1849.[18] Sewermen were less well paid than cesspool cleaners: workers earned 2F25 daily in 1842; the six or seven foremen took home 3F per day. After twenty years of service, a sewerman received an annual pension of 300F.[19] While cesspool cleaners considered themselves bound to their employer for only one night, the pension encouraged sewermen to think of their relation to the city-*patron* in more permanent terms.

Not surprisingly, the use of contractors created problems. Early in the century Bruneseau argued forcefully that the sewers could not be adequately maintained unless the city took the responsibility for cleaning them away from contractors.[20] Parent-Duchâtelet had done just this in personally overseeing work at the Amelot sewer. In the late 1830s the situation reached a nadir. The prefecture complained that the contractor had reduced the number of sewermen below the 72 set in 1830–31 and had adopted an "almost passive" role in sewer cleaning. Not only were the sewers a mess, remarked the prefecture, but the sewermen were overworked and their health was suffering[21]: the poor management of the sewer system could be read in the bodies of those who worked in it. As long as sewer cleaning was contracted out under the only sporadically vigilant eye of the Prefecture of Police—which felt itself to have more important responsibilities—Parisians were unlikely to see the sewers as an ordered world or sewermen as representatives of such a world.

The Prefecture of the Seine did not assume responsibility for cleaning the sewers from the Prefecture of Police until 1859, and the effects of the change were not visible to the public until tours began in 1867. Descriptions of sewermen penned before this date occasionally echo Parent-Duchâtelet's vision of sewermen as a special community outside of the bourgeois social order. Jules Janin, an avid reader of Parent-Duchâtelet, wrote of sewermen: "Chased from the great family which lives under the sky in the free, pure air, they have made for themselves a family in the sewer, and all the members of this family care for one another and look after one another's needs. They are in their own way great practical philosophers. Their domain is sad, it is true, but in it they are the kings."[22]

But outside those touched by Parent-Duchâtelet's account, sewermen were more often portrayed as a rough-and-tumble bunch, mirroring common perceptions of the sewers. In his widely read *Tableau de Paris* of 1853, Edmond Texier wrote, "As to the people who rule over this sub-urban city, undoubtedly it is best not to have frequent contact with their smelly rakes, their smoky lamps and their big boots."[23] The Goncourt brothers were harsher. For them, sewermen embodied the vile essence of the lower classes. In 1863 the pair went to a popular *bal*: "A man began to dance a prodigious can-can. There appeared to us, in this frenzied gymnastics, the types, the caricatures, the dreadful outlines of the crapulous movements, cartoons of sewermen *à la Daumier*, like the root of the ignoble traits of the people of the nineteenth century."[24]

Accompanying this visceral disgust was the general perception that sewermen experienced daily dangers those above ground could hardly imagine. This earned them some of the sympathy accorded cesspool cleaners in the eighteenth century. For Texier, "These obscure labyrinths have seen bloody catastrophes, terrible agonies."[25] In another journal entry for 1863, the Goncourts wrote: "I found myself on top of a coach, next to a sewerman, who was telling the coachman the perils of his profession, how many died each year, drowned in the sewers by storms, whose bodies were carried by the flow toward the Jardin des Plantes. One time, he had stayed hanging on for two hours. Just to think that men die in this way underground, in our society!"[26]

How, Texier wondered, could any salary compensate men for such work? "To spend whole days in these humid caverns, without light, without sun, and with no other air than the fetid emanation of the filth, to earn one's life stirring up the mire produced by a million people who move about above their heads, certainly the wages of those who devote themselves to such a profession are harshly earned."[27]

Emile de La Bédollière dared wonder whether the sewermen would not some day follow the example of workers above ground and rise up against those who paid them so poorly:

Are these wages proportional to the wear and tear, to the dangers? May we not one day learn that, tired of being so modestly paid, they are suddenly refusing to work? Good God, then what would happen to us? The Parisian bourgeois sees strikes of locksmiths, blacksmiths, wallpaper makers, printers, etc., without a great deal of concern. But imagine a strike of sewermen: the mire accumulates in the canals and threatens to escape to inundate Paris; filthy smells spread; the plague, typhus are going to fill the hospitals; the very life of the city is on the line; a deluge of mud is going to swallow it up.

The sewermen are, as you see, the masters of the underground city, the crowned heads of the kingdom of shadows. As such, they have a right to our respect; and if we ponder the usefulness of their job, we will reimburse them, by our esteem, for all its repulsiveness.[28]

La Bédollière's request that Janin's sad kingdom of sewermen be granted recognition took on new meaning when the social conflicts of the 1840s come to a head in the Revolution of 1848. For the literary critic Charles Augustin Sainte-Beuve, the brief emergence of sewermen into public life epitomized the demise of the monarchy and the proclamation of the republic in the world-turned-upside-down of the spring of 1848: "People were putting ridiculous inscriptions on banners. I saw one, carried in pomp by the sewer cleaners, on which read in big letters: *The Sewermen of Paris.*"[29]

Sewermen and Engineers

Nineteenth-century sanitary engineers developed an effective response to such representations of sewermen as sad sovereigns of the deep or emblems of popular disruption: in bettering the health of the city, an improved sewer system would better the sewerman. Already early in the July Monarchy, the engineer Emmery wrote that alterations in the sewer "had been able to remedy the pestilential factors, which for many years had been weighing on the unfortunate workers whose job it was to clean the sewers of Paris."[30] He was particularly proud of his policy of building all sewer mains large enough to allow sewermen to labor standing upright. Work, he argued, would be better done and better inspected if men did not have to hunch over with their nose in the mire. Any other policy, Emmery contended, was *inhumain* and *impolitique* (*barbare*, Bechmann would say later.)[31] Is it too much to see in such commentaries on the sewerman's posture the engineers' assertion of the civilizing potential of well-constructed sewers?[32]

In touting the merits of the Second Empire sewers, engineers went much further in constructing a new representation of the sewerman as an embodiment of the health, order, and civilization which modern technology could produce. The large diameter, slight incline, and multiple functions of the new Paris sewer system required a sizable labor force. This set it apart from sewer systems in other cities. The number of Paris sewermen grew to 276 in 1865 and to 627 in 1873.[33] By contrast, the narrow sewers of Frankfurt-am-Main, a city of 120,000 in 1882, required the services of only five sewermen.[34] (Marseille, Toulon, and at least one city in Italy provided the true antithesis to Parisian reliance on a large human labor force. These cities had such narrow sewer mains that small dogs were trained to drag a scrub brush from one "manhole" to the next![35])

For the engineers who built and operated the sewers of Paris, sewermen were to embody the best qualities of the new system. The engineers instituted rigorous medical screening for prospective workers. One wag wrote in 1873:

> What then is a sewerman?
> Everyday the passerby purposely avoids the sewerman. We close our eyes. We hold our nose. One must flee this worker who is always bent over pestilence, but for us a defense against it. He is covered with a dirty blouse; he has a leather cap on his head; he is outfitted in big boots, stained with filth. All that's enough not to get near him. Well, do you know who this man is you avoid with such care? An ideal of purity. Believe me, not just anyone can become a sewerman. Antinoüs, the most handsome of the ancients, might have been a sewerman, and even then it is not sure. You should know that no one becomes a sewerman without submitting to a most severe regimen. A jury examines the candidate. Not the hint of a hereditary ailment, no physical defect, no taint in the blood or skin. Very few of our contemporaries are able to offer an irreproachable appearance.
> So that one day Gratiolet said:
> "Three members of the Jockey-Club would not make one sewerman."
> Nothing is more exact than what I say here. From the point of view of the body, the sewerman is therefore the most perfect product of current civilization. Here is something to humble the pride of a lot of our fools. It also explains what a doctor in vogue told a big banker. The Croesus wanted a husband for his only daughter. Above all he wanted a son-in-law in good health, with rosy blood, appropriate for perpetuating his line.
> "Take a sewerman," the doctor responded.
> You can imagine. The banker got furious. A sewerman for son-in-law! Doesn't that come awfully close to impertinence or grossness?
> "Yes, a sewerman," the doctor repeated.

The money man did not understand. It is doubtful he understands even now.[36]

The engineers contended that sewermen would remain healthy, for work in the new sewers was no more deleterious than similar manual labor above ground. Parent-Duchâtelet had emphasized the fundamental innocuousness of the sewer's contents; the engineers who succeeded him argued that the characteristics of the sewers they had planned and built assured this. As a result of the constant circulation of air in the new sewers, the atmosphere in them varied little in temperature from that on the street. And it contained fewer microbes because these adhered to the humid sewer walls. With Parent-Duchâtelet, the engineers pointed to the long careers of selected sewermen and to sewermen's experiences during epidemics: their death rate from epidemic disease was the same or lower than that of the Parisian population as a whole.[37]

The public tour impressed upon visitors the good health of the sewermen. This image of the robust sewermen became a powerful agent in the dissemination of the idea of the sewer as a bulwark of salubrity. One visitor reported that the sewermen "are fine, stalwart-looking fellows, these toilers underground, and we are told that they are all men of perfectly healthy *physique*, as every man who applies for employment in these underground works is subjected to a rigorous medical examination, and is rejected upon the detection of the slightest infirmity or the least trace of lurking disease."[38] Another was told that it was "calculated from their days of sickness that no eight hundred men in Paris, taken from any class, enjoy, on the whole, so great a freedom from zymotic affections. By comparison they are as healthy a body of men in all respects as any in the community."[39] The public visits helped turn the idea of the sewerman's good health into a commonplace. The illustrative sentence for "sewerman" in the 1870 *Larousse* was, "One should note that sewermen generally enjoy good health."[40] For advocates of the sewers, no better evidence of their healthy nature could be offered than the condition of the men who spent their lives in them.

The engineers who constructed and operated the sewers during the Second Empire and the Third Republic sought to bring order to the sanitary system on which Parisian society depended. In Parent-Duchâtelet's day, the sewermen's job had been far less routinized than it would become during the 1860s. Second Empire engineers mechanized the flushing system and saw themselves developing a suitable labor force for such work—"numerous, supervised, ordered hierarchically," in Mille's words.[41] This new regularization of labor encouraged comparisons to the military very different from that of the cesspool cleaners' artillery of soil-tubs. Military metaphors came naturally to the engineers, descendants of the Saint-Simonians of the 1830s who had exalted the work of engineers and workers in "armies" of labor: "this legion of laborers constantly employed at flushing";[42] "this army of workers";[43] "a veritable of army of *twelve hundred* [sic] sewermen."[44] A sewer administrator at the turn of the century wrote of "an army of sewermen assuring perfect maintenance" of the sewers.[45] Parent-Duchâtelet's sewermen had transcended their work environment; the engineers' sewermen reflected theirs.

The sewer engineers succeeded in transmitting their military metaphor to the public. The tour left visitors with the impression that the army provided the model for order in the sewers: "three or four officials . . . issue to us their commands to advance, and we do advance accordingly . . . Now the process of marshaling the visitors in due order is begun . . . We dismount from our carriages at the word of command."[46] Observers of Parisian life had no trouble seeing the sewermen as "regimented."[47] Few could forego a military metaphor in describing them: "the army of labourers clad in white";[48] "the army of workmen" who cleansed the sewers.[49] "The personnel of the sewermen is now composed of a small army corps of 627 men divided into brigades," du Camp wrote in 1873. "Everyone knows them and has seen them pass in squadrons, brooms on their shoulders and big boots on their legs."[50] "La Chanson des égoutiers" from the turn-of-the-century musical *Léonard* made sewermen out to be *soldats civils* enrolled in a *régiment d'la gross'botte*.[51] Even a sewerman-songwriter of the period could not resist the association: sewermen were "worker-soldiers."[52]

The engineers' use of military metaphors marked their pride in the sewermen and their abilities, not a desperate effort to discipline through tropes. Like Parent-Duchâtelet, Belgrand recognized the importance of experimentation in the advancement of sewer technology; he pointed to the initiative of a sewerman named Louis in the development of the *wagon-vanne*.[53] Belgrand added that the key to good sewer maintenance was reliance on sewermen to report any deterioration they noted so that it could be repaired immediately.[54] Bechmann added that supervision of work in the sewers was necessarily imperfect, but that the service was able to depend on the good character of veteran workers and especially of the *chefs* promoted from their ranks (the descendants of Parent-Duchâtelet's Charpian) who led individual crews. As Bechmann wrote in 1899, "the job of flushing requires attentiveness and intelligence, and at the same time a perfect knowledge of the network. It is much preferable to entrust it to permanent workers, experienced and well-commanded, than to have it done by contractors." [55]

Healthy and disciplined, sewermen figured as model workers and public servants. One visitor referred to "the patient workmen who act as our canal-horses, and drag the boat along." [56] In the same vein as Parent-Duchâtelet, the photographer Nadar contrasted sewermen with their officious counterparts above ground: "One ought to remark on the irreproachable politeness of these workers resigned under our direction to the most humble labors and whose good behavior it would be useful sometimes to show to the officials, subaltern and superior, of our public administration." [57]

Sewermen were said to incarnate social order in other ways as well. Some saw in their apparent passivity and stoic nature a rebuke to the disintegration and confusion said to characterize contemporary society. Unlike the rowdy cesspool cleaner, the sewerman enjoyed a reputation for peaceful serenity. "I could not take my eyes off this man who, for so many years, attended every day the same performance and remained untouched by the tumult of the unruly flood." [58] The sewerman was "a philosopher," a journalist wrote in 1874, [59] but unlike the commonly depicted ragpicker-philosopher, he did not wander around muttering against society. For those who saw the hurly-burly of turn-of-the-century Paris as conducive to disease and degeneration, sewermen represented an alternative: "While . . . in our epileptic life we scurry about in pursuit of our business or our pleasures, the sewerman strolls along placidly night and day through the silent pathways of underground Paris." [60]

Nor did the army of sewerman play the part of subversives. Belgrand was credited with having used his influence to keep the sewermen calm and working during the traumatic events of 1870–71. [61] Various legends grew up about the sewermen's activities during this period. According to one report: "During the siege of Paris an armed guard was formed of the *égou-tiers*, who were obliged to be on the look-out lest the Prussian troops, making use of the entrances to these subterranean passages at Asnières, should attempt a rush into the very heart of Paris." [62] The Goncourt brothers told of a conservative woman, leader of the Société des Brassards in Paris during the Commune, who traveled daily to Versailles with the assistance of a sewerman. [63]

"The sewerman has been civilized along with the sewer; I found in him a man of the better world," wrote one of the first visitors to the new sewers. [64] The sewer engineers concurred. They were eager to spread the gospel that technology would improve not only urban sanitation, but also the material and moral conditions of the downtrodden.

modernization

Representations of Sewermen and the "Tout-à-l'égout"

Engineers and other partisans of the new sewers made the sewerman into an embodiment of the virtues of the sewer system. It is therefore not surprising that when these sanitary reformers promoted the *tout-à-l'égout*, they mobilized representations of unruly cesspool cleaners and healthy sewermen to make their case (nor that opponents of the *tout-à-l'égout* questioned elements of this comparison). The abolition of cesspools would bring not only the end of urban dumps, but of cesspool cleaners as well. French engineers agreed with Chadwick that this was not a negligible benefit of the replacement of cesspools with sewers: "it will force a change to other occupations of a less degrading character, and diminish the number of persons 'brought up' to them."[65]

In 1879, the *tout-à-l'égout* advocates conjured the by now familiar figure of the healthy sewerman to argue that the proposed change in the sewers would have no ill effects on Parisians' health. Thirteen thousand cesspools already emptied their liquid waste (unavoidably mixed with a fair amount of fecal matter) into the sewer system. Yet in comparison to the population as a whole, the sewermen of Paris seemed relatively immune to epidemic disease.[66] Why sewermen enjoyed such health was unclear. While one could find some arguing that the rotting matter in the sewers gave off vapors which destroyed noxious germs,[67] the most ardent proponents of the *tout-à-l'égout* denied that anything stayed in the sewers long enough to decay.

Critics of the *tout-à-l'égout*, led by Brouardel, were quick to challenge the engineers' position. No friend of cesspool cleaners, he refused the engineers' efforts to make opposition to the *tout-à-l'égout* equivalent to support for these outcasts. But he also questioned the relevance and reliability of statistics about sewermen's health in settling the debate over the *tout-à-l'égout*. Sewermen were not typical of the population; they were screened before being hired. Furthermore, whatever their geographic origins, long-time sewermen resembled Parisian natives in that they were less susceptible to epidemic diseases like typhoid fever because they were more likely to have been exposed to them in the past than was the Parisian population as a whole, which included many recent arrivals to the capital. Likewise, the statistics were suspect because they depended on workers' memories and encompassed only currently employed sewermen, ignoring those who had left the trade after a brief period. Brouardel concluded that even if one granted that sewermen enjoyed good health, it could be simply because the noxious odors produced in the sewers escaped through sewer vents into the atmosphere, where they threatened the populace as a whole. In this instance, what benefited the sewermen presented a menace to the city.[68]

Opponents of the *tout-à-l'égout* found sewermen too complicated a text in which to read the effects of the proposed system on the population. They preferred to revive the eighteenth-century tradition of experiments in which animals in sealed containers were poisoned by their own breath. In their most celebrated demonstration, a dog was closed up in a cage with a pile of human feces. As anticipated, the dog died before its oxygen ran out. An irritated Durand-Claye responded that the dog had succumbed because the sewage had fermented. This would not happen in the sewers where fresh air circulated constantly and the diluted sewage passed through the system before it had a chance to rot. He carried out the same experiment with fresh, diluted human sewage and reported that the dog emerged from the experience in fine condition. This, he explained, was not surprising, since sewermen toiled daily in these conditions. He pointed to two sewermen who had worked each day for months in a part of the sewers where the sewer water contained the runoff from human wastes at a proportion of one part per hundred. These workers were perfectly healthy. And to answer the objection that such workers might have recuperated during their stay above ground each night, he chained a dog to the spot for 132 straight hours. The dog survived this ordeal with no ill effects.[69]

Yet as pro-*tout-à-l'égout* forces marshaled evidence on the salubrity of the sewers, they were forced to recognize that sewermen were not the paragons of health they were often made out to be. Of the 850 sewermen at work in the years between 1882 and 1885, three contracted smallpox, three got cholera, and twenty-eight came down with typhoid fever. However, the sewermen usually recovered from these diseases; only one died of cholera and four of typhoid fever. The real bane of the sewerman's life was not water-borne disease, but the respiratory ills endemic to lower-class urban dwellers during the period.[70] While there was only one case of typhoid fever among sewermen in 1889, there were 279 cases of respiratory disease. The danger of contracting tuberculosis was very high. Between 1882 and 1885, twenty-five sewermen died of *maladies de poitrine*.[71] While debate over the health of sewermen cast doubt on the dire predictions of opponents of the *tout-à-l'égout*, it also forced a revision of the most optimistic portraits of the sewermen's health.

The mobilization of competing representations of sewermen during the *tout-à-l'égout* campaign is illustrative of a general development in the field of occupational health. Attention is drawn to a group of workers because specialists and the public see in their bodies an affirmation or denial of claims made about a potential threat to the health of the citizenry at large.[72] In the eighteenth century, cesspool cleaners' work in a mephitic environment attracted interest for this reason; in the United States today men and women in the nuclear power industry serve the same function in discussions of public health.[73]

With the construction of the Second Empire sewer system and the introduction of public tours, the characteristic representations of cesspool cleaners and sewermen diverged radically. Cesspool cleaners were impossible to ignore. They spent much of their working time above ground, but under the cloak of darkness—heard and smelled more often than seen. They worked for large, highly profitable firms, but were poorly supervised. Mercier had excused the alcoholic excesses of cesspool cleaners as necessary to allow them to face their dangerous and disgusting job, but nineteenth-century observers attributed their crapulence to the explosive combination of low character and high wages. The work seemingly necessitated a rowdy, uncontrollable labor force. For this reason, it could never be held to the standards of modern hygienic practice.

Between publication of Parent-Duchâtelet's essays and the opening of the sewers to tourists at the end of the Second Empire, sewermen were depicted as questionable figures. But in succeeding decades, sewermen seemed to acquire the traits of the new orderly, disciplined sewer system. The engineers' descriptions and the impressions gleaned during the public visit fostered an image of sewermen as a sanitary army of labor.

In the second half of the nineteenth century, cesspool cleaners came to embody the raucous, carnivalesque side of labor; sewermen became exemplars of labor's sober, civilizing mission.[74] In this context, engineers saw adoption of the *tout-à-l'égout* as more than just a technical decision; it represented a choice about the nature and meaning of labor in a future society. As such, it participated in a tradition of critical thought that discussed and evaluated society with reference to those who worked outside the mainstream—or, in this case, in an often overlooked mainstream.

• 9 •

The World Turned Upside Down

I feel this deeply. All Frenchmen are the same: engineers and street-cleaners.

—Valéry Giscard d'Estaing, quoted in *Le Nouvel Observateur*,
2 December 1974

CESSPOOL cleaners and sewermen emerged as potent signifiers for a few impertinent painters of modern life. Bringing the worlds of the cesspool and the sewer into contact with the world above elicited hidden meanings and possibilities in society. This was particularly true of radical social critics who eschewed the dichotomization of cesspool cleaners and sewermen elaborated in nineteenth-century bourgeois discourses of urban propriety. Their stock in trade was the exposé of the unacknowledged labor of all workers which underlay the social order. But perhaps the most subversive moment in their writings came when contemplation of the "degraded" labor of cesspool cleaners, sewermen, and the like challenged the normative categories through which a society understood and ordered itself.

In some social theories, the transformation of society requires the radical critique of gender relations; in others, the redistribution of political power and the products of labor. From the Renaissance through the triumphs of sanitary engineering in the nineteenth and twentieth centuries, a component of many conceptions of social change has been a revalorization of waste removal. Before work in the sewers became a clearly delineated trade, the purifying aspects of such labor were often thought to flush immorality from the criminals or saints engaged in it even as they cleansed society. Later social critics argued that the extent of a society's break with Old Regime traditions of servitude could be evaluated in terms of the treatment of those whose job it was to clean up after others.[1]

Sewermen and Social Transformation

In ancient Rome cleansing the sewers had been physically punishing and shameful labor.[2] Utopian literature of the early modern era reiterated this theme, but reinterpreted it in terms of the morally uplifting character of degrading work done for the common good. Natalie Zemon Davis, drawing on Sir Thomas More's experience on the London sewer commission, reads his comments in *Utopia* on hard labor in public works to mean that able-bodied beggars would be reformed by being set to work at jobs like flushing the sewers.[3]

At the end of the eighteenth century, a number of French social reformers developed the utilitarian aspects of this idea in some detail. The Abbé Bertholon, A. Tournon, P. Chauvet, and A. L. Lavoisier among others suggested refuse collection as useful employment for beggars and the poor.[4] For his part, Mathieu Géraud believed that not just the disposal of human waste (as fuel and fertilizer), but its collection as well could be turned to society's advantage. Criminals, he wrote, were now housed at great expense in prisons. With nothing to do, prisoners grew weak and unsuited to earn a living on their release. First-time offenders were corrupted by their association with hardened felons. All these problems would be remedied, he continued, if prisoners were made to labor at public works, and in particular "the most disgusting and the most dangerous," like cleaning out cesspools and sewers. The system would be so economical that it would allow fixed cesspools to be done away with; prisoners would remove portable ones every two days and replace them with clean ones. To prevent escapes, prisoners would wear a ball and chain and a special numbered uniform. Their prison sentences would be shortened or extended depending on their zeal at work. Géraud touted the advantages of his proposal: it would cost little to keep the city clean and free of miasmas since it was less expensive to feed two or three men than one beast of burden; prisoners would be reformed by the discipline of labor; citizens tempted by crime would be chastened by the sight of convicts performing tasks like emptying cesspools and cleaning sewers. He even argued that the presence of large numbers of prisoners performing jobs like exchanging cesspools would make the city more secure at night.[5]

Another reading of More's *Utopia* suggests that the saintly figures devoted to good works (not the beggars) were the ones that flushed the sewers in Utopia.[6] Mercier, sympathetic to the cesspool cleaners of his own day, incorporated this conception of the sanitary laborer as saint in his utopian *L'An 2440*. In this society, those who sought to achieve perfection did not lead a veiled, solitary life of prayer, but gave themselves over to a life serving the public interest: "they voluntarily assumed all the tasks which were difficult or which disgusted everyone else . . . Whether it was a matter, for example, of cleaning the sewers or cesspools, of transporting the filth, of subjecting themselves to the most demeaning, base and dangerous jobs . . . these generous victims of the public good carried them out."[7] In Géraud's and Mercier's asides to the reader, the late eighteenth-century valorization of sanitary labor was raised to a principle of individual penitentiary purging and spiritual purification.

In the nineteenth century, socialist analyses of sanitary labor turned from the individual to the explicitly social. Discussions of filth, miasmas, epidemics, and revolution buttressed the bourgeoisie's visceral disgust for the "great unwashed." French socialists confronted this aspect of class relations as well as the more conventional economic elements. Rather than asserting the moral uplift of degraded labor, they asked why society considered certain types of work undesirable and how the transformation of society might change the conception of such work in the future.

For Charles Fourier, waste disposal would offer no problems in the utopian community of Harmony. There labor would assume its true character as self-fulfillment rather than self-mortification or enslavement. In Harmony, sanitary labor would be a means for certain individuals to satisfy their inner desires and passions. Fourier placed particular reliance on the "Little Hordes," recruited from among the two-thirds of boys aged nine to fifteen and the one-third of girls that age who liked nothing better than to muck about in filth and excrement. Fourier integrated late eighteenth-century notions of the utility and honor of cesspool cleaners into a new world of sensual gratification:

> These unruly children would be venerated by the community as "guardians of social honor" and (because they would refuse to accept pay) exemplars of "the spirit of self-abnegation recommended by Christianity." [The children would cost society nothing since they would be paid in *fumées de gloire* (a pun on *fumier*).[8]] They would have their own private language or slang, their own uniforms (in the "grotesque or barbarian style"), and their own leaders, called Little Khans and Little Khantes. They would be aided by acolytes called Bonzes and Druides—older people who had never outgrown the love of filth and who would accompany them on their missions.[9]

Fourier's Little Hordes displaced the representation of the uninhibited nature of cesspool cleaners onto the naturally uncivilized exuberance of youth. (It is significant that Khans, Bonzes, and Druides evoke "primitive" societies.) Freed from the civilized world in which people's repression of their bodily functions translated into disdain for those who carried out analogous social functions, youthful waste removers would become a natural, essential part of society, like youth itself. They would shed their antisocial character and receive the accolades of society.

Socialists recognized that the very different bourgeois speculations

master/servant

about waste removal in socialist society were intended to denigrate the goal of a truly egalitarian future. On close examination, however, these dire predictions simply revealed the tenacity with which the bourgeoisie fought to maintain the most basic and basest essence of the master/servant relationship in a regime of putative equality. In "Le Communisme, avenir de la société" (1869–70), the socialist revolutionary Auguste Blanqui— the man Tocqueville had portrayed as a sewer dweller—railed against capitalist ideologues who demanded that he give detailed responses to all the problems which they imagined might arise in a communist society. Blanqui focused on the one question which seemed to concern the bourgeois the most: "Who will clean the chamber pots and see to the cesspool tubs [*tinettes*]?" Would communism liberate the already far too unrestrained cesspool cleaners? For Blanqui, such queries exposed the bourgeoisie's unwillingness to imagine a world ordered differently than the one in which they lived. "As for me, if they were to start in again at my grave on this question of the chamber pots, I would tell them plainly: 'When you don't know how to hold your nose, you hold your rear'." The vile egotism of the bourgeoisie stood unmasked: "It's an amusing thing, when one discusses communism, how the adversary's terrors instinctively bring them to this inevitable piece of furniture! 'Who will empty the chamber pot?' It is always the first cry. 'Who will empty *my* chamber pot?,' they really mean to say."[10]

The accusation that the bourgeoisie had mapped the compulsion of its anality on to the social order did not die with Blanqui. The turn-of-the-century socialist leader Jean Jaurès used the same example in his essay "Organisation socialiste" (1895–96) when describing the socialist *Etat industriel* which would succeed capitalism. This new state would not be a bloated bureaucracy which assigned people occupations.

> If a certain job is forsaken because it is either too tiring or too repugnant, [the Etat industriel] would raise the remuneration. Those who, in Blanqui's energetic expression, wish to know who will empty the chamber pots in the new society, are really hung up on very little. "Who will clean the sewers? Who will wash the dishes?" It really seems that if capitalism is not maintained, all human functions, including the digestive functions, will be suspended. What foolishness! and what misunderstanding of the way societies work! It is nowhere proven that such and such a function—cleaning the cesspools or washing the dishes (these are the bugbears of capitalism)—must be exactly disagreeable to any given individual. Nature, in its power and its variety, does not know these repugnances or these nervous timidities; it makes the flowers with dung, joy with excrement. It is no more pleasant to empty a human ulcer, which is like an excremental cesspool of the organism than to empty a

tinette; doctors are also sewermen, and surgeons are butchers, and the red nose of the gravedigger no longer knows the smell of the dead. Isn't there enough fantasy in man for all jobs? There are assuredly ragpickers by vocation.[11]

Jaurès' breathless embellishment on Blanqui's text melds Blanqui's call for an end to the capitalist caste system and Fourier's faith that all jobs fulfill the desires of certain individuals. When the world of excrement and filth erupts into Jaurès' discussion, the rational administrative order of his state (and the text itself, which seeks to exemplify this order) is disrupted. Discussion of emptying cesspools and flushing sewers becomes Jaurès' opportunity for touting the freedom which would characterize socialist society. For almost the only time in "Organisation socialiste" Jaurès finds himself truly at odds with bourgeois culture, equating sewerman with doctor and calling on the "fantasy" in man.

Sharp-eyed critics of the future socialist state noted that the most concrete suggestion socialists (including Jaurès) made when confronted with the problem a socialist society would have finding people to do jobs like cleansing the sewers was to rely on the market mechanism of better wages. For the anarchist Prince Peter Kropotkin, this question of the sewerman's pay after the revolution was a collectivist chestnut, which revealed the socialists' inability to break completely with the mechanisms of capitalism. Some socialists, Kropotkin remarked, said that all would be paid equally in a socialist society. "Some make a greater concession; they admit that disagreeable or unhealthy work—such as sewerage—could be paid for at a higher rate than agreeable work. One hour's work of a sewerman would be worth, they say, two hours of a professor's work."[12] Such a system would invert the economic relationship of sewermen and professors, but leave in place the social distinction between manual and mental labor.

The growing distance between manual and mental labor was a major concern of socialists in the first decades of the twentieth century. They saw technological change and managerial intrusion in the workplace destroying skilled workers' ability to take pleasure or pride in their craft. Writing at the end of World War I, the popular socialist author Pierre Hamp argued that mechanization and Taylorization were turning skilled craftsmen into laborers. As the joy and self-esteem they derived from work itself decreased, society would need to compensate these workers by bestowing more honor and recognition on their unappealing but socially beneficial labor. Workers would have to replace pride in their craft with pride in the social utility of their labor.

For Hamp, sewermen and streetcleaners were emblematic of the future of the working class. While their work was unquestionably useful, Hamp could not imagine that they had ever found fulfillment in the *tour de main* their jobs required. Although sanitation workers were largely unaffected by rationalization and loss of skill, the primitive, degraded nature of their labor made them the forerunners of all workers who were. A radical inversion in society's valuation of their work was the necessary prelude to a general revalorization of manual labor.

epitome of "worker"

> At a time when all crafts are losing their old reasons for being loved, the idea of nobility based on their social necessity should grow. Society itself opposes this by its disdainful prejudices against men's labor. It has contempt for what saves it and cherishes individuals according to the importance of their inutility. It is not only the psychology of the worker at his labor which must be changed, but that of society towards labor . . . For the craft to regret no longer that the work it does has ceased to be likable and to be satisfied that it is useful, social esteem must be in proportion to this usefulness. There is not as much consideration for the sweating servants of the collectivity as for the well-groomed servants of individuals. The well-groomed valet is less scorned than the street sweeper. To salute labor, we must esteem streetcleaning as we esteem the magistracy. We must decorate the man of the latrines and make it an honor to be the manual servant of the collectivity.[13]

> There have always been jobs difficult to like and which must still experience disdain. The less joy which is possible in a job, the more there grows social disdain against this thankless labor. Cleaning the streets, emptying cesspools, flushing the sewers are all trades indispensable to the public health. Does society have great esteem for the men who do these jobs? . . . Without the men who work in the collective filth, urban areas would rot away in dung and epidemics. In what disrepute are held these jobs in which love of labor not being possible, the honor of the function must take its place? The preeminence of jobs remains established not on their social utility, but on their cleanliness. The doctor is an esteemed man and the sewerman disdained, yet the urban dweller will die if the sewer is poorly cleaned just as surely as if the doctor is not diligent.[14]

Cesspool cleaners and sewermen rarely surfaced in the literature of social analysis. When they did break through, however, their untoward appearance challenged the hierarchies of social thought and the mechanisms of social differentiation. Consideration of waste workers offered social critics a potent means of assessing the value of labor and the values of society. For More, Géraud, and Mercier, jobs like cleaning sewers were the road to social order and moral perfection. Prisoners who performed these tasks would better themselves and society. Free men who did them merited the honors their societies accorded saints. For the nineteenth-century revolutionary Blanqui and the twentieth-century reformer Hamp, disdain for useful occupations like waste removal revealed the inherent moral corruption and social disfunction of the bourgeois order. Social transformation would necessarily involve a reordering of social status through a reallocation of honor and esteem as well as wages. Blanqui believed that only revolution could bring this about; Hamp argued that the ongoing transformation of the workplace required it. Fourier also proposed that society honor those who assured its cleanliness, but offered a more radical resolution of the problem of "degraded" labor. Instead of limiting himself to the idea that a future society would be structured morally and materially so as to do away with the servile and "untouchable" status of those performing even the most disagreeable tasks, Fourier questioned the essential distastefulness of any job, including waste removal. The designation of jobs as desirable and undesirable was itself a social construction which repressed the diversity of human desires.

social construction

The Madwoman of Chaillot

As figures in works of social commentary, sewermen were usually passive. Their occupation, not their actions, elicited subversive reflections. A subtle shift occurred during the first half of the twentieth century, at a time when the sewermen's union was a presence in Parisian life. The sewermen who made an occasional appearance in the literature of this period did so as social actors as well as social metaphors. Sometimes sewermen were the *vox populi*[15]; at other times they were the agents of a disquieting revolution of the marginalized and dispossessed, more disturbing than the muscular proletarians of May Day posters. Sewermen had a liminal status, recalling bygone trades, evoking contemporary workers' struggles, and incarnating avatars of an uncertain future.

20TH C.

The narrator in Jules Romains' *La Douceur de la vie* (1939) remarks, "It seems to be the turn of the plumbers, the sewermen (the former enriched by the war, the latter raised to power by the revolution), and a handful of drop-outs from the 'intelligentsia'."[16] Jacques Prévert recorded the advent of "the time of sewermen" in his 1936 dirge, "Le Temps des noyaux":

> fermez vos paupières
> le marchand de gadoue va vous emporter
> c'est fini les trois mousquetaires
> voici le temps des égoutiers.[17]

Elsewhere Prévert celebrated the *égoutier* as an embodiment of the proletarian essence. In his 1936 "La Crosse en l'air," the *camarades égoutiers* figure alongside such groups as *camarades pêcheurs de Douarnenez, camarades vidangeurs*, and *camarades mineurs d'Oviedo*.[18] And in "Salut à l'oiseau," he elaborated on the theme that birds of a feather struggle together, placing the *oiseau des égoutiers* in a flock with the *oiseau des charbonniers et des chiffonniers*, the *oiseau des casquettiers de la rue des Rosiers*, the *oiseau des prolétaires*, and the *oiseau du Premier mai*, among others.[19]

In *The Madwoman of Chaillot*, Jean Giraudoux went beyond these fragmentary evocations to create the figure of a sewerman who helps save Paris from speculators. As a personification of the world below, the Sewerman in Giraudoux's play is particularly suited to help right the world above. The play, written in 1942, but first produced posthumously after the war in 1945, tells how the Madwoman of Chaillot with the aid of two other madwomen, a sewerman, and a ragpicker, foils the efforts of a band of wily financiers, publicity men, get-rich-quick artists, politicians, and good-time girls who would destroy Paris in order to exploit the oil they believe lies beneath the city.[20]

The Madwoman of Chaillot has been interpreted in light of Giraudoux's writings of the 1930s, about the ways the "two hundred families," foreigners, and urban planners threatened his vision of France.[21] Critics have variously identified the speculators as cosmopolitan capitalists, wartime black marketeers, and German occupying forces. All agree, however, that the Madwoman and her friends represent for Giraudoux the true spirit of Paris and the essence of *la France profonde*.

The Paris underground in *The Madwoman of Chaillot*, like that in *Les Misérables*, is the site of the *nappes spirituelles* of the Parisian past.[22] The real threat, of course, is that the speculators will tap and drain this irreplaceable deposit. At the same time, the underground, like the sewer, functions as a place that renders harmless threats to the life of the city. When a young man whom the speculators have coerced to blow up the Eiffel Tower decides not to do it, he drops the bomb down a gutter.[23]

In the central action of the play, the Madwoman lures the speculators to her basement where the Sewerman has opened a passageway to a nether world (not necessarily the sewers) one can enter, but not exit. The speculators and their retinue rush in, convinced that the stairs lead to the oil deposit. They are thus disposed of, like the bomb intended for the Eiffel Tower. If the audience's primary identification of the mysterious passageway is with the slippery slope to Hell, it is not hard to see that the sewer itself—a repository of black organic liquid—is a fool's version of an oil field under Paris.

In the banter between the Madwoman and the Sewerman, Giraudoux allows free rein to Parisians' fantasies about the world of the sewer. Young children offer parents their feces. Even the most patient parents tire of such gifts, however, and socialize their children to deposit their wastes in the anonymity of the toilet. This anonymity has grown over the centuries, as chamber pots have given way to cesspools and finally to the *tout-à-l'égout*. The Madwoman joins the repressed infantile desire to offer feces as a present to the socialized repression of individual excretory functions, when she asks the Sewerman if he has received the flowers she sent his way.[24]

> Mister Sewerman, in your opinion how many Parisians have a troubled conscience? It is in your realm that they throw all the parings and all the detritus of their lives. Not me. Of all the filthy things which wash through your sewers, I am not responsible for a single one. I burn my nail clippings, I spread the ashes. Never will you find me throwing into one of your manholes, as I surprised a *conseiller d'Etat* doing, an ignoble piece of paper and its unspeakable contents. I throw nothing but my flowers, and not even faded ones. If you saw an arum floating on the waters of your gallery, I have strong reason to believe that it is mine. I don't think that there is any reason to be prouder when one does one's filth under oneself than when one does it at one's own level, and I have always arranged, as far as I am concerned, so that the sewers are clean and fragrant. If it isn't noticeable, too bad![25]

The Sewerman replies graciously that of course he notices objects like toothbrushes and popular novels "which can be thrown down only with us in mind.[26]" If there is an echo of *Les Misérables* in the Madwoman's talk of the sewer as a place where people deposit the evidence of their wrongdoing and the by-products of their wasted lives, the emphasis in her speech is on the individual fantasy that one can make an offering of feces without admitting that one has done so. And, of course, in dropping flowers in the sewer the Madwoman seemingly alludes to the use of sewage as fertilizer for the cultivation of plants.

Myths about the world of the sewers had resonance for the Madwoman and for Parisian theater-goers because they were in harmony with the mysterious world illuminated by "fairy lights" which visitors to the Parisian sewers experienced. In an early version of the play, the Madwoman evokes a tour of the sewers: "The whole grotto is covered in shimmering blue lights. One visits in a boat, without speaking. The guide coughs on purpose and all go out. Then they light up again little by little."[27]

Before addressing the question of how the Sewerman can help her rid Paris of the nefarious oil prospectors, the Madwoman insists on satisfying her curiosity about whether or not the sewermen have a king. The Sewerman replies:

> O Countess, this is another one of the municipal road-menders' stories. They don't know how to do anything except make up stories about us sewermen.

> Because they see us move about underground, they envy us. The stories they
> will tell you! They say that there is a race of girls who never come above
> ground and are reserved for the sewermen. This is completely untrue; they
> come up every month. And the orgies in the gondolas. And the rats which
> follow the piper! And the sewers which experience the effects of the setting
> and rising of the sun and which take on color in the morning and the eve-
> ning![28]

The Sewerman, otherwise reticent in his conversation with the Madwoman, warms to this topic. She cannot get him off of it.

> As to the street sweepers' slander, that we have our swimming races in the
> sewers . . . Maybe in the summer, during the dog-days . . . [29]
>
> Countess, it is like that story of the Grenelle laundry, which we are supposed
> to have set up . . . [30]

Such stories, the Sewerman tells the Madwoman, are made up by outsiders. It stands to reason that groups like street sweepers who daily send large
amounts of water and refuse into the sewers would be prone to composing
stories about what happened in them. In his eagerness to refute such accounts, however, the Sewerman confirms them: the sewermen's community of young women come up each month as if on a menstrual cycle.
(Gaston Leroux had made the community of women living in the catacombs the centerpiece of his popular turn-of-the-century novel *La Double
Vie de Théophraste Longuet*.[31]) The Second Empire miracle of clean, efficient sewers which princes and princesses could visit without discomfort
had lifted sewers out of the nightmare world of uncontrollable epidemics
and riots. The sewers in *The Madwoman of Chaillot* completed this transformation: the nightmarish visions of Thanatos gave way to a world of wonder in which Eros held sway.

Above all, the Sewerman is eager to refute the idea that his *corporation* is
ruled by a king (or a queen). He can only explain the stories about the sun
rising and setting in the sewers by saying that the sewermen shoot off fire-
works on Bastille Day and a rocket probably escaped from an open manhole: "No . . . We are more a democracy, an aristocracy, an oligarchy, as
they say. If we celebrate Bastille Day it is because we don't have a king."[32]

The political battle in *The Madwoman of Chaillot* is not over the legitimacy of kings, however, but over an illegitimate *conspiration* of Croesuses.
The play offers a twist on the cast of characters common to French political
thought in the 1930s. The enemies—get-rich-quick men and their reti-
nues—were shared by the left and the right, but the defenders of France in
The Madwoman of Chaillot were to be found on neither side. For the left,
the proletariat would lead the lower classes into battle; for the right, this

role would be played by the middle class in alliance with small property-holders. Giraudoux upsets these class-based analyses of French society by pitting *marginaux* against speculators.

Giraudoux placed the task of defending France in the hands of mad-women, a ragpicker, and a sewerman. The psychologically and economically excluded are best able to exploit the rapaciousness of the flim-flam men who threaten Paris. And as for cleaning up the filth which threatens Paris, who is better qualified than the Sewerman and the Ragpicker? The Sewerman plays a special role in *The Madwoman of Chaillot*, for he embodies the link between marginality and the working class as it is traditionally defined. (The Madwoman provides an analogous—and appropriately ten-uous—tie to the middle class.) Giraudoux's Sewerman is a proletarian, but works in a magical environment. Not feeling oppressed or alienated as is the factory proletarian, the Sewerman can converse with the Madwoman and draw on the secrets of his trade to assist her. Far from being degraded by his work, he has special powers. The company president and his immoral crew who enter the passageway are doomed; only the Sewerman has been able to descend the stairs and return alive.

Haussmann's rebuilding of Paris above and below ground ended in politically embarrassing financial scandals: the infamous "comptes d'Haussmann." Writing in the mid-twentieth century, Giraudoux resurrected the sewerman as a magical figure who could help cleanse Paris of a crass cabal of the wealthy. The city was no longer threatened by offal; the danger came now from the oxymoron of decadent developers. Giraudoux's Sewerman inverts the Haussmannization of Paris, destroying the band of speculators and hangers-on to which it had long ago given birth.

Giraudoux's Sewerman questions the typologies of sewermen found in the literatures of sanitary reform and social criticism. His moral behavior is not the expression of a natural order, but of a supernatural one. And while Giraudoux's portrayal, like those of Jaurès and Hamp, embodies a critique of the existing social order, it is not an argument for a more com-munitarian, egalitarian society. After all, it is because the Sewerman is an outsider that he has access to the secret knowledge he uses to save the city. In a society in which rational thought legitimates speculators, the purity necessary to ward them off can come only from a world set apart—the world of the mad, the female, the ragpicker, and the sewerman.

Celebration of the revealing and redemptive marginality of those who handled waste did not end with *The Madwoman of Chaillot*. However, the focus of such attention shifted away from sewermen. Alain Geismar, a stu-dent leader in May 1968, probably remembering tales of the Resistance, thought of calling on the sewermen's union to help him and his comrades escape during *la nuit des barricades*.[33] For *gauchistes* like Geismar, however, the sewermen of Paris no longer embodied the revolutionary possibilities of the marginal: they had job security and followed the dictates of the "reactionary" Confédération Générale du Travail.

Giraudoux had made the Sewerman one incarnation of the French spirit which required protection against the invasion of alien forces—not only the speculators of *The Madwomen of Chaillot*, but also the foreign workers he had described in such savage fashion in the 1930s. *Gauchistes* turned Giraudoux's cult of the Gallic on its head. Like him, they celebrated the symbolic power of socially marginal waste handlers to reveal the true nature of society. However, the standard bearers in the *gauchistes'* revolutionary scenario were not French ragpickers or sewermen, but immigrant sanitation workers.[34]

The absence of even a single non-Frenchman among the sewermen of Paris made them a corporate anomaly in the 1960s and 1970s, as more and more North Africans and Black Africans became street sweepers and garbage men. The C.G.T. saw the large presence of foreigners in these jobs as the city's way to undercut labor benefits won in the past and to facilitate privatization of urban sanitation.[35] Yet these foreigners also emerged as figures of enormous symbolic value to *gauchistes*, stymied in their efforts to establish a foothold in the native French working class. Ho Chi Minh, they believed, had once been a sweeper in the Paris *métro* and had gone on to sweep France out of Indochina.[36] *Gauchistes* interpreted the employment of African streetcleaners as a sign of France's continued colonialist mentality: "In effect, the racist prejudices inherited from the French colonialist ideology created the conditions which oriented this labor force toward the least desirable jobs, in particular trash and maintenance jobs, dirty and degrading, which public opinion, imbued with the myth of the primitiveness and the mental backwardness of Black Africa, is led to consider as quite good enough for it."[37]

Gauchistes strongly supported the strikes of garbage collectors and streetcleaners in Paris in December 1972 to demand better wages and working conditions and the same benefits for immigrant and French workers.[38] A team of *gauchiste* sociologists explained that the staging of the strike was a turning point in their thinking about the nature of the relationship between the French and immigrant labor. The government *représentation* of this conflict was disrupted by the entrance

on stage of an essential actor whom we have something of a tendency to forget: the excrements of the city. Everything then happened as if the "citizens" addressed the authorities: "Monsieur le Préfet, don't wait any longer to rid us of our garbage" and at the same time "make those people whom we could not see return again to social invisibility."[39]

Immigrants = Shit. We understand better now why it is necessary to hide them. But when the trash rises to the surface, public opinion finds itself "nose to nose" with its own feces . . . [40]

If the authorities had wanted to turn the public against the striking sanitation workers, they were foiled by Parisians' desire to repress encounters with their refuse and its social analogue, the immigrant worker. In their analyses, the *gauchistes* were faithful to a long tradition in social thought which made treatment of those who disposed of waste a crucial point of access to the fundamental nature of the society in which they lived.

The Sewermen and Their Union

In the Public Service

"You see sir, many of such like mechanics can't live above ground, so they tries to get their bread underneath it."
    —Henry Mayhew, *London Labour and the London Poor*

Qui s'y frotte, s'y pique.
    —Motto of the Paris Sewermen's Union at the turn of the century

DID THE flood of new hires during and after the Second Empire dilute the special quality Parent-Duchâtelet discerned in sewermen that made them a unique underground fraternity? For sociologists the question is familiar: can group solidarities characteristic of a community of twenty-four individuals manifest themselves in a population thirty or forty times as large? In a discussion of a public service like the sewers, this question suggests another. Should public service workers be permitted to foster such solidarities in organizations dedicated to furthering their own interests? Put more bluntly, would unionized sewermen betray the engineers' vision of an army of labor and pose a new threat to the social order?

Who Worked in the Sewers?

By the Second Empire engineers had taken responsibility for the cleaning and maintenance of the sewers away from contractors, although elements of the former system remained in the areas of labor recruitment and management. In the late 1870s there was one crew leader or foreman for every eleven or twelve sewermen[1]; he was in charge of hiring and supervision. Like subcontractors in all trades, these individuals were accused of favoritism and of making their men take meals and lodgings at their cronies' establishments.[2] The city divided sewermen into two categories. *Commissionnés* were guaranteed work each day; *auxiliaires* worked when needed. *Commissionnés* were drawn from the pool of *auxiliaires*. In 1878, there were 183 *commissionnés* and 364 *auxiliaires;* the following year there were 250 *commissionnés* and 330 *auxiliaires*.[3]

The municipal council's concern over the mysterious *odeurs de Paris* in the summer of 1880 and its commitment to the *tout-à-l'égout* project led it to almost double the credits for sewer cleaning between 1881 and 1884.[4] This allowed for a rapid increase in the number of sewermen, to 800 in 1882 and 900 in 1884–85.[5] This labor force was quite heterogeneous in terms of geographical origin, age at hiring, and job security.

When du Camp visited the sewers at the end of the Second Empire, he was told that Parisian workers shunned employment in them. Most sewermen were recent Gascon migrants. Very few lasted as long as fifteen years on the job.[6] Information gleaned from obituaries and other biographical pieces in *Le Réveil de l'Assainissement*, the union newspaper, sheds some light on the origins of men who went to work in the sewers during this period. (This small sample is unrepresentative of the labor force as a whole because it includes a disproportionate number of sewermen who worked a long period in the sewers.[7]) Of twenty-eight sewermen hired between 1857 and 1886 for whom information is available, only two came from Paris (7.1%) and none from the Seine or adjoining departments. Six of the twenty-eight came from the Haute-Garonne (21.4%). The age at which they began work varied considerably, from their early twenties to mid-forties.

By the early 1880s the labor force in the sewers seemed poised to inaugurate the future set pattern of semiskilled manual labor in twentieth-century France: when provincial workers could no longer be recruited to do the most demanding manual jobs, employers called upon foreign workers. The number of Frenchmen taking up work in the sewers had begun to fall; recent Italian immigrants to Paris replaced them. However, this situation ended abruptly in the late 1880s and early 1890s, when changes in municipal employment practices created conditions for the emergence of a stable, cohesive, and militant labor force of native French sewermen.

The Long Depression of 1873–1896 had a decisive, long-term impact on Parisian industry. In the Second-Republic tradition of the *droit au travail*, Radicals and Socialists in Paris saw municipal employment as one source of the kind of job security and benefits capitalism was failing to provide. In response to the economic crisis, the Paris municipal council approved a series of measures to improve conditions for city workers. In 1888 the council banned subcontracting and set conditions for the payment of wages, established a nine-hour workday with a mandatory day of rest, and stipulated that no more than 10 percent of the labor force could be foreign.[8]

In 1892, a proposal by the socialist Pierre Baudin that all municipal workers receive a minimum salary of 5 francs per day or 150 francs per month squeaked through the municipal council. This measure completed the transformation of employment conditions for city workers. Even street sweeping, once a poorly paid job for old men living on a meager pension or with their children, became a position sought after by young men fresh from military service.[9] The average daily wage of a sewerman rose from 3.75 francs for a twelve-hour day in the mid-1880s to 5.60 francs for an eight-hour day two decades later. While such pay was modest, Lenard Berlanstein singles out the 79 percent increase in sewermen's annual income between 1880 and 1913 as "the nearest approach to a general effort at wage restructuring" in pre-World War I Paris.[10]

Special provisions transformed work in the sewers into a career. The city reinforced the already strict standards for employment: it accepted no applicants over thirty-five (the limit had been forty); and all prospective sewermen still had to pass a rigorous medical screening when hired. A new worker served four months as a *stagiaire* and was then given a second medical examination before being offered a full-time position with the promise of no layoffs (*titularisé*).[11]

Restrictions on the hiring of foreigners and the promise of year-round employment resulted in the recruitment of an increasing number of Parisian workers from a wide variety of trades. Few of this new generation went straight from military service to work in the sewers. Most had engaged in another trade first and entered the sewers at about age thirty. For the thirty-eight sewermen about whom information is available who began work in the sewers between 1887 and 1906, twenty-one (55.3%) did so between the ages of 28 and 33. Fourteen (36.8%) had been born in Paris; three more came from adjoining departments, for a total of seventeen (44.7%). These trends continued during the prewar years. Of twenty-three sewermen who began working in the sewers between 1908 and 1914, sixteen (69.6%) were aged between thirty and thirty-three when they entered the trade. Thirteen (56.5%) had been born in Paris; eighteen (78.3%) came from Paris and adjoining departments. Occupational endogamy began to play a role in recruitment. At least one-fifth of the sewermen in the sample hired between 1900 and 1914 had a father or an uncle who had worked in the sewers.

The obituaries of sewermen hired after the change in recruitment practices suggest the diversity of occupational experiences of this new cohort. Many had been laborers before going to work in the sewers, but a number had more surprising backgrounds: an *ouvrier sommelier*, a confectioner, a saddle-maker, a shopkeeper "too upright" to succeed in business, and so forth.[12] There were numerous former plumbers, tanners, and locksmiths. "Every trade, from mechanics to gardeners, is represented among us," the union secretary told journalists before the war.[13]

The relatively advanced age at which men went to work in the sewers may indicate that many had tried and failed to find steady work in a more prestigious occupation. Over the years, however, another career pattern developed. Young men signed up to work in the sewers and then waited years to be hired. During the interim they learned another trade which they continued to do on the side as a means of earning extra money and, if still hale upon retirement, of supplementing their pension.

Organized labor has condemned such double-dipping as stealing jobs from other workers; labor historians have tacitly disapproved of it because multiple employment wreaks havoc with efforts to categorize and typify workers by occupation. Yet such practices have played and continue to play an important role in workers' lives. One might even see the exercise of two trades—one in a group and one as a lone *bricoleur* of some sort—as an instance of workers creating in their own lives the kind of diversified employment generally reserved for utopian communities.

The reconstitution of the labor force in the Paris sewers at the end of the nineteenth century is doubly significant. First, it was an instance of an unusual revalorization of manual labor which prevented a semi-skilled and socially marginal occupation from becoming the province of foreigners and turned it into an enclave of native Frenchmen. The gradual development of familial hiring patterns created conditions for the kind of kinship solidarities generally associated with elite skilled trades.

Second, many of the newly recruited sewermen were craftsmen from a wide variety of trades. The movement of these workers into the sewers was part of the remaking of the Parisian working class that took place during and after the Long Depression. The economic crisis had revealed the fundamental insecurity of a number of trades. Some of their practitioners responded by exchanging "honorable" skilled occupations for lower-status semi-skilled jobs which promised full-time employment and a modest pension. Many sewermen had been active in unions in their previous professional lives and brought this commitment to syndicalism to their new job.[14] The coming together of a wide variety of urban artisanal traditions in the sewermen's union at once upsets common stereotypes of sanitation workers and helps account for the union's vibrant corporate culture.

The Sewermen's Union

The sewermen's union developed out of the workers' concern over job security. In November 1886 a financially strapped Paris city government laid off 181 *auxiliaires*—one-quarter of the labor force—for two months. While employment in the sewers fluctuated, the magnitude of this action prompted thirty sewermen to form the first union of municipal employees in Paris in August 1887. After a rocky beginning, the union grew under the leadership of its general secretary Jules Larminier to encompass the entire labor force in the sewers.[15]

With the promulgation of new municipal regulations promising regular employment, the union's initial concern with job security shifted to hiring procedures. The union succeeded in having the foreman's right to recruit workers taken away. Instead, hiring was to be done by the date of signing up for employment.[16] Arguing the need to develop a cohesive labor force, the union was then able to convince engineers to give preference in hiring to men who were friends or relatives of sewermen.[17]

The union was particularly adamant that the sons of men who had died in municipal employ be given preference in hiring. Sewermen saw this as a customary privilege and fought vigorously to have it enforced.[18] Emile-Raymond Lefèvre's sewerman father died in January 1898, leaving him at eighteen the principal support of three siblings, an ailing mother, and an aged grandfather. In June 1898, Emile-Raymond asked to join the union to better his chances of getting a job in the sewers. The strategy worked; he was hired in 1900.[19] The union's success in influencing entry into the trade was a crucial factor in forging the social basis for solidarity in the labor force.

Union interest in employment extended to promotion. The union sought to make advancement a source of cohesion and cooperation rather than competition. It established courses to train sewermen who wanted to attain the qualifications for promotion within the ranks. Chief engineer Bechmann championed the program and the municipal council helped fund it.[20] Instructors carried the title of "professeurs à la Chambre syndicale."[21] Sewermen who received promotions to supervisory positions remained in the union. In union matters, workers and their supervisors received equal treatment.[22]

In addition to its role in hiring and promotion, the union overcame the organizational dispersion of sewermen to give them a sense of common identity. In the decades before 1914, sewermen worked in teams of from five to eight, including the *chef-ouvrier* who labored alongside the other workers.[23] These crews in turn formed bigger units, the *ateliers*. In 1899, there were 945 sewermen in thirty-five *ateliers*. Thirty-two of these *ateliers* were engaged directly in cleansing: twenty-four worked in the small galleries (637 workers) and eight in the collectors and siphon (284 workers). Each *atelier* had an underground *chambre de rendez-vous* where sewermen assembled and changed in and out of their boots.[24]

A team was responsible for all aspects of the maintenance and cleaning of a *canton* (about one-fifth of an *arrondissement*) except for removal of

12.   Sewermen put on their boots in a *chambre de rendez-vous*
(early twentieth century).

sand from the *bassins de dessablement*. The team's monopoly over knowledge of the particularities of its *canton* guaranteed it autonomy and control in the daily aspects of its work. (The organization of work also provided the rationale for union calls for a shorter work day since supervision of a *canton* required vigilance and hard work at certain times—the morning flushing in particular—but not long hours of presence.) The teams and the *atelier* constituted the horizon of most sewermen; only the constant circulation of union leaders among the *ateliers* countered this isolation. In fact, the sewermen's sense of corporate solidarity was very much a product of the union's work; the organization of work alone militated against it.

Despite the union's intervention in so many aspects of workplace life, its leadership combated the tendency toward bureaucratization which contemporaries like Robert Michels considered inevitable in the development of workers' organizations. Shunning offers from the union to pay his salary so that he could devote himself full-time to union activities, the general secretary Larminier continued to work in the sewers. (He also turned down promotion to *chef d'équipe*, wanting, he said, to remain "comrade of his comrades and not to become their boss."[25]) Larminier castigated the centralization of power in union bureaucracies and the syndical leaders in Paris who worked at no profession other than union militant. Sewermen were particularly sensitive to the dangers of bureaucratic power as a result of their daily encounters with the rigidities of the municipal administration. As Larminier explained to a reporter, "with us, the essential principle is absolute independence. We take the fear of *fonctionnairisme* so far as to not want any functionaries, even in our union. That is why the secretary is never paid. He works like the others."[26] During the war, Larminier called the German union official Karl Legien's endorsement of the Imperial war effort, before hostilities had even begun, "the most striking example" of the consequences of bureaucratization of the union movement.[27]

Public Servants

The union did not see itself solely as a defender of its members' material well-being. It sought to ensure that the *rats d'égout*, as sewermen were popularly called,[28] did not take on the moral characteristics associated with the sewer's contents. The union created a loan fund to help members avoid the typical workingman's fate of going into debt.[29] In the spirit of Fernand Pelloutier, it also tried to educate members and broaden their cultural horizons. For instance, in 1898 the union set up *cours du Syndicat*, including well-attended lectures on subjects like x-rays.[30] On other occasions, the union arranged for municipal engineers to give talks and lead special tours of the city's sanitary system.[31]

Equally important, the union constructed a moral discourse on sewermen aimed at both its members and the public. *Le Réveil de l'Assainissement* ran a column entitled "Acts of Probity" about the numerous instances of sewermen's turning in objects they had found in the sewers to the police, telling cashiers when they had been overpaid, and returning money to local merchants who had given them too much change. (But did the sewermen expect rewards? No, or so they claimed, since those rich enough to lose valuable things were usually "egotists."[32])

Most of all, sewermen wanted to shape the public representation of themselves and to obtain the recognition and recompense which they felt was their due. As public servants, they served the public, but did not want to be treated as servants. In an inversion Blanqui would have savored, the union emblem featured the booted leg of a sewerman giving a resounding kick in the pants to a bourgeois in top hat and tails.

From this perspective, the image the public took from the sewer tour was problematic. Sewermen, dressed in white to emphasize the purported cleanliness of the environment in which they worked, had long pulled the carts holding the visitors. The union succeeded in ending this humiliating practice. (A mechanical transportation system replaced it.[33]) But sewermen still resented these visits to the "nicer" parts of the sewer system because they presented their work in a false light. According to the union, the administration cleaned and disinfected the areas open to the public before tours took place.[34] (This does seem to have been the case: the engineer Will Darvillé refers to the sewers which visitors saw as *aménagés comme des salons*.[35]) The union responded by organizing its own *promenades éducatives* for other workers.[36]

From visits to the sewers and watching groups of sewermen walking along the streets with their *rabots* over their shoulders, the public came to see sewermen as not only men of mire, but as "soldiers" of order and hygiene as well. The union deployed the military metaphor differently to evoke sewermen's solidarity and combativeness. Angered at the equivocations of the municipal council over granting (and funding) the eight-hour day, sewermen emerged from the underground one day in July 1899 and marched on the Hôtel de Ville in what Larminier referred to as *une promenade d'hygiène:* the sight of all sewermen but those needed to maintain essential services marching in ranks of four won the sewermen immediate satisfaction.[37]

The Right to Organize

Such actions confirmed the fears of conservatives that unionization of public sector workers severely compromised public order by making local and national governments, expressions of the general interest, subject to the organized opposition of employees pursuing their particular interests. Sewermen, the first municipal employees in Paris to unionize, absorbed a good share of abuse on this account. Right-wing politicians challenged not only union representations of sewermen, but the union's very right to represent sewermen. Pointing to the payment of sewermen by the month (although missed time was deducted at an hourly rate), conservatives triumphantly argued that sewermen were public functionaries and as such were barred from unionizing.[38]

This challenge to the sewermen's right to organize raised a fundamental, but generally ignored, question. What did legislators have in mind when they legalized unions in 1884? According to the law, unions existed to protect the economic, industrial, commercial, or agricultural interests of their members. Opponents of public sector unionization claimed that the sewermen's union did not pursue any of these objectives. Cleaning the sewers was not a commercial activity; since sewermen worked for the city, they could have no economic interests to defend; the promise of permanent full-time employment removed sewermen from the world of the market. The only purpose which the union could serve would be to try to modify rules and regulations and to defend workers who faced punishment. A city engineer concluded in a November 1887 report, "There are neither bosses nor competition. There are only administrative regulations and if the union does not have as its objective to lean on the administration, it will not have any effect."[39] According to this interpretation, unions were permitted to play a role in the market, but not to challenge the hierarchical distribution of power within the enterprise. In the absence of normative market conditions, there was no justification for a union.

Socialists rejected this narrow rationale for unionization. Workers employed by cities and the state labored under a rigid, dehumanizing bureaucracy.[40] Unions were necessary to protect public sector workers against the excessive regimentation and arbitrary exercise of power the military metaphor of an army of sewermen suggested. Furthermore, unions could foster a community ethos: an emotional and social safety net which the public sector, whatever its other benefits, could not provide.

Despite the unresolved legal challenge to its legitimacy, the sewermen's union thrived. During its early years, sympathetic municipal councillors intervened with the prefect to assure that the union was "tolerated."[41] Some municipal sanitary engineers had originally mistrusted the union, but the chief engineers beginning with Durand-Claye supported it. After Durand-Claye's death in 1888, two socialist municipal councillors wrote: "The sewermen's union found in him a support which, although not official, was nonetheless sincere and useful."[42] Over the next decade municipal engineers came to pride themselves on the good working relationship they had developed with the sewermen's union.[43] For them it expressed the beneficial solidarity experienced by those who labored for the common good underground and served as an example of the possible corporate foundations of republican order. Whenever the union's legal status was challenged, it claimed *de facto* legitimacy based on the recognition granted it by the city council and especially the municipal engineers.[44]

Election of a right-wing municipal government in 1900 posed a serious threat to the sewermen's union.[45] Unionization and the concessions the sewermen's union had won during the 1890s seemed to shift the public conception of sewermen from a disciplined army of workers doing a demanding, if disgusting, job, to a band of disciplined shirkers, practiced in the art of "soldiering," using their quasi-military presence to win unwarranted concessions like the eight-hour day. One senator apparently told his colleagues that sewermen drank and played cards all day.[46] Just as sanitary reformers had once evoked representations of raucous cesspool cleaners to make their case for the *tout-à-l'égout,* turn-of-the-century conservatives mobilized the image of shiftless sewermen to try to break their union and ultimately to wrest responsibility for sewer maintenance from the public sector.

Conservatives' real fear was not of underground card-playing, but of public signs of the sewermen's ability to organize resistance to work. In the first years of the century, the conservative city council attempted to assert control over sewermen. It began by seeking to regulate the post of the *garde-orifice.* Each crew of sewermen was required to designate one of its number for the job. He walked the crew's path on the surface, stopping to pry off the manhole cover nearest to where the sewermen worked below in order to remain in constant contact with them. He received word of problems underground and warned of sudden rainstorms. Emblematic of the conservatives' offensive against the sewermen was their ordinance requiring *garde-orifices* to stand at their posts, when they could do their job just as well seated (and probably better, since they were closer to the manhole and therefore better able to hear their comrades below).[47] It was clear to sewermen that the sole purpose of this regulation was to impress the public. Whereas the upright sewerman below ground had earlier been a symbol of civilization, the upright sewerman of the turn of the century quite literally stood for order on the streets of Paris.

The militancy of the sewermen's union made it a particular *bête noire* of the Paris right. The sewermen's union stood out from other municipal workers' unions. In 1897, it had seceded from the general union of municipal workers when the latter accepted a city council plan that required municipal workers to pay a portion of the cost of increased pension benefits.[48] For the next decade and a half, other municipal union leaders castigated the sewermen's union for its all-or-nothing stance.[49]

Conservative newspapers launched a campaign against the union at the turn of the century, asserting that it cost Parisian rate-payers dearly. *La Presse* charged that the union controlled advancement with obvious unfortunate consequences.[50] According to *L'Eclair*, the union had ordered a slowdown among sewermen after the sewer administration received funding for only twenty of the seventy-two new workers it had asked for to compensate for introduction of the eight-hour day. The newspaper quoted a hostile municipal councillor's claim that the new workers were unnecessary since teams of fewer than five men were often sufficient to get the work done. *L'Eclair* went on to suggest that in addition to the slowdown, the union organized workers to take full advantage of paid sick days; each worker took about twenty-eight sick days per year as if he had received a *mot d'ordre* to do so.[51] The union vigorously denied these accusations and brought a libel suit against *L'Eclair*. To the sewermen's consternation, the courts threw the case out, on the grounds that unions of municipal workers were not legal and therefore could not bring suit.[52]

The attacks in the press were part of a concerted effort by conservatives to break the union and place sewer maintenance in private hands. In 1902 the city punished three union members for articles they had written in *Le Réveil de l'Assainissement*. It turned over a portion of the extraction of sand to private contractors[53] and announced plans to put cleaning of the Left Bank sewers up for bids and to lay off all sewermen over age sixty and all who were not *titularisés*. (The *L'Eclair* article published shortly before this initiative had suggested that private enterprise would soon take over sewer maintenance.) Although the union threatened to strike over the issue, the deciding factor in the resolution of the conflict was the steadfastness of the chief engineer Bechmann. He convinced the municipal council that the sewers were a public service which should not be turned over to private enterprise.[54] Following the *L'Eclair* court case, municipal engineers went out of their way to reiterate their endorsement of the existing system of labor relations in the sewers, including the legitimacy of the union.[55]

Bechmann's crucial intervention was one of a number of instances, including cases of promotion and hiring, in which municipal engineers voiced support for sewermen and their union. While there were, of course, numerous conflicts between engineers and their subordinates, these examples of cooperation reveal the engineers' Saint-Simonian expectation that technological and social progress would march in tandem. Sanitation engineers shared neither the conservatives' desire to cut the costs of cleaning sewers in the short term nor their long-term aim of turning government services over to capitalist entrepreneurs. On the contrary, they considered these projects to be against both the efficient and humane operation of the sewers and the best interests of the collectivity.

The union appreciated instances of engineers' sympathetic solidarity. However, it came to see the city-*patron,* with its meddling rules and medical bureaucracy, as epitomizing the worst elements of a rigid, hierarchical regime with no respect for workers like sewermen. How, the union asked, could municipal councillors pass a resolution against spitting in public and not fund medical facilities for sewermen? In his comments on the January 1910 flood in Paris, Larminier fused the themes of bourgeois egotism and the need to respect labor found in Blanqui's and Hamp's comments on sanitary work. He turned the "solidarist" ideology of class cooperation and social harmony preached by bourgeois republicans back upon itself. "Parisians do not know us or know us only through popular songs, that is to say very badly." No one acknowledged that sewermen had put in twenty-four-hour days like the policemen and soldiers. "And yet, we were the ones who carried the policemen on our backs across the flooded streets."[56] Without their efforts to protect the Palais National, he reminded the president of the Republic, the water "would have made your situation one with that of a lot of proletarians, from an aquatic point of view, of course": "Usually disdained by all, bourgeois or representatives of society, we would like to point out to its supreme head that, despite all, we are conscious of our social role and that, struggling against nature's angry floods, we struggle against the rising waters of social demoralization, caused particularly by the lack of solidarity of the upper reaches of society with the humble classes to which we belong."[57] Through their union, sewermen laid claim to the status of moral proletarians, at once echoing Parent-Duchâtelet's representation of their predecessors and endowing the concept with new social and political meanings.

11

The Body of Sewermen

There is something barbaric in making a man live a large part of his
life . . . under the thumb of a pile of regulations and then to tell him
[when he retires] that the only answer is to be subject to another set
of regulations like that which exists in old-age homes.

—Jules Larminier, "La Colonie"

IN PARENT-DUCHÂTELET'S gloss of the sewerman's body, a man's
health was one signifier of his moral behavior. In comparison to his predecessors, Parent-Duchâtelet downplayed the inherent danger of locales like
sewers; they were most dangerous to individuals weakened by dissolute
living. In the decades before World War I, the union offered a different
reading of the corpus of the sewermen's work. The union had been born
in response to the insecurity of keeping a job in the sewers; it soon turned
its attention to the insecurity inherent in that job. The union emphasized
that the myriad perils of work in the sewers were largely independent of
the individual sewerman's control. For the union, the morality of sewermen was reflected not in their individual health, but in their realization of
Parent-Duchâtelet's dream of a collective response to injury and illness.

Dangers

Sewermen daily faced the risk of accidents from strenuous labor in damp,
poorly lit tunnels. Like other workers engaged in heavy manual labor in
humid, cramped quarters, they suffered frequent hernias and lumbagos
and were prone to arthritis. Many took serious falls in the dark subterran-
nean corridors.[1] And despite the presence of *gardes-orifices* on the street and
shelters in the larger sewers, sewermen occasionally asphyxiated or
drowned when sudden downpours generated raging underground torrents.

The fauna of the sewers presented another set of dangers. Poisonous
centipedes and spiders ("sometimes as large as a hand") which lived on the
ceiling of the sewers dropped down on sewermen and gave nasty bites
which could easily become infected. The knotted rag which sewermen to

13.   The death of two sewermen by asphyxiation at the
Boulevard Rochechouart in 1880.

this day wear around their necks provided only partial protection. Swarms
of flies around rotting matter sometimes forced sewermen to the surface.
Rats (*gaspards* in the sewermen's argot) were both a nuisance and a serious
health hazard. One sewerman estimated in 1897 that each sewerman killed
two hundred to three hundred rats annually.[2] When cornered, the rats
turned vicious. They could jump and inflict nasty wounds on the hands

14. A sewerman poses; photograph by Boyer (1911).

15.   A sewerman ascends with a box of rats; photograph by Boyer (1911).

and face. Although this was not known until well into the twentieth century, rats' urine carries a sometimes fatal virus.[3]

The sanitary engineers argued that in a properly functioning sewer, sewage did not present a health hazard. But even they had to admit the growing danger which the byproducts of new industries and services posed. Garages illegally disposed of unwanted oil and fuel in the sewers. Without warning, laundries released withering blasts of scalding steam into them. Sewermen endured fires, explosions, steam and chemical burns, blindness, eczemas, and infections from their contact with often unidentifiable elements in the sewage. (It is dangerous for sewermen to have colds, since they depend on their noses to warn them of dangerous substances.[4])

The union publicized the risks sewermen faced. It drew up reports on serious accidents and outlined the measures necessary to prevent their recurrence.[5] To honor sewermen and other municipal workers who died from work accidents, the union lobbied the city to build a large monument in Père Lachaise. In the first four years of the memorial (1889–1892), four of the eleven municipal workers who died from injuries sustained on the job were sewermen.[6] Their names adorn the top of the pillar.

Tuberculosis

Parent-Duchâtelet had been enamored of social statistics. In the introduction to his study of prostitution, he rejected the notion that social scientists could be satisfied any longer with terms like *"many, often, sometimes, very often, etc."*[7] It was in the spirit of this form of social representation that the sewermen's union analyzed the health of its members. Where Parent-Duchâtelet had offered the lengthy careers of certain workers as evidence of the salubrity of the sewerman's job, the union took advantage of the regularization of employment to compile data to rebut generalizations drawn from individual cases. It made this data available to would-be industrial hygienists like Dr. Foveau de Courmelles, who presented a paper on sewermen to the Société française d'hygiène in January 1903.[8] The health of sewermen seemed to have worsened during the union's first decades (although rising mortality rates may reflect a growing percentage of career sewermen): 1.8 percent of sewermen died annually during the period 1886–1894; 2.5 percent for 1894–1900; and 3.6 percent during the first years of the twentieth century.[9]

Yet the mortality rates of active sewermen were misleading. They were even used by contemporary observers to support the engineers' view of the labor force's overall healthiness and to deny the sewermen's claim to special compensation for their work: "the mortality among the thousand workmen who spend most of their lives in [the sewers] is about the same as that of the same number who follow trades above ground. Many of these fellows are old men who have never done any other kind of work; they labour in the sewers until they die of old age or are pensioned off."[10] Such an interpretation was misleading because it ignored the turnover among sewermen created by injury and illness. At the turn of the century, Larminier estimated that one-third of sewermen died after ten years of work; only 3 percent remained on the job the twenty years required to earn a full pension.[11]

The wear and tear of work in the sewers was reflected in a high incidence of pulmonary disease (revealed earlier in debates over the *tout-à-l'égout*) and especially tuberculosis. This disease took an enormous toll on Frenchmen during this period. In 1911–1913 it killed 2,136 inhabitants per million in France, a significantly higher rate than in Germany (1,519) or Great Britain (1,397).[12] Two-thirds of the thirty-five to forty sewermen who died annually at the beginning of the twentieth century were said to be victims of tuberculosis.[13]

Men who worked in the sewers were particularly susceptible to tuberculosis. Tubercular bacilli from a variety of sources were flushed into the sewers. While Bechmann argued that "the uniformity in temperature undoubtedly compensates in part" for the difficulties of work in the sewers,[14] sewermen pointed to the humidity of the air in the workplace and to what they felt to be the unhealthy effects of the abrupt changes in temperature between the sewers and the street. Although Bechmann claimed that the air quality in the sewers was not much different than on the street, one team of scientists found that installation of the *tout-à-l'égout* had rendered ventilation "almost insufficient."[15] Because sewermen often had to share protective headgear, contagious diseases such as tuberculosis spread rapidly in their midst.[16]

Alain Cottereau has shown that the statistics drawn up by social reformers in the late nineteenth century, which attributed the high incidence of tuberculosis among the poor to inadequate housing, obscured the role of working conditions in the spread of the disease.[17] Sewermen were cognizant that their family economy suggested a more complicated connection between occupational and domestic factors in the transmission of tuberculosis than that proposed by supporters of one or the other theory. Sewermen with large families could afford less for food; they were therefore more susceptible to tuberculosis in the workplace and more likely to pass it on to their children at home.

Through much of the nineteenth century, the sewers had been presented as a potential source of disease to the inhabitants of Paris. In contrast, since the opening of the sewers to visitors, sewermen had enjoyed a reputation for remarkable health. When the public was finally coming to trust that disease would not emerge from the sewers to threaten the city's population, sewermen demanded recognition that the sewers were in fact a breeding ground of disease for those who worked in them. The statistics the union produced were hardly the stuff of epidemiologists' dreams; they are better understood as one effort by the union to intercede in medical debates in which sewermen's lives were increasingly inscribed and represented.

The Politics of Employees' Health

The sewermen's union offered an early and particularly successful example of both semi-skilled-worker and public-employee unionism in France. Although sewermen shared in the advantages granted all municipal workers, the authority wielded by their union gave them a privileged position among the city's manual laborers.

Sewermen made significant gains with regard to sick days, length of the work day, and pensions. In 1893, the city decided to pay all municipal workers full salary for sick days, instead of the half-pay it had allotted before. In the decade after 1887, the number of sewermen rose only slightly (from 950 to 985), but the sick days they took almost doubled (from 11,348 to 22,004).[18] One need not accept *L'Eclair*'s explanation of this phenomenon as syndicalist-inspired shirking. The sewermen's rigorous schedule suggests an equally compelling explication in terms of a high incidence of illness in their ranks. In the 1890s, sewermen worked ten-hour days with only a fifteen-minute break to eat; they alternated weeks of day and night work.[19]

Not surprisingly, reducing the work day was one of the union's primary demands. The union's efforts were crowned with success in 1899 when the Paris sewermen became one of the first groups of manual laborers in France to receive the eight-hour day. The hours of effective labor were significantly less—five hours according to critics. Sewermen worked in two four-hour shifts with a two-hour break at midday; the time to put on boots, to go to and from work sites in the sewers, and to unboot was included in the eight hours.[20] Sewermen also obtained an end to Sunday work and an annual vacation of twelve days.

Sewermen received partial pensions calculated at a rate of 24 francs per year of service up to ten years; after ten years, the city council added another 100 francs. Above age fifty, a sewerman who had put in at least twenty years of service received a full pension of 600 francs when the doctor appointed by the city declared him no longer fit to work. (The full pension was later increased to 700 francs; payroll deductions financed this raise.) The widow of a retired sewerman received half of his pension and orphans under age eighteen were also given assistance.[21] The union established a legal service to assure that sewermen and their families obtained the full compensation owed them for occupational illness, injury, and death.

In tandem with the increased medical and retirement benefits accorded sewermen and other municipal workers, the administration developed the capacity of its medical services to sift, classify, and monitor as well as to care for workers well beyond the Second Empire's rigorous physicals. Parent-Duchâtelet's individual initiative in this direction became bureaucratized. For semi-skilled workers like sewermen, the goal of collective control of the labor process included exercising the means to restrict labor or to apportion it among individuals according to aptitude and abilities, limited as these might be by age, illness, and injury. Despite frustration with the rules and regulations of the municipal regime, turn-of-the-century sewermen exercised real autonomy in their work. This made them all the more adamant in their run-ins with the form of labor management embedded in the practices of occupational medicine. While workers had always resisted individually and collectively the wear and tear of work, the emergence of unions and "company doctors" institutionalized struggles over the sewerman's body.

Doctors played a crucial role throughout a sewerman's career, from hiring through retirement. Each step of the way had a potential for conflict. A prospective sewerman had to pass a rigorous physical examination to qualify for the *stage* and again when he completed it. The administration saw the *stage* as a period in which to weed out malcontents and potential tuberculars. The doctor had to decide whether the *stage* revealed any signs that the worker was unsuitable for *titularisation*. In controversial cases, the union might throw its weight behind a *stagiaire*. In 1898, for instance, the union petitioned the municipal council in favor of the *stagiaire* Legay whose index finger had been crushed while working in the sewers and who had failed the medical exam for *titularisation*, despite fellow workers' claims that he could do his job perfectly well.[22]

More serious were the conflicts which arose over the granting of sick days, for which the city paid full wages after 1893. As a consequence of this policy, sewermen claimed, doctors refused to grant sick days until workers were very ill. This was particularly serious for workers in the early stages of tuberculosis, who were sent to work until they could no longer do so. When the doctor finally recognized their illnesses, they were so sick that they had to take extended sick leaves. If they were not able to return to work in a year, they were retired and given their pensions.[23]

From the sewermen's perspective, the administration doctor monitored the worker's ability to work rather than his health. Instead of encouraging workers to conserve their health by liberally granting sick days, the doctors made sewermen work until they dropped and could be pensioned off. This was hardly economical, the sewermen argued, since the city gave the incapacitated worker sick pay for up to a year before making him retire. (Such medical policies may also account in part for the increase in sick days that raised the suspicions of turn-of-the-century conservatives.) Larminier summed up the union position: "the worker educated in his social duties, and as a result a supporter of public services, has no need for other censors than his conscience" to decide whether he is too ill to work.[24]

Workers were acutely aware that their ill comrades required a flexible employment policy in order to survive. One finds an occasional instance of an individual bucking the system and taking matters into his own hands. In the late 1890s Arthur Hardouin, a six-year veteran of the municipal sanitation services, arranged to switch jobs with his friend, the tubercular sewerman Nicod, in hopes that work above ground would return the sick man to health. Nicod died, however, and after eight years in the sewers Hardouin himself retired from the sewers with tuberculosis. Bedridden for twenty-two months, he too eventually succumbed to the disease.[25]

Doctors entered into a further debate over alcoholism. The question of drunkenness was both an issue of corporate pride and a matter of individual survival. Sewermen resented the widespread bourgeois belief in endemic lower-class alcoholism. When the city offered temperance medals to selected workers, the union declined them as an affront.[26] The label "alcoholic" was not simply a social insult for individual sewermen, however, but often a matter of life or death. The union charged that the administration doctor frequently told sick workers that their illness was due to "alcoholism," and that they were therefore ineligible for sick pay. The union rallied around workers in this situation, soliciting the testimony necessary to prove that a sick worker was not a heavy drinker.[27]

The greater intrusion of medicine into labor management was a constant source of such incidents. From the workers' point of view, both occupational diseases and personal behavior were relative concepts which could not be grasped in terms of rigid typologies. However, the remuneration of worktime and the allocation of pensions encouraged doctors to differentiate workers into able workers and workers to be retired; temperate and alcoholic individuals, and so on. In light of the modest pension awarded those who retired before twenty years of service, the sewermen considered policies which forced workers into early retirement to be immoral.[28] When unions sought more liberal sick leave and pension decisions, their efforts naturally brought them into conflict with the medical authorities introduced to supervise these very programs.

"Our Second and Real Syndical Family"

Owners often use familial metaphors to describe their relationship to their employees. This discursive device to legitimate the economic enterprise as a "natural" form of social relations frequently overlaps and conflicts with a counterdiscourse generated from below by workers who speak of their workmates in familial terms. The workers do not attribute patriarchal authority to a manager or an employer. Instead, the neighborhood, the shop floor, or the union is thought of as an extension or an enlarged version of the family.[29] For turn-of-the-century sewermen, syndical life formalized such a living community and attested to a belief in the permanency of the sewermen's commitments to one another after death.

The conception of the sewermen's union as a family evolved out of the increasingly cooptative and sometimes familial recruitment of sewermen and the bonds which united sewermen in their teams and *ateliers*. Yet the union was not simply a superstructure built upon those relationships. Union activities created new affective relationships of trust and responsibility by extending familial and workplace solidarities to encompass the labor force as a whole.

Family life and syndical life overlapped in many ways. The person of Larminier provided an important point of contact. Union members frequently came to the crowded apartment where he lived with his wife and three children not only to conduct union business, but also to ask his help in solving family problems.[30] Larminier was known for having refused on principle a small inheritance which once came his way; yet he was so respected by union members that some fifty of them left their wills in his hands.[31]

The union's familial concerns extended well beyond the world of Larminier's flat. Having obtained security of employment and improvements in pay and working conditions, the union addressed the situation of retired workers and of sewermen's widows and orphans. At the turn of the century thirty-five to forty sewermen died each year and another forty or so retired, many because of ill health.[32] Retired sewermen found that the pensions allotted by the city were insufficient. In Paris, in the words of a sympathetic municipal councillor, "they could only vegetate miserably."[33] Retired sewermen had to take odd jobs or worse yet, to turn to the Assistance publique.

Worn-out men in their forties and fifties, the pensioned-off sewermen had difficulty getting jobs in the private sector. Their status as *réformés des services de la Ville* was said to be as much of an impediment to finding work as their health.[34] Consequently, retired sewermen were forced to turn to the municipality for employment. The sewerman Charles Franck went blind working in the sewers and received a partial pension in 1895. The sum was not enough to live on, so he had to take a job as a brushmaker for the city.[35] The union looked covetously at the ubiquitous *gardiens* of parks and promenades in Paris, recruited from among veterans, and sought to have retired sewermen considered for these posts.[36]

For sewermen who were no longer able to work and did not have families to look after them, the only recourse seemed to be city-run old-age homes. As these institutions would take only the indigent, a retired sewerman who entered a home had to forfeit his pension. This seemed particularly unfair to municipal employees; because their pensions were paid by the city, they had no way of hiding or transferring their assets as did others who entered the homes. Places were scarce, so even if a sewerman was willing to give up his pension, he often required personal connections to be admitted.[37] In any case, to the retired sewerman an old-age home was another form of disciplinary institution, like the municipal bureaucracy he had just left. Going to a "hospice" was a "difficult extremity for a man who, having spent his life under the discipline of rules, under the weight of a hierarchical order, cannot even hope to die an independent man."[38]

The widows and children of sewermen who had passed away presented the union with an equally serious problem. Municipal benefits were often not enough for them to live on. In the early years union members had passed the hat, but found that this method was too slow to provide assistance to families when they were most in need. Therefore the union established a fund for the families of deceased sewermen in 1895,[39] and held an annual Fête de la Caisse des Veuves which attracted thousands.[40] The union could not, however, afford to pay for the upkeep of all the children left by its members. Indigent widows were threatened with having to turn their children over to the Assistance publique if they could not care for them.[41] Occasionally, the union was able to intervene with municipal authorities to get jobs for sewermen's widows. For instance, the union assisted one widow in obtaining a permit to work as a street vendor and another a job as a seamstress for the Assistance publique.[42] Yet such ad hoc solutions were insufficient to help the families of most deceased sewermen.

The union condemned the institutional alternatives available to children whose families could not take care of them. It hated the idea of seeing them go to the Assistance publique, but was no more enthusiastic about other possibilities. The union found public facilities for tubercular children who had been infected by their sewermen fathers woefully inadequate. It had an even lower estimation of Church-run social services for children.[43] As a result, the union devoted considerable effort to the placement of its needy orphans. Larminier explained that "the sentiments of sincere solidarity [which linked sewermen] cannot just disappear when one of us dies. When he goes, those who remain [his family] must be our own; when one of us disappears, we consider ourselves as the father of his children."[44]

Individual union members had long acted on this sentiment. Jean Badognani, a sewerman from 1880 until his death in 1904, took the three children left by a close friend who died in 1886 and raised them as his own.[45] In the spring of 1902, the union militant Péquignot saw his father die and his wife and son take ill. Yet when his brother-in-law died, he assumed charge of his nieces and nephews because his sister lacked the means to raise them. Proceeds from a union collection aided Péquignot with the financial, if not the emotional, burden this must have placed on him.[46]

Yet the placement of children was not often amenable to such individual solutions. The union found that relatives outside the *métier* were often unwilling to take children of deceased sewermen, even when the union offered financial support.[47] The union also became dissatisfied with the expedient of placing orphans with peasant families; the peasants charged an exorbitant amount, skimped on the food given the children, forced them to do heavy labor, and did not give them what Larminier called a "familial education."[48]

The case of young Théophile Corbel exemplified these problems. The sewerman Théophile-Yves-Marie-Corentin Corbel, originally a sailor from the Côtes-du-Nord, went to work in the Paris sewers about 1890. He had three children, the youngest of whom, Théophile, was in born in 1895. A few years later, disaster struck. Corbel's wife died in 1899 and he passed away the following year. He had been a member of the union; after his death, the union board of directors went before the local justice of the peace to request guardianship of the three children. The two eldest were aged twenty and eighteen at the time of their father's death, but young Théophile required the union's immediate attention. As a temporary expedient, the union treasurer paid the boy's teen-aged niece out of his own pocket to care for him, but this could not be a permanent solution. The union then placed Théophile with an uncle, an employee of the Compagnie des Chemins de fer de l'Ouest in the Maine-et-Loire. The man complained that he already had five children, and in view of the high cost of living in the area, he would be hard-pressed to support young Théophile without being relocated and promoted, if possible. Larminier then arranged an interview with the general secretary of the Chemins de fer de l'Ouest and received assurances from the company that it would make the necessary arrangements with its employee. The placement did not work out, however, because of the aunt's fears that the boy would bring evil to the house. (Young Théophile did not know the sign of the cross and cried when taken to mass.) The union then placed Théophile with relatives in the Beauvaisis. Some time later union members made an unannounced visit to this family. They found that Théophile was poorly treated and removed him immediately, to a family in the Paris suburbs where the sewermen could look after his upbringing more closely.[49]

The union took seriously the idea that it was "our second and real syndical family,"[50] responsible for the care of sewermen who could no longer work and for the families of sewermen who had died. In most cases, however, the union lacked the resources to do so. Sewermen, like other working-class groups of the period, had an intense dislike for the kind of public and private institutional options offered to those unable to provide for themselves. While the union could (and did) demand higher pensions, even these would not solve the problems involved in the placement of orphans. And as the experience of young Théophile Corbel suggested, the urban orphan would likely receive better care from the new "family" created by his father's former workmates than from blood relations in the provinces.

The Magic Mountain of the Sewermen

The community formed by the sewermen's union faced two dangers. First, the vision of the union as an "enlarged family"[51] threatened to disintegrate to the extent that the lives of members and their families were repeatedly disrupted by injury, illness, and death. Second, the union's very success at winning compensation for sewermen and their families might eventually spawn selfish individualism on the one hand, and dependence on municipal welfare benefits on the other, both attitudes antithetical to the professed working-class values of mutual aid and suspicion of authority. This is how the Paris police analyzed the situation on the eve of May Day 1910: "As for the municipal workers, nothing to fear for May Day . . . Without being enviable, the fate of municipal workers is preferable to that of their brothers in private industry, and if they obtain a few more improvements, they will become pure social conservatives, the reserve army of the bourgeoisie, having every reason to protect a guaranteed salary without layoffs, the eight-hour day and a pension."[52] In fact, it was the extent and nature of the social welfare benefits granted by the city—at once highly valued, but inadequate—which acted as the catalyst for new forms of corporate solidarity among sewermen.

In 1900 Larminier proposed a solution to the problems faced by invalids and retirees, widows and orphans. Their various pensions and indemnities were insufficient for each to live on, but if they could live together rent-free in an agricultural "colony" outside Paris, their lot would improve both financially and emotionally. "The old would raise the young; the young would find their parents again; for both, it would be the *foyer relevé*, the family reconstituted."[53] A restorative rural order would overcome urban dissolution. Speaking to the general assembly of the union in 1901, Larminier concluded: "Those who pass on would know that those they leave behind would not lose the tender embraces of their first family. Gathering them in, the big family would assure that they receive everything they need."[54] The colony he envisaged would also allow retirees "to spend the end of their lives freely."[55] The union enthusiastically endorsed Larminier's idea.

Under Larminier's leadership, the sewermen's union had invested in a number of worker institutions, including the Verrerie Ouvrière at Albi, the Palais du Travail, and the Palais Syndical.[56] The colony project partook of this general wave of turn-of-the-century syndical institution building, yet it differed as well.[57] Although the idea of the colony originated with the union, it complemented the strategy of Third Republic social reformers to encourage the development of working-class institutions within the republican framework. René Waldeck-Rousseau's 1884 law governing unions did not permit them to hold more than a minimal amount of property, and certainly not the land and buildings required by the kind of settlement which Larminier and the sewermen envisaged. The turn-of-the-century Waldeck-Rousseau cabinet, which included the Socialist Alexandre Millerand as Minister of Commerce, proposed to amend the 1884 law to permit unions to own property. Workers' organizations gave a lukewarm response to the government's proposal. At the Paris *bourse du travail* only forty-two unions (of the six hundred in the city) came to a meeting called to discuss the measure. Of these, twenty-five opposed it and only seventeen, including the sewermen's union, approved it. The majority feared that outright property ownership (unlike cooperatives or syndical "palaces") would divert unions from the primary struggle with employers. The government responded by dropping the bill in favor of more pressing matters.[58]

Unable to buy, the union asked the Paris city council to rent it a piece of land outside the city for a nominal fee. The union argued that the transaction would save money in the long run by reducing the number of orphans and aged for whom the Assistance publique would have to care. The union initially suggested that the city lease it land in the area near the irrigation fields where liquid sewage was treated.[59] The municipal council, by this time no longer favorably disposed to the sewermen's interests, refused this site and dragged its feet on the matter for several years.

The project might have gone nowhere if sympathetic engineers had not taken an interest in it.[60] Bechmann applauded the enterprise and announced to the sewermen at their annual *fête* that he would try to help them find land. In July 1905 he arranged for the city to rent seven hectares of city land in La Ville-sous-Orbais (Marne) to a union-operated joint-stock company for an annual fee of five francs.[61] The land had been bought during the Second Empire as part of Belgrand's project to bring fresh water to Paris. Its rocky soil was largely uncultivable; the only buildings on the plot were a few decaying dwellings and an abandoned mill.[62]

The sewermen joined enthusiastically in building the colony. As the union could not own property, many sewermen—two hundred and fifty within a few months—agreed to invest 100 francs each, payable in installments, in the company-colony.[63] The union also contributed the funds it had previously used to aid needy sewermen and their families. The union newspaper *Le Réveil de l'Assainissement* carried frequent mention of collections and memorial gifts for the colony. Such contributions could be a way for sewermen to deal with loss in their own families: when E. Lamblin's daughter died, he gave all her toys, clothes, and furniture to the colony.[64]

Groups of sewermen—many of whom were former construction workers—volunteered one week of their vacation to clear the land, start gardens and orchards, and build barns, stables, a henhouse, and housing for the colony. For some bachelors, this work "was only an extension of what they were practicing personally" with respect to the orphans of comrades.[65] The union took advantage of the experience which many sewermen had gained in other occupations before beginning to work in the sewers. As Larminier explained, "when we need masons, ditch diggers or carpenters, I spread the word, 'We need so many men exercising the following skills at the colony.' And the carpenters, ditch diggers and masons sign up; they ask for their annual vacation—in the middle of winter, if necessary—and come to spend it [at the colony]."[66] A sewerman with a background in metalworking devoted several years of vacations to building staircases.[67] Retired sewermen living in the colony occupied themselves with gardening and tending livestock as much as their health permitted. Most of the food consumed at the colony was grown there.[68]

The goal was to create a familial atmosphere for the several dozen residents who settled in during the first years of the community. The union's first step was to remove orphans from the peasant families who had been

raising them and to bring them to the colony.[69] Widows took in these orphans; adults punished children who misbehaved by refusing to hug them
for half a day.[70] Orphans were raised "according to exclusively lay principles."[71] At age fourteen they left to undertake an apprenticeship in whatever profession suited them best. While serving their apprenticeship they
still lived with "tutors" drawn from the ranks of the sewermen's union.
This allowed the union to continue to look after their charges' well-being.
The colony also assured that orphans would accumulate a nest egg by de-
positing a portion of the money which the city provided for their upkeep
in individual accounts in their names.[72]

Young Théophile Corbel, whose unhappy experiences were chronicled
earlier, thrived at the colony. Sickly as a youth, he became a healthy, even
heroic adolescent, having rescued a paralyzed old woman at the colony in
the midst of gunfire during 1914. Eventually he went into the army and
died in battle in 1917.[73] Alumni of the colony formed a group, Le Liseron,
which met regularly and reported on the whereabouts of its members in
the union newspaper. The *liseron* (a bind-weed), Larminier explained, "is a
creeper which, in spite of adverse conditions and age, coils around trees
and keeps going to the top without ever breaking."[74]

The colony was a working-class alternative to the Third Republic's conception of welfare benefits as individual in nature, to be used collectively
only in state, municipal, or Church-sanctioned institutional settings. Sewermen stressed repeatedly that the colony allowed them to escape the rules
and regulations of the administrative hierarchy under which they worked
and which characterized all welfare institutions. And because retired sewermen were lodged rent-free and continued to receive their individual pension payments, they enjoyed much more independence than they would
have retained in an old-age home.[75]

For ailing sewermen the colony was, in the words of Cottereau, "une
sorte de pratique de sanatorium sauvage."[76] Turn-of-the-century hygienic
theory focused on the design of housing for the urban lower classes as the
key to limiting the ravages of tuberculosis. Recent research has argued that
such an approach was necessarily insufficient: "[tuberculosis], the double
effect of malnutrition and under-nutrition, and of rickets caused by a lack
of irradiation of the body by ultra-violet rays, would be unlikely to disappear with a change in the shape of houses . . . It is above all the fact of
having enough to be able to eat a good balanced diet, and of taking in the
sun a few hours per day which is the veritable cause of the disappearance
of tuberculosis."[77] From this perspective, the colony arguably put into
practice a more efficacious mode of checking tuberculosis than did many

of the more narrowly focused urban renewal projects of contemporary public hygienists.[78]

One measure of the colony's success was the decision by the Paris municipal workers' union to create a similar institution, despite decades of troubled relations with the sewermen's union. The sewermen's union had joined the municipal workers' "central" on the eve of World War I under pressure from the C.G.T., which was seeking to consolidate individual unions into industrial federations.[79] Despite the merger, the sewermen's union continued to incur frequent reproaches for its efforts to maintain a separate identity.[80] The sewermen must therefore have experienced some satisfaction when, in 1916, the Paris municipal workers opened a Colonie-Orphelinat des Travailleurs Municipaux on five hectares of abandoned land near Epinay-sur-Orge owned by the department of the Seine. This colony followed the model set by the sewermen and used the same familial rhetoric to describe its mission.[81]

Like so much else in France, the sewermen's union and its colony never recovered from the effects of World War I. By the end of 1915, some six hundred sewermen had been called into service. At the front, many continued to think of their union as a second family. They kept up their dues, wrote ironically cheerful letters to *Le Réveil de l'Assainissement*—a common subject was the continuity in their lives from the *chasse aux rats* in the sewers to that in the trenches—and attended union meetings when on furlough. Some took their leaves at the colony.[82] Sewermen turned soldiers continued to depend on the union to look after their wives and children and instructed their wives to pay their union dues while they were at the front.

By the end of 1915, twenty-eight sewermen had died in the war, seventy-one had been injured, seventeen taken prisoner, and another seventeen were missing in action. Those who had died left behind twenty-eight widows and forty-five orphans. The union kept its commitment to care for them. Seventeen orphans were placed at the Colony; the rest received financial assistance from the union.[83] At the end of 1916, thirty orphans lived at the Colony.[84] In June 1917, the union reported that thirty-two sewermen had died so far in the war; the union was paying between 2,500 and 2,800 francs each month to widows and caring for up to thirty-five orphans at the Colony.[85] In December 1917, Larminier reported that the number of sewermen who had died in combat had risen to fifty-three.[86]

The war interrupted construction of the colony; it would never come near its goal of accommodating all members of the sewermen's family in need. In the fall of 1914 the Germans occupied and pillaged the colony. After the French retook the site, the sewermen fixed it up as best they could. During the war, the union expanded the facilities at the colony several times to accommodate the children of sewermen who had died in combat.[87] Much of this work was undone in 1918, when French troops ransacked the place and took numerous vital items.[88]

The damage done to the colony during the conflict was emblematic of that experienced by the sewermen as a group. The war decimated the generation succeeding Larminier and the founders of the union and the Colony.[89] It radicalized the sewermen who remained at work during the war. Many protested Larminier's practice of including selections from the army's *ordre du jour* in the obituaries of fallen sewermen and their sons.[90] In June 1921, the sewermen voted unanimously to align themselves with the radical *minorité* in the C. G. T.[91] After the C.G.T. split at the end of the year, the majority of unionized sewermen formed a pro-Communist *unitaire* union; a minority affiliated with the anti-Communist *confédérés*. The *unitaires* controlled the colony.[92]

The nature of the colony's activities changed during the interwar years. The French state assumed greater responsibility for the care of individuals with tuberculosis. (The prewar colony prefigured, as it were, the movement in the 1930s for more humane treatment of patients and their reintegration into society.[93]) In the 1920s, the colony came to be used as a vacation center for sewermen and their families; each summer fifty adults and sixty children spent their vacations there in the company of the retired sewermen who were permanent residents.[94] World War II delivered a death blow to the colony. The occupying German forces used it as a prisoner-of-war camp in 1940. When the Germans retreated, they destroyed as much of the colony as they could. After the war, the union was too poor to rebuild the settlement and turned it over to the prefecture of the Seine to serve as a summer camp.[95]

During the short life of the colony, the Paris sewermen's union creatively grafted forms of community cooperation characteristic of working-class life onto the nascent social welfare system of the Third Republic. The sewermen rejected as immoral and inhumane the placement of orphans with rapacious peasants and infirm sewermen in old age homes. They proposed their colony as a way to make whole again shattered lives threatened by further fragmentation in the welfare bureaucracy. Workers, widows, orphans, invalids, and retirees pooled their resources and talents to create an explicitly familial structure to replace the ones that had been broken by the hardships of the job. In so doing, workers echoed the technology of the Second Empire sewers which used the wastes of society to grow produce in the irrigation fields outside of Paris; the sewermen took the social wastage of the workplace and set out to transform it into an enlarged, caring family.[96]

In the century after Parent-Duchâtelet first wrote of the sewermen of Paris, the occasional professional from the upper classes periodically contrasted the sewermen's corporate solidarity with bourgeois (and worker) egoism. Parent-Duchâtelet hoped to find an outlet for this *esprit de corps* in the Catholic Société philanthropique; Bechmann in the lay republic. The Bonneff brothers, early twentieth-century socialist journalists who specialized in occupational health issues, wrote of Larminier, in a phrase reminiscent of Parent-Duchâtelet, "The life of this worker is beautiful and simple like that of a wise man of antiquity"[97]; the exemplary accomplishments of the sewermen's union made it their model for all workers.[98] (In fact, as with Parent-Duchâtelet for an earlier period, too much of what we know of turn-of-the-century sewermen comes from their enthusiastic accounts.) Doctor Foveau de Courmelles, who cooperated with the sewermen's union in the preparation of a report on occupational health in the profession, celebrated the sewermen's corporate unity. Writing in 1917, he argued that the middle classes had to unify in order to claim their rightful place in society. He presented the sewermen and their union as a model for the middle classes to follow.[99] The word of a different life Foveau de Courmelles and others brought forth from the underground sounded the discordant note which celebration of the marginal could introduce into the everyday reaffirmations of the social hierarchy. Through the voice of a few bourgeois mavericks, the message from below took the form of a moral lesson in which a representation of the communitarian other challenged the interplay of aggrandizement and repression of self in liberal, bourgeois society.

Turn-of-the-century republican social reformers incorporated elements of this challenge in the ideology of solidarism. Solidarists contended that classical liberalism had failed to come to grips with the interdependence of modern society and the fundamental inequalities among its members. The solidarist response was that all would have to restrict their individual self-interest in order to further the social good: people enter the world indebted to society and must discharge that debt by insuring one another against the insecurities of existence. In theory, solidarism offered a counter to both liberal individualism and socialist collectivism by positing a way in which the social order could be sustained without succumbing to the devastating disruptions of *laissez-faire* economic crises or the ultimate cataclysm of socialism. In practice, solidarists promoted a variety of social reforms, including limitation of the working day, social insurance, and assistance to those in need.[100]

However, such benefits were not necessarily "consumed" as those who doled them out expected. The usual manner of disposing of orphans, the aged, the infirm, victims of industrial accidents, and so on, was to establish a combination of individual benefits and institutions set apart from the social mainstream. The sewermen's union offered an alternative to this policy of marginalization. Within their colony, the sewermen proposed to live the solidarist philosophy of social indebtedness in a way alien to the lifestyle of its bourgeois exponents. There they opposed a community culture to the individualism and social differentiation embedded in the social security systems not just of France, but of most Western societies.

The sewermen's union was neither revolutionary nor reformist in the way these terms have come to be understood during the twentieth century. While the activities of the union had their own distinctive quality, they were also exemplary of the blend of anti-bureaucratic socialism, syndicalism, and cooperativism which characterized important elements of the European labor movement at the turn of the century.[101] Unlike political revolutionaries or revolutionary syndicalists, the sewermen's union did not seek the overthrow of the state. Yet its ultimate goal was not reformist either, in the sense of exchanging workers' autonomy and control over their lives for greater rewards from capitalism or the state. The union's aim was, on the contrary, to win concessions which it used in a subversive manner to alter the nature of institutional intervention in the lives of workers and their families. The origins of this innovative praxis must be sought not only in the cultural and material conditions of the sewermen's world, but also in the ways in which sewermen represented these conditions to themselves and others.

12

Sewermen Today

You don't heed the squalid work of sewermen, though you approve of
it as necessary.

—Antoine de Saint-Exupéry, *Citadelle*

FOR THE first two decades of the Fifth Republic the sewermen of Paris
remained a group apart, with their own traditions and culture. In a rapidly
changing society, a confluence of practices dating from the turn of the century sustained sewermen's representations of themselves: influence in hiring decisions; a large degree of autonomy in the workplace; public sector
employment; a strong union; and an unusual degree of rapport between
engineers and workers. Since the 1970s changes in each of these areas have
initiated a radical transformation which threatens the unique position of
sewermen in the social landscape of Paris.

Recruitment

Although the length of the Paris sewers grew over the course of the twentieth century, the number of sewermen remained fairly constant: 799 in
1935; 786 at the end of the 1970s—108 *chefs égoutiers* and 678 *égoutiers*.[1]
While other branches of Paris sanitation were increasingly staffed by immigrant labor in the 1960s and 1970s, recruitment into the sewers continued to be restricted by custom to French citizens. A man who signed up to
work in the sewers in the late 1970s generally had to wait two years to be
hired; in 1983, four years. [2]

No one entered the *corps* who was not *pistonné* by family, neighbors, or
the union.[3] In 1979, when the union official Sarrazin undertook a survey
of the background of sewermen, he found that hereditary endogamy
among them persisted. The link of kinship and employment applied to the
extended rather than the nuclear family: although Sarrazin encountered
fourth-generation sewermen, sewermen were, as a rule, not the sons of
sewermen. Workers were more commonly introduced into the service by

another relative who had been or was a sewerman—nephew, uncle, cousin, brother-in-law, and so on.[4] Membership in the C.G.T. and neighborhood ties provided other entrées into the trade. One worker, writing in 1983, reported that at least sixty sewermen had been born in the Ménilmontant district of Paris.[5] A municipal administrator explained, "There were hardly any free candidacies, that is to say an individual spontaneously presenting himself and being hired under these conditions . . . Candidates were generally more or less 'recommended' by a relative, a friend inside the service. One could almost speak of cooptation."[6]

Like their predecessors, most sewermen hired in the decades after World War II had left school early and worked in other trades before entering the sewers. A survey of sewermen in the 1950s revealed that the average age at hiring was between thirty and thirty-five. The sewermen's backgrounds remained as diverse as ever: "head cook, woodcutter, bookkeeper's assistant, butcher, truck driver, customs agent, insurance company employee." Like their predecessors, however, most incoming sewermen had worked in the building trades. Frustrated with the cyclical employment in construction, they accepted lower wages in exchange for the guarantee of regular employment. Forty percent of the sewermen in Sarrazin's 1979 survey originally came from the countryside. For them, use of urban contacts to find jobs in the sewers often crowned a successful entry into the world of the city. The Paris street-cleaning department served as a way station for many workers moving from the private sector to work in the sewers. After the statutory three years, they sought a transfer to the sewers to take advantage of the higher pay, the shorter work day, and earlier retirement offered sewermen.[7]

In answer to Sarrazin's question why they had chosen to work in the sewers, 80 percent of sewermen pointed to the stability of employment and another 10 percent to layoffs or dead-ends in their previous job. Sewermen had obtained the six-hour day in 1936 (six hours and forty minutes including the time to change and shower). Most sewermen worked in a single shift from 6:30 A.M. to 12:30 P.M. to take advantage of the maximal flow of water from morning street-cleaning.[8] Sarrazin hypothesized that an increasing number of men were drawn to work in the sewers because of the short work day, which gave them an opportunity not only to take a second job, but to participate in various cultural and sports activities as well.[9] (One sewerman I met is the sighted member of the world champion tandem mixed *voyant/non-voyant* cyclist team—one cyclist is male and one female; the lead is sighted; the back rider is blind. He trained each afternoon in order to retain his title.)

The Job

Work in the sewers and the dangers it presented likewise changed remarkably little until the late 1970s. Teams of five to seven men, who often worked together for years, continued to patrol their own designated areas of the sewer system.[10] The close bonds formed among workers on these teams remained the basis of safety in the sewers. One sewerman, recently retired after twenty years of work, commented, "A corporative spirit perhaps, but it was thanks to that we saved our skins."[11] The crews of sewermen worked largely free of supervision. A sewerman explained the appeal of the work: "There reigns a certain liberty. We are responsible for our own work from A to Z."[12]

If Belgrand or Bechmann was to visit the sewers today, he would still feel quite at home. The major technical change in cleansing and maintenance has been the introduction of trucks with large vacuum pumps to empty the *chambres de dessablement*. The trucks remain on the street while crews working in the *chambre* manipulate a hose extending from the truck down into the sewers. Workers no longer shovel sand manually, but they still have to walk around bent over in the muck holding the vacuum tube.

Sewermen recognized the antiquated nature of sewer technology and described their work in preindustrial terms. One sewerman remarked in 1977, "Our grandfathers, they did the same operations we do. The tools have not changed in one-hundred years."[13] Sewermen working the small galleries used a modified form of the *rabot* "which had to be pulled with a rope a little like the *laboureurs* of the Middle Ages who pushed the plough along by their own power."[14] The system of *wagons-vannes* and *bateaux-vannes* was (and is to this day) used to clean the larger sewers. Because of the continuing danger of using electric power in the sewers, workers still hauled these carts and "boats" back to their places. "Men pull the wagon in the same way as they moved stone blocks to build the pyramids."[15] "With a cadenced step, recalling the Volga boatmen, the men pull, one touching the other, against the raging water."[16]

The first portent of change was a new spirit among the engineers who supervised the sewers. The city of Paris established its own engineering school which began turning out graduates in the 1960s. These young engineers had a reputation for being "innovative." One official high in the municipal administration compared them to their predecessors: "It is well-known that engineers of the older generation were certainly more 'understanding,' laxer than their successors in the face of the workers' ways of doing things, and that this attitude came from the fact that they had been perfectly integrated into the organization for a long time."[17] The C.G.T. complained that "the [new] engineers are parachuted in."[18] Both management and the union agreed that the new cohort of engineers threatened to upset the kind of labor relations which had characterized the sewers in the past.

Health and Welfare

Recent medical studies have shown that Parisian sewermen carry intestinal parasites at five to six times the level of other individuals from the same socioeconomic background[19]; sewermen have been officially recognized to be at risk for three occupational diseases (including tetanus and anthrax).[20] In addition to illness, sewermen today face increased dangers from the dumping of hazardous chemicals, service station oil, and wastes from hospitals and laboratories. Despite ordinances forbidding the disposal of noxious substances in the sewers, the nature of the sewers (and popular perception of the *tout-à-l'égout* as a place impossible to pollute) has made illegal dumping particularly difficult to control. To take one example, dry cleaners and industrial dye shops send large quantities of chlorinated products into the sewer. Sometimes this causes a fog so thick that sewermen's lamps cannot pierce it. Because chlorinated products are denser than water, they settle in the sand at the bottom of the sewers. When sewermen disturb these deposits during cleansing, they release dangerous clouds of toxic fumes.[21]

As in the past, sewermen as a group have had to pick up the slack for their colleagues who were sick or injured. In the late 1970s, 30 percent of sewermen missed work each year due to accidents and 74 percent due to illness.[22] Many of these absences were for extended periods: sewermen averaged about two months of lost work time annually due to injuries and illness during this period. Because so many sewermen were injured or ill at any one time, teams were often short-handed. This caused further strain on the sewermen who continued to work. As a result, many ill sewermen balked at taking time off. With this in mind, the chief medical officer at the Prefecture of the Seine briefly revivified the long-standing representation of Parisian sewermen as a heroic breed apart—"aristocrats of the prefecture"[23]—an image the engineers had abandoned.

Throughout the twentieth century, sewermen have fought to protect and expand the prerogatives granted them in recognition of the particular dangers of their work. They rarely resorted to strikes, preferring instead to *faire banquette*, quite literally to remain on the sides (*bancs*) of the sewers. During such job actions, sewermen typically performed urgent work, but not daily maintenance tasks.[24] In 1934, sewermen thwarted the prefecture's attempt to cut expenses by pushing back the age at which workers could retire with a full pension. Five years later, however, this measure was incorporated into the emergency decrees instituted on the eve of World War II. The C.G.T. reported in 1946 that only 7 percent of sewermen who retired after at least twenty years of service lived more then five additional years.[25]

Sewermen struck for the first time in April 1949 to get their prewar pension plan back; the following year legislation reestablished their privileged position with respect to other municipal workers.[26] Sewermen with twenty years of service could retire at fifty with a pension set at 2 percent of the base salary for each year of service. Sewermen who worked more than five consecutive years were given credit for an additional half-year of work for each of their first twenty years of service; this provision did not hold for additional years of service. A sewerman who retired after twenty years therefore received 60 percent of his base salary; a sewerman who retired after thirty years received 70 percent of his base salary.

The 1977 Strike

In 1859 the Prefecture of the Seine had assumed responsibility for maintenance and cleaning of the sewers. Despite sometimes bitter conflicts between the sewermen and the prefecture, this relationship had helped assure the security and continuity of the sewermen's corporation. This situation changed with the law of 31 December 1975 which gave the city of Paris the right to self-governance. It placed sewermen under the *tutelle* of three ministries (Finances, Interior, and Health), but under the day-to-day control of city hall. Adding this change to the shift in recruitment of engineers created the conditions for an unprecedented conflict.

With the election of the conservative Jacques Chirac as mayor of Paris, the sewermen faced a situation similar to the one their predecessors encountered at the turn of the century. As a result of the 1975 municipal reform, however, Chirac's administration had much greater power to carry out a program of cost-cutting in municipal services. Furthermore, sewermen no longer presented a fully united front. Support for the majority C.G.T. union had declined since World War II. It had received 90 percent of votes to the Comité administratif paritaire in 1951, but only 77.65 percent in 1976. (The more moderate Force Ouvrière, F.O., and Confédération Française des Travailleurs Chrétiens, C.F.T.C., received most of the other votes.)

Sewermen had been feeling the pinch even before the election of the

Chirac government. In 1975, they had demonstrated at the Elysée Palace for better protective gear and a more regular supply of soap and towels in their locker rooms.[27] With the Chirac administration in power, the C.G.T. called on sewermen to *faire banquette* beginning 19 October 1977 to force the city to open negotiations over a range of issues involving remuneration, working conditions, creation of a health and safety committee, and payment of a bonus "thirteenth month." Beyond these demands, the C.G.T. had wider aims in unilaterally launching the strike. It sought to use the movement to mobilize popular support against the Chirac government and to create a climate for national negotiations on issues like payment of the bonus month. For years, the French left had been cooperating in preparation for the legislative elections in the spring of 1978. In September 1977, disagreement over the specifics of the Common Program scuttled the alliance. In the period following the demise of the Common Program, the Communist-led C.G.T. hoped that a show of militancy against a prominent leader of the conservatives would allow it to solidify its leading position nationally and to recoup the losses it had experienced among sewermen since the 1950s.[28]

In calling the strike, the C.G.T. proffered a challenge to sewermen, competing unions, and the public, as well as to the Chirac administration. Would sewermen rise to the occasion and play a vanguard role, reaffirming the public presence of French labor, doing what striking sanitation workers had done for immigrant labor a few years earlier? Drawing on their corporate identity and deploying their reputation as a group apart, the majority of sewermen followed the order to strike. At the outset, the C.G.T. claimed 80 percent participation; the municipal administration set the figure at 65 percent. The other unions kept their distance, however; the C.F.T.C. left the decision to strike up to its members; the F.O. opposed the movement.

The C.G.T. anticipated—even expected—these responses. What disheartened it was the public apathy to the sewermen's cause. The sewermen held twenty-three street demonstrations during the sixty-two day strike; some were quite picturesque, as when the striking sewermen marched through the city blowing their *trompettes de sécurité* or carrying dead rats on poles and chanting, *Chirac t'es foutu/les égouts sont dans la rue* (Chirac, you're beat/The sewers are in the street[29]). Yet these actions generated little passion among Parisians: neither the angry denunciations nor the deep expressions of solidarity which had characterized earlier strikes of immigrant sanitation workers. Nor was Paris overcome with anxiety about the consequences of untended sewers. The taming of the sewers had ultimately tamed the popular imagination. To paraphrase Blanqui and Jaurès, the public now seemed little concerned about who would flush *their* sewers. Even the inconvenience created by the strike was minimal. When street-cleaners walk off the job, the public daily experiences the growing accumulation of trash. The sewers slowly silted up during the sewermen's strike, but this happened far from the public view.

The split in the labor movement and a lack of public pressure to end the strike permitted the municipal authorities to let the conflict drag on. From the beginning, the Chirac administration questioned the representation of sewermen by the majority C.G.T. The municipality rejected the C.G.T.'s call to *faire banquette* as a subterfuge[30]; it considered the action an illegal strike and thereby justified its refusal to meet with representatives of the sewermen until the twenty-fifth day of the strike. Even then, it agreed to talk only with delegates from the C.F.T.C. and the F.O. The Chirac administration finally ended the strike after sixty-two days by agreeing to sit down with the C.G.T. as well, but it left no doubt who would have the upper hand in the future.

Since the Strike

The strike marked a turning point in the history of Paris sewermen. Demoralized by the defeat, large numbers quit the union. The sewermen's impulse to direct their sons into other lines of work strengthened: when Sarrazin asked in his 1979 survey if sewermen would like their sons to become sewermen, 82 percent responded "no" and only six percent said "yes." (The others expressed no opinion.)[31] The Chirac regime capitalized upon this disillusion and doubt among sewermen to consolidate its victory along several fronts. While letting it be known that some municipal services—sand extraction was frequently mentioned—might eventually be better handled by private contractors,[32] the administration acted forthwith in the domains of hiring and labor process.

The municipal administration took control of recruitment after the strike. One official explained: "During the period 1977/82 'union recommendations' were replaced with 'political recommendations' as a result of the change in the status of the City of Paris which became a municipality with an elected mayor. In my opinion it is very important to underscore this fact."[33] The administration took advantage of its new power to break with precedent and hire men as young as eighteen in order to compensate for the aging of the labor force. At the end of the decade, up to eighty new sewermen a year entered the service and the average age of a sewerman dropped to thirty-five.[34] Although these recruitment practices lasted only a short time, they were sufficient to dilute the longstanding sociocultural homogeneity of the sewermen.

In 1983–84 the city began systematically to reduce the size of the labor force by restricting hiring to a limited number of individuals coming from other municipal services. By 1 July 1988, the maximum number of sewermen was set at 611 (499 *égoutiers* and 112 *chefs égoutiers*); the actual figures were 450 and 105. As of that date, the administration reported that "*No hiring is anticipated* although there do exist positions to be filled." The city's projection for the future suggested a staff of only 200 *égoutiers* and 50 *chefs égoutiers* by the year 2000.[35]

In addition to taking control of hiring and sharply reducing the size of the labor force, the Chirac administration altered the way work was done in the sewers. The physical labor sewermen performed remained largely the same. They continued to employ the system of moving barrages inherited from the Second Empire.[36] It was the organization of labor that fell into disfavor. Municipal administrators strongly criticized the longstanding practice of giving a team of five to seven workers responsibility for all aspects of maintenance and cleaning of a *canton* (except for removal of sand from the *bassins de dessablement*). The administration felt this system did not allow it to allocate resources in the most efficient manner:

> The big problem with this organization is that it does not permit any evolution. Without constantly changing the boundaries of the *cantons* we came to see that certain crews were being transformed into simple sentinels as a result of the self-cleaning of the works, while others lacked the means to complete their tasks.[37]

Because sewermen knew their work areas far better than the engineers who supervised them, municipal administrators felt that they could not closely monitor what work the teams of sewermen were doing[38]: soldiers of hygiene threatened to become "simple sentinels." The key to reformed work in the sewers, the Chirac administration decided, was the introduction of computer science: *l'informatique.* This would, in turn, require a transformation of the organization of work in the sewers. "In effect, it was impossible to conceive of this technique while maintaining the old organization. In our case, we can consider that the appearance of this tool entailed an overturning of the existing structures."[39]

With this in mind, the Chirac administration broke the sewermen's control over their work by replacing the system of *cantons* with a new division of labor. All workers were asked to choose one of three specializations: inspection, flushing, or extraction of sand. Instead of having responsibility for both inspecting and cleansing a designated area, sewermen were assigned to specialized teams in charge of one job or the other. They now carry out these functions over a larger portion of the sewer network, moving about the city in mini-vans. Performing fewer tasks, in a wider area, sewermen have lost some of the power which intimate knowledge of a small section of the sewer had previously afforded them. And by separating the functions of inspection and cleansing, the administration has assured that one group of sewermen checks on the work of another, whereas in the past the same team had both identified problems and responded to them.[40]

The administration is now introducing hand-held computer units which maintenance teams use to enter information as they do their rounds. This information is relayed in turn to a computer covering the sewer system as a whole.[41] One of the goals of this technology is to reduce the autonomy which the sewermen's knowledge of the particularities of the system had given them. Quite simply, the sewermen's work culture proved an impediment to realization of the Chirac administration's post-Haussmannian conception of the sewers as organs of a body in which there would be a constant and unimpeded flow of information to a cranial center, which would distill it and disseminate commands to its members: "Analyses and decisions are made at the level of the system as a whole. The overall appraisals allow elected officials to be presented with a full picture of the patrimony they manage."[42] Of course, this reduction in the sewermen's control over their workplace has been represented by the administration as a positive revalorization of their work: "The sewerman is no longer isolated in his *canton*. The information he gathers makes its way to the decision-makers. The job of inspection [*surveillance*] is thus considerably up-graded."[43]

The Chirac regime has developed the public spectacle of urban cleansing aboveground, not below. In this *représentation* of the drama of Paris life, street-cleaners, dressed in bright, fashionable ecology-green jumpsuits, offer something for every taste. Traditionalists can watch the majority-French workforce[44] sweep the streets with replicas of the famous twig brooms (the "twigs" are now plastic); youth can spot street-cleaners zooming about town on green vacuum-equipped motorbikes on the lookout for dog droppings. Sewermen have only a small role to play in this show. The Chirac government has succeeded in giving a new representation of them: they are laborers like other laborers. The administration's programs for rationalization and cost cutting have involved not simply application of new forms of management to sewer maintenance and cleaning, but a de-mythification and demystification of sewermen as well. As is true for all

Foucault

social representations, the Chirac regime's banalization of sewermen seeks to transform power relations by challenging the terms in which social actors see themselves and are interpreted by others.

The C.G.T., left to lament the effacement of sewermen in the occasional journalistic resurrections of the mysterious world below Paris ("romanticized reporting, delirious articles which refer to fabulous treasures discovered in the miasmas of the sewer system"[45]), has responded by assuming curatorship of the specters of plague and sedition that once haunted Paris sewers. When the city announced plans in 1985 to reduce the number of sewermen, the union predicted that the cutbacks would lead to a rise in the rat population; "the dangers of cholera could appear within seven years." Furthermore, a smaller labor force would necessitate "abandoning daily surveillance of the sewers around ministries, embassies, banks, consulates, *maisons de la culture*, UNESCO, etc.; this could lead to a recrudescence of the risk of *attentats*."[46] Through these dire predictions, the union reiterated the representation of sewermen it had made to the president of the Republic in 1910. In itself, sewer technology, whether Second Empire boats or Fifth Republic computers, has not saved Paris from disease and sedition; sewermen have.

Conclusion

> I learned that the peasant cleaning sewers can be just as good as the professor . . . I began to believe in *liberté, egalité, fraternité*.
> —Carlos Guerreiro, quoted in Jane Kramer, *The Europeans*

real vs. imagined

THE EXPANSION of the Paris sewer system during the Second Empire and Third Republic responded to real and imagined threats which the bourgeois of Paris saw haunting their city: real and imagined, for real threats are also conjured in the imagination and imagined threats are real for those who imagine them. The renovated sewer system provided an exemplary instance of a technological solution to a nexus of social problems: *ordure* and *odeur* gave way to *ordre*. A healthier, more livable Paris resulted. Yet this technology was conceived, implemented, and interpreted not only in technical terms, but in political, economic, social, moral, and aesthetic ones as well. Juxtaposing these, sanitation experts and engineers were able to articulate a "public" interest which ultimately triumphed over the "private" interests of individual property owners and companies and even the professed scientific disinterestedness of medical authorities in the conflict over the *tout-à-l'égout*.

Accompanying discussions of sanitary practices was a disparate body of literature on the people who performed them. While bourgeois Bohemians of nineteenth-century Paris philosophized about ragpickers,[1] a few of their contemporaries sought to analyze society through its cesspool cleaners and sewermen. In their representations of such figures, social scientists and socially minded engineers joined literati and politicos in exploring fundamental questions about the relationship of labor to morality; the ability of technology to harness not only the material world, but the social world of labor as well; and the division of labor in their society and in the world of the future.

Equally important was the way in which such representations of social groups were brandished in battles over public policy. Democracies have the need to make "technical" debates over subjects like sanitary reform or municipal economics meaningful to the public. The formulation and dissemination of social representations are thus not just a means for the public health reformer or engineer to deal with an ultimately unknowable "other" (the ragpicker, cesspool cleaner, or sewerman), but serve to forward far reaching social visions as well.

Through their language and practices, the sewermen and their union put forth their own broad vision of social life: a counterculture to that of the middle-and upper-class opinion makers of the Third Republic. These workmen bestowed meaning on the particular methods of recruitment, organization of labor, and hazards of their trade. The sewermen of Paris were pioneers both in demanding the right to unionize for "public servants" and in securing social welfare measures. Working for the city of Paris, they were among the first French manual laborers to receive the eight-hour day, paid vacations, and other benefits. For their employer, these benefits were intended to foster stability and social harmony in an era of widespread conflict between workers and employers. But for the sewermen the benefits facilitated an alternative interpretation: the union used them collectively to undermine the statist/individualist premises of the nascent social security system.[2]

The contemporary transformation of work in the Parisian sewers involves both the introduction of new technologies and conflicts over how work is to be represented and interpreted. We are witnessing today the effacement of the Parisian sewermen's particularity and the disappearance of their world, a world which has fascinated outsiders from Parent-Duchâtelet to myself. Yet it is important to reflect on the legacy of the sewers and sewermen of Paris. In France and throughout the West, environmentalism and the welfare state are under urgent discussion. The challenges today are to rethink the blend of expediency and ecology which inspired sanitation engineers and to reclaim the sense of solidarity which permitted sewermen to incorporate the social security system into community life, while retaining a large degree of autonomy from state and employer.

Notes ♦ Index

Notes

Unpublished documentation for the kind of study of sewers and sewermen I have done is scattered. I found pertinent materials in the Archives départementales de la Seine (ADS), the Archives départementales de la Marne, the Archives nationales (AN) and the Archives de la Préfecture de Police (APP). I made greater use of materials not located in public archives: documentation provided by the Service technique de l'assainissement de la Ville de Paris; the records of the C.G.T. sewermen's union (Archives Syndicat); the papers of the former union leader Sarrazin (Archives Sarrazin); and the unpublished essay by the sewerman Lucien Gauchet, "Les Egouts de Paris." In addition, I interviewed and later corresponded with individual sewermen and administrators. In gathering material on sewers and sewermen in literature, I used the data base of the American and French Research on the Treasury of the French Language project.

Introduction

1. Cited (from Karl Marx, *The Economic and Philosophical Manuscripts*) with this interpretation by Lloyd Kramer, *Threshold of a New World: Intellectuals and the Exile Experience in Paris, 1830–1848* (Ithaca: Cornell University Press, 1988), p. 149. Alain Corbin's pathbreaking *The Foul and the Fragrant: Odor and the French Social Imagination,* trans. Miriam Kochan (Cambridge: Harvard University Press, 1986) is the fundamental work on odor in the nineteenth century; in it he perceptively addresses many of the subjects discussed in this book.
2. Karl Marx and Friedrich Engels, *The Communist Manifesto,* ed. Frederic L. Bender (New York: Norton, 1988), p. 60. "Civilization," François Guizot had divined during the 1832 cholera epidemic, "sleeps on an immense mine of barbarism." J. Lucas-Dubreton, *La Grande Peur de 1832 (le choléra et l'émeute)* (Paris: Gallimard, 1932), p. 82.
3. Sigmund Freud, *Civilization and Its Discontents,* trans. James Strachey (New York: W. W. Norton, 1962).
4. Mary Douglas, *Purity and Danger: An Analysis of the Concepts of Pollution and Taboo* (London: Ark Paperbacks, 1984). See also Mary Douglas and Aaron Wildavsky, *Risk and Culture* (Berkeley: University of California Press, 1982).

5. In handouts given the public today, Paris sanitation officials invariably describe the length of the city's sewers as the distance from Paris to Istanbul, implicitly suggesting that the sewers put this much distance between Paris and supposed sites of Oriental contagion.

6. The fears and fascinations which the sewers once generated reappear, for example, in tales like that of alligators in the New York sewers evoked by Thomas Pynchon in *V.* According to this myth, tourists brought baby alligators from Florida to New York. When they grew tired of their new pets, they put them down the toilet. These alligators are said to flourish in the sewers, sometimes along with "New York White," marijuana flushed down the toilet during drug busts. Robert Daley and others have tracked the story back to a 1935 *New York Times* article and to the reminiscences of the New York Sewer Commissioner in the 1930s. Jan Harold Brunvand, *The Vanishing Hitchhiker* (New York: Norton, 1981), pp. 90–98. Robert Daley, *The World beneath the City* (New York: Lippincott, 1959), pp. 187–189.

   Brunvand classified "alligators in the sewers" as one of several tales on the theme of "animals contaminating the human environment" (p. 98). (The idea is in line with Mary Douglas, *Purity and Danger.*) However, sewers are not usually considered part of the human environment. I think this story can be just as easily interpreted as a guilt-laden fantasy about the destruction of beings for which people once took responsibility. Owners of baby alligators may feel some guilt and remorse at flushing their pets down the toilet when they become too boring or burdensome to care for. The belief that the alligators continue to live in the sewers is a form of wish fulfillment. But in the psyche the guilt born of the original wrongful act grows. The alligator fantasized through this guilt is no longer a small baby, but a large, threatening albino adult, the Moby Dick of the city.

   Harlan Ellison offers a similar interpretation of sewer life in "Croatoan," the story of a man whose many girlfriends have had abortions. The tale begins with the narrator flushing an aborted fetus down the toilet. His distraught girlfriend then makes him metaphorically invert the abortion by descending into the sewers and finding the "child." After a long underground trek, he comes upon alligators and a colony of children. He ends up staying with the children, who call him father. *Strange Wine* (New York: Harper and Row, 1978), pp. 17–34.

   For the ephemeral existence of sewer alligators conceived outside of the sewers, see "Alligators," *The New Yorker* (28 March 1988), pp. 20–22.

   Underground reptilian fantasies persist, at least among the nonantediluvian. Kevin Eastman and Peter Liard's Teenage Mutant Ninja Turtles reiterate the story of pet alligators' "afterlife" in the New York sewers. Playmate Toys explains, "A boy's bowl of pet turtles falls into the stench of an underground city sewer. They land on Splinter, a penniless but powerful Ninja master who lives in the muck. Splinter's enemy Shredder (leader of the evil Foot clan), pours a disgusting green ooze over Splinter (and accidentally, the Turtles!), hoping to zap him dead. Instead, the Turtle pets mutate into Turtle teens, and Splinter turns into the biggest rat ever to face a trap. Splinter, the big cheese leader, teaches the Turtles the ways of the Ninja! Together they form a kick-stomping fighting team for the side of good against the deadly Foot clan!" The four Turtles' Renaissance names evoke their rebirth: Leonardo, Donatello, Michelangelo, and Raphael. This creation myth suggests that the nineteenth-century fear of sewage as a factor in illness, and denizens of the sewer as either abased or exalted breeds apart, has been largely displaced in the United States today by phobias (the 1984 film, "C.H.U.D.") and fantasies about the very real dangers existing in underground chemical and nuclear pollution. My thanks to Charles Reddy, an expert on the Turtles, for insights into their lives. See also "On and Off the Avenue," *The New Yorker* (11 December 1989), pp. 141–143; and, for the real turtles in the New York sewers, *The New York Times*, 6 April 1990, p. B1.

7. Peter Stallybrass and Allon White, *The Politics and Poetics of Transgression* (London: Methuen, 1986), p. 196 (in italics in the original). This provocative study includes a section on sewers in nineteenth-century literature. It is surprising that no one has written on the role of sewers and sewermen in comtemporary literature and films (including Andrzej Wajda's film "Kanal"). Although Graham Greene denied there was anything symbolic about the Vienna sewers in *The Third Man* (London: Heinemann, 1950), the sewer is the place in the tale where identity can be resolved in a divided city: there Rollo shoots his doubleganger Harry.

In *It* (New York: Signet, 1987), Stephen King makes the sewer the locus of a variety of sociopathic practices in American society, including child abuse, child abduction, wife abuse, juvenile delinquency, gay bashing, and racism. Through the unifying metaphor of the sewer, he attributes a single nature to these activities. This in turn suggests a liberal policy of social tolerance: the universal condemnation of child abuse in American society stigmatizes the tacitly accepted practices of homophobia.

Margaret Drabble's *The Middle Ground* (New York: Alfred A. Knopf, 1980) draws parallels between the feminist Kate Armstrong and her father, a London sewer worker and ardent union man, to explore the politics of class and gender. Kate is surrounded by an "underground world" (p. 189) of eccentrics— including one Hugo Mainwaring ("Hugo" as in the author of *Les Misérables;* "Main" as in sewer main; and "Waring" as in George Waring, leading proponent of a sewer system in which human waste was separated from storm sewers.) Kate is suspicious of feminists who lament women's lot as "shit and string beans"; her father's work with "shit" had been much worse (pp. 58–59). And her feelings about her long commitment to feminism are reminiscent of those of a disillusioned union stalwart: "I'm beginning to think I feel the same way about women that my father feels about the unions. That it was a good cause in the old days" (p. 8).

8. Wendy Lesser, *The Life below the Ground: A Study of the Subterranean in Literature* (Boston: Faber and Faber, 1987). Rosalind Williams' *Notes on the Underground* (Cambridge: M.I.T. Press, 1990) appeared too late for me to use it in this study.

9. Louis Chevalier, *Laboring Classes and Dangerous Classes in Paris during the First*

Half of the Nineteenth Century, trans. Frank Jellinek (Princeton: Princeton University Press, 1973). In this book I have not examined representations of sewage, sewers, sewermen and cesspool cleaners among the lower classes. For this, one could begin with Corbin's comments on their attitudes to odors and excrement. See *The Foul and the Fragrant,* pp. 211–221.

10. Victor Hugo, *Œuvres complètes,* ed. Jean Massin (Paris: Club Français du Livre, 1969), 11:823. See also Roland Barthes on the disruptions caused by the January 1955 flood in Paris and the political gloss given them. "Paris Not Flooded" in *The Eiffel Tower and Other Mythologies,* trans. Richard Howard (New York: Farrar, Straus and Giroux, 1979), pp. 31–34.

11. David Pinkney, *Napoleon III and the Rebuilding of Paris* (Princeton: Princeton University Press, 1958), pp. 127–145 (and the map of the collector sewers on p. 149). More recently, Wolfgang Schivelbusch has examined diverse facets of another nineteenth-century urban innovation—the spread of artificial light. See his *Disenchanted Night: The Industrialization of Light in the Nineteenth Century,* trans. Angela Davies (Berkeley: University of California Press, 1988).

On the transformation of Paris during the second half of the nineteenth century, see, in addition to Pinkney, Jeanne Gaillard, *Paris, la ville, 1852–1870: l'urbanisme parisien à l'heure d'Haussmann* (Paris: Champion, 1977); Anthony Sutcliffe, *The Autumn of Central Paris: The Defeat of Town Planning 1850–1970* (London: Edward Arnold, 1970); and T. J. Clark, *The Painting of Modern Life: Paris in the Art of Manet and His Followers* (Princeton: Princeton University Press, 1984).

12. Marx and Engels, *The Communist Manifesto,* p. 58.

13. Gertrude Himmelfarb, "Denigrating the Rule of Reason: The 'New History' Goes Bottom-Up," *Harper's* 268 (April 1984): 84–90.

14. "All practices, whether economic or cultural, depend on the representations individuals use to make sense of their world." Lynn Hunt, "Introduction," in *The New Cultural History* (Berkeley: University of California Press), p. 19.

1. The Old Regime

1. André E. Guillerme, *The Age of Water: The Urban Environment of the North of France A.D. 300–1800* (College Station: Texas A & M University Press, 1988), pp. 95–101, 116. Guillerme concentrates on a dozen northern French cities, but does not include Paris.

2. A. Mille, *Assainissement des villes par l'eau, les égouts, les irrigations* (Paris: Dunod, 1885), p. 98.

3. Guillerme, *The Age of Water,* pp. 118–74 (quotes on pp. 171, 138, 136). On industrial wastes in eighteenth-century Paris, see Pierre-Denis Boudriot, "Essai sur l'ordure en milieu urbain à l'époque pré-industrielle. De quelques réalités écologiques à Paris aux XVII et XVIIIèmes siècles. Les déchets d'origine artisanale," *Histoire économie et société* 7 (1988):261–281.

4. Charles Kunstler, *Paris souterrain* (Paris: Flammarion, 1953), p. 189.

5. Pierre Saddy, "Le Cycle des immondices," *Dix-huitième Siècle* 9 (1977):203–

214, presents a good overview of waste disposal in eighteenth-century Paris. See also Richard Etlin, "L'Air dans l'urbanisme des lumières," ibid., 123–134; and Jacques Guillerme, "Le Malsain et l'économie de la nature," ibid, 61–72.

6. Alfred Franklin, "Etude sur la voirie et l'hygiène publique à Paris depuis le XIIe siècle" in Anne de Beaulieu, *Estate, Noms et Nombre de toutes les rues de Paris en 1636* (Paris: Léon Willem, 1873), p. 19.

7. Simon Lacordaire, *Les Inconnus de la Seine. Paris et les métiers de l'eau du XIIIe au XIXe siècle* (Paris: Hachette, 1985), p. 258.

8. Pierre Chauvet, *Essai sur la propreté de Paris* (Paris, 1797), p. 14.

9. Pierre-Denis Boudriot, "Essai sur l'ordure en milieu urbain à l'époque pré-industrielle. Boues, immondices et gadoue à Paris au XVIIIe siècle," *Histoire économie et societé* 5 (1986): 516–519, 522.

10. E. Imbeaux, "Evacuation des immondices liquides: Egouts et vidanges" in A. Calmette, E. Imbeaux and H. Pottevin, *Egouts et vidanges* (Paris: J.-B. Baillière, 1911), p. 183. Catherine de Silguy, *La Saga des ordures du Moyen Age à nos jours* (Paris: Editions de l'Instant, 1989), pp. 36–37.

11. Boudriot, "Essai sur l'ordure," 519–520. A. Alphand, *Note du directeur des travaux de Paris. La Situation du service des eaux et égouts. Les Mesures à proposer au conseil municipal* (Paris: A. Chaix, 1879), p. 60.

12. Mille, *Assainissement,* pp. 98–99. Eugène Belgrand, *Les Travaux souterrains de Paris,* 5 vols. (Paris: Dunod, 1887), 5:258. Louis Chevalier made Montfaucon a centerpiece of his *Laboring Classes and Dangerous Classes in Paris during the First Half of the Nineteenth Century,* trans. Frank Jellinek (Princeton: Princeton University Press, 1973).

13. Jean-Noël Hallé, *Recherches sur la nature et les effets du méphitisme des fosses d'aisance* (Paris: Ph.-D. Pierres, 1785), pp. 69–70.

14. A.-J.-B. Parent-Duchâtelet, "Des Obstacles que les préjugés médicaux apportent dans quelques circonstances à l'assainissement des villes et a l'établissement de certains manufactures" in *Hygiène publique,* 2 vols. (Paris: J. B. Baillière, 1836), 1:14. Alain Corbin, *The Foul and the Fragrant: Odor and the French Social Imagination,* trans. Miriam Kochan (Cambridge: Harvard University Press, 1986), p. 31 (quoted). Corbin reviews the gamut of sanitary practices of the era and their olfactory consequences in sparkling fashion.

15. Franklin, "Etude," pp. 137–145. H. Lemoine, "Les Egouts de Paris du XIVe siècle à 1825," p. 4. This is a reprint of an article from *La Revue de la Chambre syndicale de maçonnerie, ciments et beton armé de la Ville de Paris et du Département de la Seine* (1929–1930). Hurtaut and Magny, *Dictionnaire historique de la ville de Paris et de ses environs* (Paris: Moutard, 1779), 2:725.

16. A.-J.-B. Parent-Duchâtelet, "Essai sur la cloaque ou égouts de la ville de Paris" in *Hygiène publique,* 2 vols. (Paris: J. B. Baillière, 1836), 1:185–186, 233. Préfecture du département de la Seine, Direction des eaux et des égouts, *Renseignements généraux sur les eaux et les égouts de la Ville de Paris* (Paris: Gauthiers-Villars, 1875), p. 36.

17. Maxime du Camp, *Paris. Ses organes, ses fonctions et sa vie dans la seconde moitié du XIXe siècle,* 6 vols. (Paris: Hachette, 1869–1875), 5:416. Franklin, "Etude," p. 19. Parent-Duchâtelet, "Essai sur la cloaque," 1:186. Belgrand, *Les Travaux,* 5:23.

18. Augustin Pierre Perrot, *Dictionnaire de la voirie* (Paris: Prault, Onfroy, Belon, Perrot, 1783), pp. 111–112. Parent-Duchâtelet, "Essai sur la cloaque," 1:232–233. Belgrand, *Les Travaux*, 5:169.

19. Parent-Duchâtelet, "Essai sur la cloaque," 1:188, 281. Lemoine, "Les Egouts de Paris," pp. 5, 53.

20. Lemoine, "Les Egouts de Paris," p. 5. Simon Lacordaire, *Histoire secrète du Paris souterrain* (Paris: Hachette, 1982), pp. 148–149.

21. Nicolas-Edmé Restif de la Bretonne, *Les Nuits de Paris or the Nocturnal Spectator: A Selection*, trans. Linda Asher and Ellen Fertig (New York: Random House, 1964), p. 93. Elsewhere, however, Restif expresses approval of "subterranean conduits for gutters" (p. 83).

22. Kunstler, *Paris souterrain*, pp. 193–195. Belgrand, *Les Travaux*, 5:27–28n1.

23. Louis-Sébastien Mercier, *Tableau de Paris*, 12 vols. (Amsterdam: n.p., 1782), 7:138–139.

24. Victor Hugo, *Œuvres complètes*, ed. Jean Massin (Paris: Club Français du Livre, 1969), 11:877.

25. Hurtaut and Magny, *Dictionnaire historique*, 2:725–731.

26. Baudriot, "Essai sur l'ordure," 518.

27. Lemoine, "Les Egouts de Paris," 39.

28. Corbin, *The Foul and the Fragrant*, p. 58, identifies the end of the eighteenth century as characterized by "a reduced threshold of tolerance among the masses, who made a direct connection between odors and death."

29. Hugo, *Œuvres complètes*, 11:877, 878.

30. Pliny, *Natural History*, trans. D. E. Eichholz (Cambridge: Harvard University Press, 1962), p. 83 (bk. XXXVI, ch. xxiv).

31. Bernardini Ramazzini, *Diseases of Workers*, trans. Wilmer Cave Wright (Chicago: University of Chicago Press, 1940), p. 107. For a recent evaluation of sanitary practices in ancient Rome, see Alex Scobie, "Slums, Sanitation, and Mortality in the Roman World," *Klio* 68 (1986): 399–433.

32. Chevalier de Jaucourt, "Cloaque" in *Encyclopédie ou Dictionnaire raisonné des sciences, des arts et des métiers* (Paris/Amsterdam: various publishers, 1751–1772), 3:538–539. Saint Augustine, *The City of God against the Pagans*, 7 vols., trans. William M. Green (Cambridge: Harvard University Press, 1963), 2:28 (Green's commentary on bk. 4, ch. 8).

33. Guillerme, *The Age of Water*, p. 174.

34. John McManners, *Death and the Enlightenment* (Oxford: Oxford University Press, 1981), pp. 315–317. René Suttel, *Catacombes et carrières de Paris* (Paris: Editions S.E.H.D.A.C.S., 1986).

35. McManners, *Death*, pp. 307, 315.

36. Owen Hannaway and Caroline Hannaway, "La Fermeture du cimetière des Innocents," *Dix-huitième Siecle* 9 (1977): 181–191. Madeleine Foisil, "Les Attitudes devant la mort au XVIIIᵉ siècle: sépultures et suppressions de sépultures dans le cimetière parisien des Saints-Innocents," *Revue historique* 510 (April-June 1974): 303–330.

37. Voltaire, "Préface de Catherine Vade" in *Oeuvres complètes de Voltaire* (Paris: Garnier Frères, 1877), 10:5 (cited in part by McManners, *Death*, p. 307).

38. Philippe Ariès, *L'Homme devant la mort* (Paris: Seuil, 1977), pp. 488–493.
39. Maurice Barrois, *Le Paris sous Paris* (Geneva: Hachette, 1964), p. 33.

2. Sewers and Social Order

1. Louis Chevalier, *Laboring Classes and Dangerous Classes in Paris during the First Half of the Nineteenth Century,* trans. Frank Jellinek (Princeton: Princeton University Press, 1973). Catherine Kudlick, "Disease, Public Health and Urban Social Relations: Perceptions of Cholera and the Paris Environment, 1830–1850" (Ph.D. diss., University of California at Berkeley, 1988), pp. 159–165.
2. H. Lemoine, "Les Egouts de Paris du XIV^c siècle à 1825," pp. 40–41. This is a reprint of an article from *La Revue de la Chambre syndicale de maçonnerie, ciments et beton armé de la Ville de Paris et du Département de la Seine* (1929–1930).
3. Louis R. Gottschalk, *Jean Paul Marat: A Study in Radicalism* (New York: Greenberg, 1927), pp. 78–79. For a recent description of Marat hiding in the sewers, see Christopher Hibbert, *The French Revolution* (New York: Penguin Books, 1982), p. 142.
4. Paul Fassy, *Marat. Sa mort, ses véritables funérailles* (Paris: Libraire du *Petit Journal,* 1867), pp. 24–26, 36–40. Alfred Bougeart, *Marat. L'Ami du peuple,* 2 vols. (Paris: Librairie internationale, 1865), 2:330.
5. A.-J.-B. Parent-Duchâtelet, "Essai sur la cloaque ou égouts de la ville de Paris" in *Hygiène publique,* 2 vols. (Paris: J. B. Baillière, 1836), 1:297. In 1848, British authorities uncovered a plot to plant explosives in the London sewers to blow up parliament and government offices. R. A. Lewis, *Edwin Chadwick and the Public Health Movement 1832–1854* (London: Longmans, Green, 1952), p. 90n4.
6. Alexis de Tocqueville, *Recollections,* trans. George Lawrence (Garden City, N.Y.: Doubleday, 1971), pp. 147–148. I would like to thank John Headley for bringing this reference to my attention.
7. See especially Hugo's "L'Egout de Rome" (1853) in *Œuvres complètes,* ed. Jean Massin (Paris: Club Français du Livre, 1969), 8:746–747. Chevalier, *Laboring Classes,* pp. 107–110, looks at Hugo's discussion of sewers in *Les Misérables.*

   The American and French Research on the Treasury of the French Language project searched the texts of over 1,500 classics of French literature since the eighteenth century for the words *égout* and *égouts.* Of the 542 references, 189 were in the works of Hugo, including 172 in *Les Misérables.*
8. Charles Baudouin suggests that Hugo's history of sewer exploration in *Les Misérables* reenacts the author's infantile search for his origins—the child's digestive theory of pregnancy and cloacal theory of birth through the anus. Hugo refers to the overflowing of the Paris sewers in 1802—the year he was born. *Psychoanalyse de Victor Hugo* (Geneva: Editions du Mont-Blanc, n.d.), esp. pp. 78–87. The years of Bruneseau's exploration of the sewers (1805–

1812) coincide with the years when Hugo too was investigating the mystery of his origins (p. 155n3).

9. Eugène Sue, *Les Mystères de Paris* (Paris: Jean-Jacques Pauvert, 1963), p. 1.

10. Hugo, *Œuvres complètes*, 11:622; see also 11:859. The name Gueulemer is itself evocative: *gueule* means big mouth; *mer* means sea.

11. Ibid., 11:497, 503, 794.

12. Ibid., 11:902. Hugo edited out a reference to Cartouche, the most famous criminal of the Old Regime, escaping to his lair in the sewers and leaving the police dumbfounded. *Un Carnet des 'Misérables', octobre-décembre 1860: notes et brouillons,* ed. Jean-Bertrand Barrère (Paris: Lettres modernes, 1965), p. 184 (f° 107).

13. Hugo, *Œuvres complètes*, 11:876.

14. Henry Mayhew, *London Labour and the London Poor*, 3 vols. (London: Griffin, Bohn, 1861), 2:446.

15. Hugo, *Œuvres complètes*, 11:876. Charles Baudelaire wrote in "La Fanfarlo" (1847) of "le ruisseau, lit funèbre où s'en vont les billets doux et les orgies de la veille, charriait en bouillonnant ses milles secrets aux égouts . . ." *Œuvres complètes* (Paris: Pléiade, 1961), p. 506.

16. Hugo, *Œuvres complètes*, 11:877.

17. Ibid., 11:880. Gaston Leroux repeated Hugo's technique of citing an early nineteenth-century explorer of the Paris sewers in this manner. In *La Double Vie de Théophraste Longuet,* in Leroux, *Romans fantastiques* (Paris: Robert Laffont, n.d.), 3:320n2, Leroux wrote that the official report of 1823 [*sic*] on cleaning the Amelot sewer revealed that the *chambre à coucher de Cartouche* had been discovered in the sewers. (See n. 12 above.) Just as Hugo's supposed borrowings from Bruneseau cannot be traced, no reference to Cartouche is to be found in Parent-Duchâtelet's 1826 report on the Amelot sewer. What is important is the belief among readers that such things could very well have been found in official reports (and perhaps in the sewers themselves).

18. Hugo, *Œuvres complètes*, 11:532.

19. Ibid., 11:882. H. C. Emmery, "Statistique des égouts de la ville de Paris (année 1836)," *Annales des ponts et chaussées* 7 (1837), was Hugo's major source of information on the sewers of Paris. In a footnote (p. 268n4), Emmery praises the "courage and zeal" of Bruneseau and his son-in-law Félix Nargaud and commented that their work had prepared the way for cleaning the city's sewers and that it had not received the recognition it deserved. This passage was probably the inspiration for Hugo's account of Bruneseau in *Les Misérables*.

20. Hugo, *Œuvres complètes*, 11:878–879.

21. A.-J.-B. Parent-Duchâtelet, "Rapport sur le curage des égouts. Amelot, de la Roquette, Saint-Martin et autres" in *Hygiène publique*, 1:313, 426–427.

22. Emmery, "Statistique des égouts," 268, 270 (quoted).

23. A. Chevallier, "Mémoire sur les égouts de Paris, de Londres, de Montpellier," *Annales d'hygiène publique et de médecine légale* 19 (1838): 366.

24. ADS VO³17, Bruneseau, "Renseignements sur la situation actuelle des égouts de Paris," 27 December 1806.

25. AN F⁸95, Bruneseau, "Observations sur la salubrité de Paris," n.d.

26. ADS VO³17, Bruneseau, "Renseignements."

27. Bruneseau wrote of his exploration of the sewers: "Many times I have travelled through the Paris sewers, most often bent over, my nose in the offal, and most often suffocating from *méphitisme* to the extent of having to ascend periodically to breathe." AN F⁸95, Bruneseau, "Observations."

28. See Erwin H. Ackerknecht, "Anticontagionism between 1821 and 1867," *Bulletin of the History of Medicine* 22 (1948): 562–593; William Coleman, *Death is a Social Disease: Public Health and Political Economy in Early Industrial France* (Madison: University of Wisconsin Press, 1982); and Kudlick, "Disease," pp. 18–61.

29. A.-J.-B. Parent-Duchâtelet, *De la Prostitution dans la Ville de Paris*, 2 vols., 2nd. ed. (Paris: J. B. Baillière, 1837), 1:7. See Alain Corbin's excellent "Présentation" in A.-J.-B. Parent-Duchâtelet, *La Prostitution à Paris au XIXᵉ siècle* (Paris: Seuil, 1981), pp. 9–55. While Parent-Duchâtelet paralleled his own experiences in exploring brothels and other sites of filth in Paris, he clearly set prostitution apart from these subjects of investigation as potentially more dangerous to the moral and medical order of society. On this theme, see the illuminating studies of Charles Bernheimer, *Figures of Ill Repute: Representing Prostitution in Nineteenth-Century France* (Cambridge: Harvard University Press, 1989), pp. 8–33; and Jill Harsin, *Policing Prostitution in Nineteenth-Century Paris* (Princeton: Princeton University Press, 1985), pp. 104–113.

30. Parent-Duchâtelet, *De la Prostitution*, 1:21.

31. Ibid., 2:526.

32. The best recent histories of the epidemic are Kudlick, "Disease" (which brings out the conjunction of revolution and cholera) and Patrice Bourdelais and Jean-Yves Raulot, *Une Peur bleue. Histoire du choléra en France 1832–1854* (Paris: Payot, 1987). See also Louis Chevalier, *Le Choléra. La Première épidémie du XIXᵉ siècle* (La Roche-Sur-Yon: Imprimerie Centrale de l'Ouest, 1958); and François Delaporte, *Disease and Civilization: The Cholera in Paris, 1832*, trans. Arthur Goldhammer (Cambridge: M.I.T. Press, 1986).

33. *Rapport sur la marche et les effets du choléra-morbus dans Paris et les communes rurales de la Seine. Année 1832* (Paris: Imprimerie royale, 1834), pp. 35–36. See also Georges Vigarello, *Le Propre et le sale. L'Hygiène du corps depuis le Moyen Age* (Paris: Seuil, 1985), pp. 191–206.

34. Stéphane Flachat [Mony], *Religion Saint-Simonienne. Le Choléra-Assainissement de Paris* (Paris: Evarat, 1832). On the Saint-Simonians, see Robert Carlisle, *The Proffered Crown: Saint-Simonianism and the Doctrine of Hope* (Baltimore: The Johns Hopkins University Press, 1987).

35. Erwin Ackerknecht, "Hygiene in France, 1815–1848," *Bulletin of the History of Medicine* 22 (1948): 140. Coleman, *Death*, pp. 284–302.

36. J.-B. Monfalcon and A.-P. I. de Polinière, *Traité de la salubrité dans les grandes villes* (Paris: J. B. Baillière, 1846), p. 101.

3. Engineering and Empire

1. A.-J.-B. Parent-Duchâtelet, "Essai sur la cloaque ou égouts de la ville de Paris" in *Hygiène publique*, 2 vols. (Paris: J. B. Baillière, 1836), 1:194. *L'Hermite de*

la Chaussée d'Antin, quoted in Léon de Lanzac de Laborie, Paris sous Napoléon, 8 vols. (Paris: Plon-Nourrit, 1905–1913), 2:212–213.

2. In 1835 the aging Talleyrand complained to the prefect Count Rambuteau that the laying of sewers under both the Rue St. Honoré and the Rue St. Florentin at the same time trapped him in his house. Unless work at one site was stopped, the only way for him to exit would be through the window. ADS, D³A, no. 312 pièce 9, Talleyrand to Rambuteau, 25 October 1835. Rambuteau himself noted that each hole or trench dug in Paris during his tenure as prefect was known as "un Rambuteau." Comte de Rambuteau, Mémoires du Comte de Rambuteau publiés par son petit-fils (Paris: Calmann-Lévy, 1905), p. 376.

3. H. C. Emmery, "Egouts et bornes-fontaines," Annales des ponts et chaussées 4 (1834): 255–256n15. Emile Gérards, Paris souterrain (Paris: Garnier Frères, 1908), p. 486. Georges Eugène Haussmann, Premier mémoire sur les eaux de Paris présenté par le préfet de la Seine au conseil municipal (4 août 1854) (Paris: Charles de Mourgues Frères, 1858), pp. 44–45.

4. Rambuteau, Mémoires, p. 376.

5. Hector Noreau, Nouveaux égouts proposés à la ville de Paris (Paris: Firmin Didot Frères, 1831), p. 4n1.

6. Adolphe Joanne, Paris illustré en 1870 (Paris: Hachette, 1870), p. 1035.

7. Préfecture du département de la Seine, Direction des eaux et des égouts, Renseignements généraux sur les eaux et les égouts de la Ville de Paris (Paris: Gauthiers-Villars, 1875), p. 37.

8. Louis-Sébastien Mercier, Tableau de Paris, 12 vols. (Amsterdam: n.p., 1789), 12:72.

9. H. Lemoine, "Les Egouts de Paris du XIVᵉ siècle à 1825," p. 43n3. This is a reprint of an article which appeared in La Revue de la Chambre syndicale de maçonnerie, ciments et beton armé de la Ville de Paris et du Département de la Seine (1929–30).

10. Parent-Duchâtelet, "Essai sur la cloaque," 1:229–230.

11. A.-J.-B. Parent-Duchâtelet, "Rapport sur le curage. Amelot, de la Roquette, Saint-Martin" in Hygiène publique, 1:339–42, 432.

12. Georges Bechmann, Notice sur le Service des eaux et de l'assainissement de Paris (Paris: Ch. Béranger, 1900), pp. 43–44.

13. Quoted in John von Simson, "Water Supply and Sewerage in Berlin, London, and Paris: Developments in the Nineteenth Century" in Urbanisierung im 19. und 20. Jahrhundert (Cologne: Böhlau Verlag, 1983), p. 430. For the history of water use in France, see Jean-Pierre Goubert's excellent The Conquest of Water: The Advent of Health in the Industrial Age, trans. Andrew Wilson (Princeton: Princeton University Press, 1989).

14. Benjamin Ward Richardson, The Health of Nations: A Review of the Works of Edwin Chadwick, 2 vols. (London: Longmans, Green, 1887), 1:lxvii.

15. Georges Eugène Haussmann details the parallels between the sewers he constructed and those built by the Romans in his Mémoires du Baron Haussmann, 3 vols. (Paris: Victor-Havard, 1893), 3:351–352. The best account of the transformation of Paris during the Second Empire remains David Pinkney,

Napoleon III and the Rebuilding of Paris (Princeton: Princeton University Press, 1958).

Many engineers wrote detailed technical works on the Paris sewer system and these form the basis for the following description of the sewer. See in particular A. Alphand, *Note du directeur des travaux de Paris. La Situation du service des eaux et égouts. Les Mesures à proposer au conseil municipal* (Paris: A. Chaix, 1879); Bechmann, *Notice sur le service des eaux;* Bechmann, *Salubrité urbaine. Distribution d'eau. Assainissement,* 2 vols. (Paris, Ch. Béranger, 1899); Eugène Belgrand, *Les Travaux souterrains* (Paris: Dunod, 1887), 5 vols., vol. 5.; Will Darvillé, *L'Eau à la ville, à la campagne et dans la maison* (Paris: Libraire de la construction moderne, n.d.); A. Debauve, *Distributions d'eau. Egouts,* 2 vols. (Paris: P. Vicq-Dunod, 1897); Gérards, *Paris souterrain;* M. Humblot, *Les Egouts de Paris à la fin de 1885* (Paris: Imprimerie Chaix, 1886); A. Mille, *Assainissement des villes par l'eau, les égouts, les irrigations* (Paris: Dunod, 1885); A. Wazon, *Principes techniques d'assainissement des villes et habitations suivis en Angleterre, France, Allemagne, Etats-Unis et présentés sous forme d'etudes sur l'assainissement de Paris* (Paris: J. Baudry, 1884); Paul Wéry, *Assainissement des villes et égouts de Paris* (Paris: Dunod, 1898). Gabriel Dupuy and Georges Knaebel's illuminating *Assainir la ville hier et aujourd'hui* (Paris: Dunod, 1982) examines the theory and practice of sewer construction and operation in France since the beginning of the nineteenth century, with an emphasis on the period after 1940.

16. Georges Eugène Haussmann, *Mémoire sur les eaux de Paris* (Paris: Vinchon, 1854), pp. 52–53.

17. Haussmann, *Mémoires,* 3:111–119.

18. Dupuy and Knaebel, *Assainir la ville,* p. 18.

19. Thomas Rammell, "Report on the Cesspool System in Paris." Appendix 4 to General Board of Health, *Report on the Supply of Water to the Metropolis* (London: W. Clowes, 1850), p. 1.

20. Léon Colin, *Paris. Sa Topographie, son hygiène, ses maladies* (Paris: E. Masson, 1885), p. 211.

21. R. Baumeister, *The Cleaning and Sewerage of Cities,* trans. J. M. Goodell (New York: Engineering News Publishing, 1895), p. 79.

22. Henry Haynie, *Paris Past and Present,* 2 vols. (New York: Frederick A. Stokes, 1902), 2:292–294.

23. Bechmann, *Notice sur le service des eaux,* pp. 44–45.

24. Maxime du Camp, *Paris. Ses organes, ses fonctions et sa vie dans la seconde moitié du XIXe siècle,* 6 vols. (Paris: Hachette, 1869–1875), 5:450.

25. J. J. Waller, "Under the Streets of Paris," *Good Words* 35 (1894):493.

26. Humblot, *Les Egouts de Paris,* pp. 6–7.

27. Victor Hugo, *Œuvres complètes,* ed. Jean Massin (Paris: Club Français du Livre, 1969), 11:881.

28. Daniel Bellet and Will Darvillé, *Ce que doit être la Cité moderne* (Paris: H. Nolo, n.d.), p. 124. Philippe Lefrançois, *Paris souterrain* (Paris: Editions internationales, 1950), p. 92.

29. See, for example, F. Liger, *Les Egouts de Paris* (Paris: Guillaumin, 1883), pp. 232–238.

30. Contemporaries interpreted several of these auxiliary functions as promoting a personalization and decentralization of social life seemingly at odds with the technocratic nature of the sewer system itself. Pneumatic letters, for instance, were recognized as "more secret than the telegram proper . . . and, best of all, preserving the caligraphy of the sender." (Waller, "Under the Streets," 494). Workers engaged in the production of *articles de Paris* made use of compressed air to power machines and lathes in small shops and apartments. While extension of the sewer system unified the circulatory functions of the city, it (like electricity) also allowed for dispersal of industrial production.

31. A. Chevallier, "Mémoire sur les égouts de Paris, de Londres, de Montpellier," *Annales d'hygiène publique et de médecine légale* 19 (1838):366.

32. A. Mille, "Assainissement de la Seine," c. 1875 [translation of an unidentified article into English, at the New York Public Library].

33. Victor Fournel, *Paris nouveau et Paris futur* (Paris: Jacques Lecoffre, 1865), p. 17.

4. The Visit

1. Frances Trollope, *Paris and the Parisians in 1835* (New York: Harper and Brothers, 1836), pp. 132–136.

2. Emile de La Bédollière, *Les Industriels. Métiers et professions en France* (Paris: Veuve Louis Janet, 1842), p. 178. It is true that an English-language guidebook published the previous year had bothered to inform tourists that the Paris sewers harbored "a prodigious number of rats" and "very abundant" fungi. *Galignani's New Paris Guide* (Paris: A. and W. Galignani, 1841), p. 129.

3. A. Daverton, *Assainissement des villes et égouts de Paris* (Paris: Dunod, 1922), p. 393.

4. Henri Malet, *Le Baron Haussmann et la rénovation de Paris* (Paris: Editions municipales, 1973), p. 268.

5. Pierre Larousse, *Grand Dictionnaire universel du XIXᵉ siècle* (Paris: Administration du *Grand Dictionnaire universel*, 1879), 7:263. Eugène Belgrand, *Les Travaux souterrains de Paris*, 5 vols. (Paris: Dunod, 1887), 5:209.

6. Georges Bechmann, *Notice sur le service des eaux et de l'assainissement de Paris* (Paris: Libraire polytechnique, 1900), p. 300. Alphand covered the Canal Saint-Martin with little gardens which hid the air vents, and offered tours of it before the sewers were opened to the public. Victor Fournel, who considered the project an example of the Empire's wasteful, ostentatious approach to the reconstruction of Paris, described the canal and the boat ride through it: "The devotees of new emotions will no more be able to do without a trip through the Saint-Martin canal than a balloon trip . . . This expedition is interesting to do once, but after a while it lacks picturesqueness, or at least the picturesqueness is too uniform and smacks too much of the engineer's hand." *Paris nouveau et Paris futur* (Paris: Jacques Lecoffre, 1865), pp. 98–99.

7. Belgrand, *Les Travaux souterrains*, 5:209.

8. J. J. Waller, "Under the Streets of Paris," *Good Words* 35 (1894):493.

9. Ibid., 494.

10. "The Paris Sewers," *The Illustrated News,* 29 January 1870, p. 129.
11. A. Mille, *Assainissement des villes par l'eau, les égouts, les irrigations* (Paris: Dunod, 1885), p. 145. Henry Haynie, *Paris Past and Present,* 2 vols. (New York: Frederick A. Stokes, 1902), 2:303.
12. "The Paris Sewers," p. 129.
13. Lucy H. Hooper, "A Visit to the Sewers of Paris," *Appleton's Journal* 13 (3 April 1875): 430.
14. Waller, "Under the Streets," 494.
15. Maxime du Camp, *Paris. Ses organes, ses fonctions et sa vie dans la seconde moitié du XIXe siècle,* 6 vols. (Paris: Hachette, 1869–1875), 5:445.
16. Karl Baedeker, *Paris and Environs,* 13th ed. (Leipzig: Karl Baedeker, 1898), p. 64.
17. Paul Joanne, *The Diamond Guide for the Stranger in Paris* (Paris: Hachette, 1889), p. 343.
18. Francis White, "A Visit to the Paris Sewers," *Harper's Weekly* 37 (29 April 1893):395.
19. Thomas W. Knox, *The Underground World* (Hartford: J. B. Burr Publishing, 1880), p. 528.
20. "The Paris Sewers," p. 129.
21. White, "A Visit," 395.
22. Paul Wéry, *Assainissement des villes et égouts de Paris* (Paris: Dunod, 1898), p. 402.
23. X. Feyrnet, "Courrier de Paris," *L'Illustration* 44 (10 December 1864):371.
24. Ibid.
25. Walter Benjamin, "Paris, Capital of the Nineteenth Century" in *Reflections,* trans. Edmund Jephcott (New York: Harcourt Brace Jovanovich, 1978), p. 150.
26 Nadar [Gaspard Félix Tournachon], *Quand j'étais photographe* (Paris: Ernest Flammarion, 1899), pp. 126–129. Nadar's photographs of the sewers and catacombs are available in *Le Paris souterrain de Félix Nadar 1861* (Paris: Caisse nationale des monuments historiques et des sites, 1982). For a recent discussion of photographs of workers (including Nadar's), see André Rouillé, "Les Images photographiques du monde du travail sous le Second Empire," *Actes de recherche en sciences sociales* 54 (September 1984):31–43.
27. *Galignani's New Paris Guide,* p. 129.
28. Bechmann, *Notice sur le service,* pp. 301, 332, 334. A. Debauve, *Distributions d'eau. Egouts,* 2 vols. (Paris: P. Vicq-Dunod, 1897), 2:482.
29. Waller, "Under the Streets of Paris," 494.
30. Bechmann, *Notice sur le service,* p. 301.
31. White, "A Visit," 395 (quoted). Charles Kunstler, *Paris souterrain* (Paris: Flammarion, 1953), p. 229.
32. Kunstler, *Paris souterrain,* p. 219.
33. Hooper, "A Visit," 430.
34. White, "A Visit," 395.
35. Pliny, *Natural History,* trans. D. E. Eichholz (Cambridge: Harvard University Press, 1962), p. 85 (bk. XXXVI, ch. xxiv).

36. Ibid., p. 83. Alfred Meyer, "La Canalisation souterraine de Paris," in *Paris Guide par les principaux écrivains et artistes de la France,* 2 vols. (Paris: Librairie internationale, 1867), 2:1606.

37. Fournel, *Paris nouveau,* p. 100. Writing during the Third Republic, F. Liger— one of the few vociferous critics of the new sewers—claimed that their renown was the work of those who wanted to keep alive the reputation of the "mythological reign" of Napoleon III. *Les Egouts de Paris* (Paris: Guillaumin, 1883), p. 229.

38. Victor Hugo, *Œuvres complètes,* ed. Jean Massin (Paris: Club Français du Livre, 1969), 11:881.

39. Du Camp, *Paris,* 5:430–431.

40. Maxime du Camp, *Les Convulsions de Paris,* 4 vols. (Paris: Hachette, 1878).

41. Du Camp, *Paris,* 5:457, 510–512.

42. Louis Veuillot, *Les Odeurs de Paris* (Paris: Georges Crès, n.d.), p. 8.

43. Ibid., pp. 1–2.

44. Ibid., p. 1.

45. Ibid., p. 2.

46. *Grand Larousse encyclopédique en dix volumes* (Paris: Librairie Larousse, 1961), 4:391. See the reference to "the comparison, too often repeated, and which is beginning to tire, of naturalist literature with the sewers" in "Courrier de Paris," *Illustration* 77 (29 January 1881):66.

47. Bloy was a master of the scatological comment. Referring to a book he did not like as *crapule,* he wondered how he should dispose of it since it might block up his toilet and he was too far from a sewer grate. *Journal de Léon Bloy,* 3 vols. (Paris: Mercure de France, 1963), 2:285.

48. Haynie, *Paris,* 2:305–306. Haussmann had envisaged placing gas mains in the sewers but abandoned this plan for fear of accidents. Adolphe Laurent Joanne, *Paris illustré. Nouveau guide de l'étranger et du parisien* (Paris: Hachette, 1867), p. 1037.

49. Jean Raymond Tournoux, *L'Histoire secrète* (Paris: Plon, 1962), p. 105.

50. Ibid., p. 16. Deloncle and the leadership of the Cagoule were clearly fascinated with the subversive possibilities of refuse and disease. They planned to transform garbage trucks into armored vehicles (ibid., p. 17) and attempted to steal the germs which cause botulism from the Institut Pasteur for use in assassinating dissidents who left the Cagoule for Colonel de La Rocque's Parti Social Français (ibid., pp. 54–57).

51. Raymond Massiet, *La Préparation de l'insurrection et la bataille de Paris* (Paris: Payot, 1945), pp. 99–100; and Georges Verpraet, *Paris. Capitale souterraine* (Paris: Plon, 1954), pp. 155, 284–286.

52. Tournoux, *L'Histoire secrète,* pp. 13, 16, 26.

53. Richard Saul Wurman, *Paris Access* (New York: Access Press, c. 1986), p. 163.

5. The Irrigation Fields

1. Maxime du Camp, *Paris. Ses organes, ses fonctions et sa vie dans la seconde moitié du XIXe siècle,* 6 vols. (Paris: Hachette, 1869–1875), 5:455. At the time, "écu-

meurs de la Seine," authorized by the Prefecture of the Seine, skimmed a wide variety of items from the river for resale. Jules Brunfaut, *Hygiène publique. Les Odeurs de Paris,* 2nd ed. (Paris: Veuve Ambroise LeFèvre, 1882), pp. 149–150.

2. *La Lanterne,* 1 February 1902 (reprinted in *Le Réveil de l'Assainissement,* 16 February 1902, p. 2).

3. Du Camp, *Paris,* 5:455; 460 (quoted).

4. Mathieu Géraud, *Essai sur la suppression des fosses d'aisance, et de toute espèce de voiries, sur la manière de convertir en combustibles les substances qu'on y renferme, etc.* (Amsterdam: n.p., 1786).

5. Nicolas-Edmé Restif de la Bretonne, *Les Nuits de Paris or the Nocturnal Spectator. A Selection,* trans. Linda Asher and Ellen Fertig (New York: Random House, 1964), pp. 92–93. See ch. 6, n. 48 below.

6. For a good exposition of Leroux's ideas on the "circulus," see Armelle Le Bras-Chopard, *De L'Egalité dans la différence: Le Socialisme de Pierre Leroux* (Paris: Presses de la Fondation nationale des sciences politiques, 1986), pp. 296–302. On plans for the utilitarian use of waste during this period, see the perceptive comments of Alain Corbin in *The Foul and the Fragrant,* trans. Miriam L. Kochan (Cambridge: Harvard University Press, 1986), pp. 114–121.

   Many social reformers in Great Britain conceived of the use of human refuse as fertilizer as a refutation of Malthus. See, for instance, Henry Mayhew, *London Labour and the London Poor,* 3 vols. (London: Charles Griffin, 1861), 2:177–182. For George Burges, an individual's waste provided "more than enough to fertilise the soil requisite for his food." Great Britain's urban concentrations gave it an advantage over other countries in the efficient collection of human manure. Burges concluded that its use could save British agriculture from the effects of free trade:

> The bane and antidote before us lie;
> Spread Free-Trade poison, and the farmers die;
> God's gift Guano spread; the poorest soil
> With smiling crops Free-Traders' aim will spoil.

   Native Guano: The Best Antidote against the Future Fatal Effects of a Free Trade in Corn (London: Effinham Wilson, 1848).

7. Pierre Leroux, *Aux Etats de Jersey* (London: Universal Library, 1853), p. 12.

8. Quoted by Roger Guerrand, "Petite histoire du quotidien: L'Avènement de la chasse d'eau," *Histoire* 43 (March 1982): 97.

9. Jean-Pierre Lacassagne, "Victor Hugo, Pierre Leroux et le Circulus," *Bulletin de la Faculté des Lettres de Strasbourg* 48 (1970): 389–400; and Dominique Laporte, *Histoire de la merde* (Paris: Christian Bourgois, 1978), pp. 97–117. However, Hugo had been attracted to the idea that the inexpensive production of fertilizer was an important step in the suppression of hunger before his trip to Jersey. See "Journal de ce que j'apprends chaque jour," 21 July 1846, cited by René Journet and Guy Robert, *Le Mythe du peuple dans "Les Misérables"* (Paris: Editions Sociales, n.d.), p. 195n62.

10. Victor Hugo, *Œuvres complètes,* ed. Jean Massin (Paris: Club Français du

Livre, 1969), 11:873. Nineteenth-century novelists used statistics primarily for their descriptive force. The figures Hugo cited in *Les Misérables* were one-quarter of those he came up with in his original notes. *Un Carnet des "Misérables," octobre-décembre 1860: Notes et brouillons,* ed. Jean-Bertrand Barrère (Paris: Lettres modernes, 1965), pp. 222–229 (f° 141–143).

The estimated value of an individual's daily waste products when used as fertilizer was between $1.64 and $2.01 in the United States in 1873. Joel A. Tarr and Francis C. McMichael, "The Evolution of Wastewater Technology and the Development of State Regulation: A Retrospective Analysis" in *Retrospective Technology Assessment—1976,* ed. Joel A. Tarr (San Francisco: San Francisco Press, 1977), p. 176.

11. Hugo, *Œuvres complètes,* 11:874.

12. Ibid.

13. Ibid.

14. Ibid.

15. Ibid., 11:875.

16. Paul Claudel, "Réflexions et propositions sur le vers français," *Nouvelle Revue française* (1 October 1925): 440–441.

17. S. E. Finer, *The Life and Times of Sir Edwin Chadwick* (London: Methuen, 1952), p. 222. On the relationship of scientific and nonscientific discourse about sewage treatment in Great Britain, see Christopher Hamlin, "Providence and Putrefaction: Victorian Sanitarians and the Natural Theology of Health and Disease," *Victorian Studies* 28 (1985):381–411.

18. Edwin Chadwick, *Report on the Sanitary Condition of the Labouring Population of Great Britain* (Edinburgh: Edinburgh University Press, 1965), pp. 120–123.

19. Finer, *The Life and Times,* p. 300. On Liebig, see Benjamin Ward Richardson, *The Health of Nations: A Review of the Works of Edwin Chadwick,* 2 vols. (London: Longmans, Green, 1887), 2:18–19.

20. Quoted in John von Simson, "Water Supply and Sewerage in Berlin, London, and Paris: Developments in the Nineteenth Century" in *Urbanisierung im 19. und 20. Jahrhundert* (Cologne: Böhlau Verlag, 1983), p. 432.

21. Karl Marx and Friedrich Engels, *Marx and Engels on Ecology,* ed. Howard Parsons (Westport, Conn.: Greenwood Press, 1977), p. 176.

22. Chadwick favored separate systems for disposal of storm water and human sewage; he was sorely disappointed by London's decision to build a unitary sewer. Richardson, *The Health of Nations,* 2:204–205, 208.

23. Leroux, *Aux Etats de Jersey,* p. 5.

24. R. Baumeister, *The Cleaning and Sewerage of Cities,* trans. J. M. Goodell (New York: Engineering News Publishing, 1895), p. 114.

25. Préfecture du département de la Seine, Direction des eaux et des égouts, *Renseignements généraux sur les eaux et les égouts de la Ville de Paris* (Paris: Gauthiers-Villars, 1875), p. 44.

26. Préfecture de la Seine, *Assainissement de la Seine. Epuration et utilisation des eaux d'égout* (Paris: Gauthiers-Villars, 1876), p. 3.

27. Ibid., p. 98.

28. A. Debauve, *Distributions d'eau. Egouts,* 2 vols. (Paris: P. Vicq-Dunod, 1897), 2:514.

29. AN F^{14} 2283^2, Mille to Secrétaire général du Ministère des Travaux Publics (MTP), 23 June 1864; 4 September 1872; Mille to MTP, 22 January 1871.

30. A. Mille, *Assainissement des villes par l'eau, les égouts, les irrigations* (Paris: Dunod, 1885), pp. iii-iv.

31. Georges Bechmann, "Notice biographique sur M. Mille," *Annales des ponts et chaussées* 7th series 7 (1894):723.

32. Mille, *Assainissement,* p. iii. Pierre Pierrard describes the *bernatiers* (or *berneux*) who went through Lille in the early morning buying excrement from house-wives and servants for sale to farmers. *La Vie ouvrière à Lille sous le Second Empire* (Paris: Bloud et Gay, 1965), p. 54.

33. A. Mille, *Rapport sur le mode d'assainissement des villes en Angleterre et en Ecosse* (Paris: Vinchon, 1854).

34. Francisque Sarcey, *Les Odeurs de Paris. Assainissement de la Seine* (Paris: Gauthiers-Villars, 1882), p. 14.

35. Préfecture de la Seine, *Assainissement de la Seine,* pp. 3–41.

36. *Le Temps,* 14 November 1867, p. 3.

37. Richardson, *The Health of Nations,* 2:216. Paul Vincey carried out a similar experiment with equal success as part of an effort to encourage dairy farming on sewage farms. "Les Champs d'Epuration de la Ville de Paris et le lait de L'Assistance publique," *Mémoires de la société nationale d'agriculture de France* 138 (1899): 403–417.

38. Ernestine A. Durand-Claye, *Alfred Durand-Claye 1841–1888* (Paris: Imprimerie Chaix, n.d.), p. 102.

39. Ibid., pp. 1–5.

40. Alfred Durand-Claye, *Titres et travaux scientifiques de M. Alfred Durand-Claye* (Paris: Imprimerie Chaix, 1883), p. 7.

41. Durand-Claye, *Alfred Durand-Claye,* p. 5.

42. Georges Bechmann, *Salubrité urbaine. Distributions d'eau et assainissement,* 2 vols. (Paris: Ch. Béranger, 1899), 2:230. Durand-Claye, *Titres et travaux,* pp. 33–34.

43. Préfecture de la Seine, Direction des Eaux et des Egouts, *Transformation de la vidange et suppression de la voirie de Bondy. Achèvement des égouts et emploi de leurs eaux dans l'agriculture. Mémoire de l'Inspection générale des Ponts et Chaussées.* (Paris: Charles de Mourgues Frères, 1875), pp. 71–72.

44. Sarcey, *Les Odeurs de Paris,* p. 9.

45. Alfred Durand-Claye, *Réponse à l'article publié dans la Revue des Deux Mondes par M. Aubry-Vitet sur la question des égouts de Paris* (Paris: Chaix, 1882), pp. 31–32.

46. Alfred Durand-Claye, "L'Assainissement municipal de la Ville de Paris. Droits, devoirs et réformes" [1871] (Handwritten manuscript, copy at the Boston Public Library), p. 43. Préfecture de la Seine, *Assainissement,* p. 33.

47. Société impériale et centrale d'horticulture de France, *Utilisation des eaux d'é-gout de la ville de Paris* (Paris: E. Donnaud, 1870), p. 22.

48. Michel Phlipponneau, *La Vie rurale de la banlieue parisienne* (Paris: Armand Colin, 1956), p. 488.

49. Sarcey, *Les Odeurs de Paris*, pp. 21–22.

50. Roger-Henri Guerrand, "La Bataille du tout-à-l'égout," *Histoire* 53 (February 1983):70.

51. Louis Gauthier, *Le Tout-à-l'égout et l'assainissement de la Seine par l'utilisation agricole des eaux d'égout de Paris* (Paris: Georges Chamerot, 1888), p. xi.

52. *Discours prononcé par M. Frédéric Passy. Séance du 19 janvier 1888* (Paris: Imprimerie des *Journaux officiels*, 1888), p. 26.

53. See Paul Hayes Tucker, *Monet at Argenteuil* (New Haven: Yale University Press, 1972), pp. 151–152, 176–181.

54. Daniel Bellet and Will Darvillé, *Ce que doit être la Cité moderne* (Paris: H. Nolo, n.d.), pp. 131–132. Paul Joanne, *Paris* (Paris: Hachette, 1908), p. 394.

55. Georges Bechmann, *Notice sur le Service des eaux et de l'assainissement de Paris* (Paris: Ch. Béranger, 1900), p. 306. Durand-Claye, "L'Assainissement," p. 43. Edward Conner, "The Paris Municipality and its System of Irrigating Land by Means of the City's Sewage," *Land Magazine* 4 (1900):21.

56. Paul Vincey, "La Digestion de Paris," *Mémoires de la Société nationale d'agriculture de France* 138 (1899):228.

57. Bechmann, *Notice*, p. 400.

58. J. Schlœsing, *Irrigation à l'eau d'égout dans la plaine de Gennevilliers* (Paris: Chaix, 1892), pp. 18–19. The engineer Paul Vincey carefully worked out the total amount of azote, phosphoric acid, and potash consumed in Paris. Fifty-six percent of these materials returned to the soil through liquid sewage in 1895; the rest ended up in night soil, dung, and street sweepings. Vincey estimated the total value of these materials at 28,053,094 francs. "La Digestion de Paris," *Mémoires de la Société nationale d'agriculture de France* 138 (1899): 219–247.

59. Du Camp, *Paris*, 5:466–467. Préfecture de la Seine, *Assainissement*, p. 33.

60. Henry Haynie, *Paris Past and Present*, 2 vols. (New York: Frederick A. Stokes, 1902), 2:289n1.

61. Ardouin-Dumazet, *Voyage en France*, vol. 65 (Paris: Berger-Levrault, 1921), pp. 190–199.

62. Bechmann, *Salubrité urbaine*, 2:234–235. Durand-Claye, *Titres et travaux*, p. 17.

63. Gustave Jourdan, *Etudes d'hygiène publique* (Paris: Berger-Levrault, 1892), p. 36.

64. Raymond Quinot, *Gennevilliers*, 2 vols. (Gennevilliers: Ville de Gennevilliers, 1966), 2:20.

65. Conner, "The Paris Municipality," 20.

66. Ardouin-Dumazet, *Voyage*, pp. 188–192.

67. Sarcey, *Les Odeurs de Paris*, pp. 21–22.

68. Phlipponneau, *La Vie rurale*, p. 491. See Chadwick's criticism of French peasants' use of sewage. Richardson, *The Health of Nations*, 2:208.

69. Bechmann, *Notice*, pp. 307, 309.

70. Eugène Tisserand and E. Hardy, *Rapport de la Commission chargée de décerner*

des récompenses aux cultivateurs de la plaine de Gennevilliers qui auront justifié du meilleur emploi des eaux d'égouts (Paris: Lahure, 1874), p. 7.

71. Ministère de l'Agriculture et du Commerce. Commission de l'assainissement de Paris, *Rapports et avis de la Commission* (Paris: Imprimerie nationale, 1881), p. 214n1.

72. Edmond Garnier, *L'Agriculture dans le département de la Seine et le marché parisien du point de vue ravitaillement alimentaire* (Poitiers: Imprimerie L'Union, 1939), p. 13.

73. Ardouin-Dumazet, *Voyage*, pp. 192, 200–201. See the map in Emile Gérards, *Paris souterrain* (Paris: Garnier Frères, 1908), p. 499.

74. Lewis Mumford, *The City in History* (New York: Harcourt Brace Jovanovich, 1961), p. 478. Robert Auzelle, "Haussmann et les cimetières. Le projet de Méry-sur-Oise" in Louis Réau et al., *L'œuvre du Baron Haussmann. Préfet de la Seine 1853–1870* (Paris: Presses Universitaires de France, 1954), pp. 124–130.

75. Durand-Claye, *Alfred Durand-Claye*, p. 95.

76. Du Camp, *Paris*, 5:464.

77. Karl Baedeker, *Paris and Environs*, 18th ed. (Leipzig: Karl Baedeker, 1913), p. 347.

78. Sarcey, *Les Odeurs de Paris*, p. 17.

79. Bechmann, *Salubrité urbaine*, 2:355.

80. Jean de Mollins, *Hygiène publique. Les Eaux d'égout industrielles et ménagères* (Lille: L. Danel, 1891), p. 88.

81. Bechmann, *Notice*, pp. 309 (quote), 341.

82. Haynie, *Paris*, 2:300–305.

83. Charles Kunstler, *Paris souterrain* (Paris: Flammarion, 1953), p. 205.

84. Lucy H. Hooper, "A Visit to the Sewers of Paris," *Appleton's Journal* 13 (3 April 1875):430.

85. By the late nineteenth century sewage farming was practiced in cities throughout France, including Reims, Perpignan, and Saint-Etienne, and in 150 towns and cities in Great Britain. The United States boasted numerous enthusiastic supporters of sewage farming. For France, see Debauve, *Distributions*, 2:512–513. For Great Britain, see Hamlin, "Providence and Putrefaction"; G. E. Fussell, "Sewage Irrigation Farms in the Nineteenth Century," *Agriculture* 64 (1957–58):138–141; and Nicholas Goddard, "Nineteenth Century Recycling: The Victorians and the Agricultural Use of Sewage," *History Today* 31 (June 1982):32–36. For the United States, see Joel A. Tarr, "From City to Farm: Urban Wastes and the American Farmer," *Agricultural History* 49 (1975):598–612.

86. Durand-Claye, *Titres et travaux*, p. 13.

87. Robert C. Brooks, "The Sewage Farms of Berlin," *Political Science Quarterly* 20 (1905):308.

88. Ibid., 309.

89. Ibid., 306–307.

90. Quoted in Jean-Baptiste Martin, *La Fin des mauvais pauvres* (Seyssel: Champ Vallon, 1983), p. 37.

91. Jules Verne, *The Begum's Fortune,* ed. I. O. Evans (Westport, Ct.: Associated Booksellers, 1958), p. 125. The model company town of Pullman near Chicago operated a very successful sewage farm. Richardson, *The Health of Nations,* 2:217–218.

92. Peter Kropotkin, *The Conquest of Bread* (London: Penguin Press, 1973), pp. 103–104. Elsewhere, Kropotkin mentions the successful use of sewage as fertilizer in Milan (p. 218). See also his comments on "the valley of the Seine [where] the value of the land was doubled by irrigation." *Fields, Factories and Workshops* (London: Thomas Nelson and Sons, n.d.), p. 175.

93. Kropotkin, *The Conquest of Bread,* p. 104.

94. Such aspirations notwithstanding, small farmers from the sewage-fertilized fields around Arpajon struck back at the city in 1936, closing down Les Halles under the leadership of Henri Dorgères and his Greenshirts. Robert Paxton to Author, 17 November 1988.

95. Paul Vincey, "Les Grèves agricoles récentes et leur influence sur l'économie rurale," *Bulletin des séances de la Société nationale d'agriculture de France* (1909), pp. 784–794. Phlipponneau, *La Vie rurale,* pp. 495–496, 498.

96. Phlipponneau, *La Vie rurale,* p. 496.

97. Well into the twentieth century, Parisian engineers continued to pursue the alchemical aim of turning refuse to social advantage. When the city switched from horse-drawn garbage trucks to electric ones, the batteries were charged at plants powered by the incineration of garbage. M. L. Girard, *Le Nettoiement de Paris* (Paris: Librairie de l'Enseignement technique, 1923), p. 32. Although gasoline engines replaced electric engines in these vehicles after 1920, sanitation engineers never lost sight of "the dazzling revenge which modern industry has won over refuse," burning garbage for power and using the ash for bricks: "We expel [garbage] with disgust from our houses. It returns, furnishing the materials to build them, the motor force to relieve our manpower and the electric light to increase our comfort" (ibid., p. 52).

98. Ch. Rouchy, *Les Eaux d'égout de Paris* (Paris: Jules Rousset, 1907), p. 104.

99. Georges Verpraet, *Paris. Capitale souterraine* (Paris: Plon, 1954), p. 143. Syndicat interdépartemental pour l'assainissement de l'agglomération parisienne, "L'Assainissement de l'agglomération parisienne," p. 13.

100. Phlipponneau, *La Vie rurale,* p. 492.

101. Ibid., p. 493.

102. C. Veron, "L'Epuration des eaux usées de Paris et de l'agglomération parisienne," p. 10 in pamphlet prepared by Mairie de Paris, Le Service technique de l'assainissement [1983].

103. P. Fauveau, "Le Service technique de l'assainissement," p. 2 in ibid. See also Gérard Bertolini, *Eau, déchets et modèles culturels. Alternatives au tout-à-l'égout* (Paris: Editions Entente, 1983), p. 104.

104. *New York Times,* 16 November 1987, pp. 1, 11.

6. Montfaucon Liquidated

1. A. Mille, *Assainissement des villes par l'eau, les égouts, les irrigations* (Paris: Dunod, 1885), pp. 99–100. Henri Joseph Gisquet, *Mémoires de M. Gisquet*

écrits par lui-même, 4 vols. (Paris: Marchant, 1840), 4:300–301. Thomas Rammel, "Report on the Cesspool System in Paris." Appendix 4 to General Board of Health, *Report on the Supply of Water to the Metropolis* (London: W. Clowes, 1850), pp. 17–18 (quoted).

2. A.-J.-B. Parent-Duchâtelet, "Rapport sur les améliorations à introduire dans les fosses d'aisances, leur mode de vidange, et les voiries de la ville de Paris" in *Hygiène publique*, 2 vols. (Paris: J.-B. Baillière, 1836), 2:354–355.

3. A.-J.-B. Parent-Duchâtelet, "Recherches pour découvrir la cause et la nature d'accidens très graves développés en mer, à bord d'un bâtiment chargé de poudrette" in *Hygiène publique*, 2:271.

4. Gisquet, *Mémoires*, 4:306–307.

5. Ibid., 4:308.

6. In 1844 Dr. Louis Roux portrayed Montfaucon as a "reversal" of good administration. *De Montfaucon, de l'insalubrité de ses établissements et de la nécessité de leur suppression immédiate* (Paris: Delaunay, 1841), p. 4. He described what he saw at the slaughterhouses in terms of inversions of gender norms, family relations, and the natural order: "To understand Montfaucon and the slaughterhouses, and the horror which they must inspire, one has to imagine a woman got up as a slaughterhouse worker, holding a bloody knife between her teeth, while she whets another one beside a horse she is about to carve up. Never have the most hideous conceptions of novelists of the charnel house of the Innocents ever produced anything as repulsive as an androgyne done up so. Her pores exude murder; her eyes breathe ferocity; she stops from time to time to threaten her old father who works a little ways away with a knife. It would be difficult to say exactly how many degrees such a creature has fallen below the animals she dissects" (pp. 12–13n1).

7. Ibid., p. 32. Roux was most appalled by the slaughterhouses.

8. The obsessive introduction of new techniques to discipline and correct Montfaucon and its contents recall contemporaneous penal projects. Michel Foucault, *Surveiller et punir* (Paris: Gallimard, 1975).

9. Pierre Giraud, *Mémoire et projet sur les voiries, les boyauderies, les ateliers d'écarissage, les manufactures de brique et de carreau, les fabriques de vernis gras, de colle forte, de minium, des nitrières artificielles* (Paris: 1809?), p. 7.

10. Ibid, p. 10.

11. Jules Garnier, *Une Visite à la voirie de Montfaucon* (Paris: Méquignon-Marvis Fils, 1844), p. 34.

12. Ibid., p. xii.

13. François Leuret, "Notice historique sur A.-J.-B. Parent-Duchâtelet" in *Hygiène publique*, 1:vi. See also Ann Fowler La Berge, "A.-J.-B. Parent-Duchâtelet: Hygienist of Paris, 1821–1836," *Clio Medica* 12 (1977):279–301.

14. Baron des Genettes, *Eloge de M. Hallé* (Paris: Didot le Jeune [1822]), p. 15.

15. Leuret, "Notice historique," 1:vii.

16. Ibid., 1:xii–xiii.

17. John Hubbel Weiss, *The Making of Technological Man: The Social Origins of French Engineering Education* (Cambridge: M.I.T. Press, 1982), p. 125.

18. Parent-Duchâtelet, "Recherches pour découvrir," 2:259–260.

19. Parent-Duchâtelet, "Rapport sur les améliorations," 2:396.

20. Ibid., 2:386.

21. Ibid., 2:392.

22. A.-J.-B. Parent-Duchâtelet, "Des Obstacles que les préjugés médicaux apportent dans quelques circonstances à l'assainissement des villes et à l'établissement de certains manufactures" in *Hygiène publique*, 1:14–15. The tale bore repeating. The deputy Bourneville reported that Montfaucon was closed in 1849 after a "memorable session, held on the very grounds by the city council, attended by the Prefect of the Seine and the Prefect of Police." *Rapport fait au nom de la commission chargée d'examiner le projet de loi ayant pour objet l'utilisation agricole des eaux d'égout de Paris et l'assainissement de la Seine* (Paris: Imprimerie de la Chambre des députés, 1887), p. 16n1.

23. A.-J.-B. Parent-Duchâtelet, "Rapport sur les nouveaux procédés de MM. Salmon, Payen et Compagnie pour la dessiccation des chevaux morts et la désinfection instantanée des matières fécales; précédé de quelques considérations sur les voiries de la ville de Paris" in *Hygiène publique*, 2:288–289; "Rapport sur les améliorations," 2:354–355.

24. Ibid., 2:395. Parent-Duchâtelet, "Des Obstacles," 1:15.

25. Jules Janin, "Les Egouts," *Revue de Paris* 34 (1836):251.

26. Parent-Duchâtelet, "Des Obstacles," 1:49–50. These were the ancestors of the bourgeois who blocked extension of irrigation fields around Paris at the end of the century.

27. Ibid., 1:51–52.

28. Ibid., 1:12. Doctors were not in good repute. Three years earlier, mobs had seen doctors as doing the bourgeoisie's genocidal work in the 1832 cholera epidemic.

29. Ibid., 1:51–52.

30. Parent-Duchâtelet, "Rapport sur les améliorations," 2:396–397.

31. Rammell, "Report," p. 24.

32. J.-B. Monfalcon and A.-P. I. de Polinière, *Traité de la salubrité dans les grandes villes* (Paris: J.-B. Baillière, 1846), p. 75.

33. Mille, *Assainissement*, p. 123.

34. A. Alphand, *Note du directeur des travaux de Paris. La Situation du service des eaux et égouts. Les mesures à proposer au conseil municipal* (Paris: A. Chaix, 1879), p. 61. Aimé Girard, *Rapport préliminaire présenté à la Commission d'assainissement pour servir de base à des délibérations sur la nocuité des établissements que reçoivent ou manipulent les matières de vidange* (Paris: Imprimerie nationale, 1880), p. 9.

35. Alphand, *Note du directeur*, p. 56. Eugène Belgrand, *Les Travaux souterrains de Paris*, 5 vols. (Paris: Dunod, 1887), 5:302. A. Durand-Claye, "L'Assainissement municipal de la Ville de Paris. Droits, devoirs et réformes" [1871] (reproduction of handwritten manuscript, at the Boston Public Library), pp. 32–33.

36. Mille, *Assainissement*, pp. 124–125. Léon Colin, *Paris. Sa Topographie, son hygiène, ses maladies* (Paris: E. Masson, 1885), p. 229. Of these twenty-four dumps, eighteen were begun after 1850; ten manufactured ammonium sulfate. Girard, *Rapport préliminaire*, pp. 3–4.

37. Emile Raspail, *Des Odeurs de Paris,* 2nd. ed. (Paris: n.p., 1880), pp. 9–10.

38. Garnier, *Une Visite,* p. 5.

39. Girard, *Rapport préliminaire,* p. 1.

40. Parent-Duchâtelet, "Rapport sur les améliorations," 2:352, 366, 384, 386, 388, 390. Ironically, greater water use could make the fixed cesspool more ill-smelling. Landlords had little incentive to repair cesspools which leaked their contents into the ground. Furthermore, contemporaries reported that increased amounts of water in cesspools promoted the formation of "sulphuretted hydrogen gas." Rammell reported that in Paris, "The foulness of the cesspools, therefore, would appear to be in direct proportion to the cleanly habits of the inmates of the houses to which they respectively belong." "Report," p. 6.

41. Emile Gérards, *Paris souterrain* (Paris: Garnier Frères, 1908), p. 486. Durand-Claye, "L'Assainissement municipal."

42. Roger Guerrand, "Petite histoire du quotidien: l'avènement de la chasse d'eau," *Histoire* 43 (March 1982): 98–99.

43. Justus Liebig, *Organic Chemistry in Its Applications to Agriculture and Physiology,* trans. John Webster (Cambridge, Mass.: John Owen, 1841), pp. 188–189. J.-B. Boussingault, *Economie rurale considérée dans ses rapports avec la chimie, la physique et la météorologie,* 2 vols. (Paris: Béchet Jeune, 1844), 2:142–143.

44. *Tout-à-l'égout,* the method that prevailed, refers to evacuation of human and urban sewage through the same system. See Gérard Jacquemet, "Urbanisme parisien: La Bataille du tout-à-l'égout à la fin du XIXᵉ siècle," *Revue d'histoire moderne et contemporaine* 26 (1979):505–548; and Roger-Henri Guerrand, "La Bataille du tout-à-l'égout," *Histoire* 53 (February 1983):66–74.

45. Ernestine A. Durand-Claye, *Alfred Durand-Claye 1841–1888* (Paris: Imprimerie Chaix, n.d.), p. 11. G. E. Haussmann, *Mémoires du Baron Haussmann,* 3 vols. (Paris: Victor-Havard, 1893), 3:115–117, 362–366. Edmond Badois and Albert Bieber, *L'Assainissement comparé de Paris et des grandes villes de l'Europe* (Paris: Baudry, 1898), p. 185.

46. Belgrand added that household rubbish could be similarly disposed of in the sewers using hoppers in the courtyard. Subterranean trash removal is carried out through systems of underground pneumatic tubes in certain urban centers today, most notably in Disney World. The rush of air performs the same functions as water in the sewer, both removing the waste and cleansing the tube.

47. G. E. Haussmann gave his technical appraisal of the *tout-à-l'égout* in *Mémoire sur les eaux de Paris* (Paris: Vinchon, 1854), pp. 46, 52–53, 58–59. See Durand-Claye, "L'Assainissement," pp. 57–58.

48. The Paris municipal council's decision to support the *tout-à-l'égout* in 1880 (and reconfirmed in 1883) accompanied a series of refuse removal reforms undertaken after the particulary malodorous summer of 1880. Like establishment of the *tout-à-l'égout,* these assertions of public authority in the name of hygiene challenged the rights of individual property owners and threatened the way of life of a legendary occupational group. In 1883 the city imposed a mandatory street-sweeping tax which ended the anarchic practice of having property owners assume this responsibility themselves. The same year the Pre-

fect Poubelle made obligatory the use of segregated trash containers in Paris (one each for garbage, papers and rags, and glass and pottery). While the first measure replaced individual initiative with a tax, the second raised the ire of landlords, concierges, and ragpickers, who saw their freedom as urban gleaners vanishing. Ragpickers who stayed in the trade increasingly took employment as aides to late-rising concierges (taking the cans out and in in exchange for the right of first removal) or as members of garbage truck crews. Catherine de Silguy, *La Saga des ordures du Moyen Age à nos jours* (Paris: Editions de l'Instant, 1989), pp. 23–26.

49. Ministère de l'Agriculture et du Commerce. Commission de l'Assainissement de Paris. *Rapports et avis de la Commission* (Paris: Imprimerie nationale, 1881), pp. 43–45.

50. AN F⁸208, "Renseignements recueillis sur l'état des égouts au point de vue des odeurs qu'ils répandent, par le Docteur Brouardel," presented to the Commission d'assainissement de Paris, 7 October 1880.

51. M. Humblot, *Les Egouts de Paris à la fin de 1885* (Paris: Imprimerie Chaix, 1886), p. 57. See Parent-Duchâtelet, "Essai sur la cloaque ou égouts de la Ville de Paris" in *Hygiène publique*, 1:165.

52. Jean de Mollins, *Hygiène publique. Les Eaux d'égout industrielles et ménagères* (Lille: L. Danel, 1891), p. 119. But was there any more ingenious scheme than Antoine Maurel's proposal to pump sea water to Paris for sanitation purposes? A big advantage of this solution, Maurel suggested, was that it would make "bains d'eau de mer" available to all Parisians. The revenues collected from these baths would quickly pay the costs of installation. *Assainissement des villes en général et de Paris en particulier par l'eau de mer* (Nice: V.-Eug. Gauthier, 1894), pp. 6–7.

53. Georges Bechmann, *Salubrité urbaine. Distributions d'eau et assainissement*, 2 vols. (Paris: Ch. Béranger, 1899), 2:357.

54. Alain Corbin, *The Foul and the Fragrant: Odor and the French Social Imagination*, trans. Miriam Kochan (Cambridge, Mass.: Harvard University Press, 1986), p. 226.

55. Louis Gauthier, *Le Tout-à-l'égout et l'assainissement de la Seine par l'utilisation agricole des eaux d'égout de Paris* (Paris: Georges Chamerot, 1888), p. vii.

56. Max de Nansouty, "Tout à l'égout?-rien à l'égout?," *L'Illustration* 100 (15 October 1892):302.

57. Edward Conner, "The Paris Municipality and Its System of Irrigating Land by Means of the City's Sewage," *Land Magazine* 4 (1900):18, 22. "L'Assainissement de la Seine," *L'Illustration* 114 (15 July 1899):48. Although one-fifth of the contents of the city's sewers continued to pour into the Seine in 1911, the remainder was purified through irrigation. Will Darvillé, *L'Eau à la ville, à la campagne et dans la maison* (Paris: Librairie de la Construction moderne, n.d.), p. 466. Daniel Bellet and Will Darvillé, *Ce que doit être la Cité moderne* (Paris: H. Nolo, n.d.), pp. 124–125.

58. Georges Bechmann, *Distributions d'eau et assainissement*, 2 vols. (Paris: Baudry et Compagnie, 1898), 1:71.

59. Gabriel Dupuy, "La Science et la technique dans l'aménagement urbain. Le

Cas de l'assainissement," *Annales de la recherche urbaine* 6 (January 1980):11–12.

60. More than half the dwellings in Paris were hooked up to the *tout-à-l'égout* by 1905. However, it took several decades to complete the process. Alphonse Gaston Colmet-Daâge, "Notice biographique sur Georges Bechmann," *Annales des ponts et chaussées* 7 series, 5 (1927):118. See the recollections of the photographer Brassaï [Gyula Halasz]: "A Night with the Cesspool Cleaners" in *The Secret Paris of the 30's,* trans. Richard Miller (New York: Pantheon Books, 1976), unpaginated.

61. Georges Bechmann, *Notice sur le Service des eaux et de l'assainissement de Paris* (Paris: Ch. Béranger, 1900), pp. 335–338. Gabriel Dupuy and Georges Knaebel, *Assainir la ville hier et aujourd'hui* (Paris: Dunod, 1982), pp. 22–23.

7. Cesspool Cleaners and Sewermen

1. Mary Douglas, *Purity and Danger: An Analysis of the Concepts of Pollution and Taboo* (London: Ark Paperbacks, 1986), pp. 124–125.

2. My editor, Anita Safran, suggests that *maîtres fi fi* gave way to *mesdames pipi*—yet one more trade in which gender and de-skilling have gone hand in hand.

3. Maxime du Camp, *Paris. Ses organes, ses fonctions et sa vie dans la seconde moitié du XIX⁰ siècle,* 6 vols. (Paris: Hachette, 1869–1875), 5:422–423. Pierre-Denis Boudriot, "Essai sur l'ordure en milieu urbain à l'époque pré-industrielle. Boues, immondices et gadoue à Paris au XVIII⁰ siècle," *Histoire économie et société* 5 (1986):522.

4. Simon Lacordaire, *Histoire secrète du Paris souterrain* (Paris: Hachette, 1982), pp. 179–180 (quote on p. 180) and Boudriot, "Essai sur l'ordure," 521. One nineteenth-century author spoke of nighttime strolls through the streets of Paris "perfumed by the triumphal chariot of the cesspool cleaners"; Amédée de Tissot, *Paris et Londres comparés* (Paris: A. J. Ducollet, 1830), p. 10.

5. Louis-Sébastien Mercier, *Tableau de Paris,* 12 vols. (Amsterdam: n.p., 1782), 1:78. Bricheteau, Chevallier, and Furnari, "Note sur les vidangeurs," *Annales d'hygiène publique et de médecine légale* 28 (1842):47.

6. Alfred Franklin, *La Vie privée d'autrefois: L'hygiène* (Paris: Plon, 1890), pp. 115–119. Alain Corbin, *The Foul and the Fragrant: Odor and the French Social Imagination,* trans. Miriam Kochan (Cambridge: Harvard University Press, 1986), p. 93.

7. Boudriot, "Essai sur l'ordure," 521. When, however, the *compagnons* launched a strike in 1734 for better pay, the masters crushed it by hiring workers outside the guild to do the work. Franklin, *La Vie privée,* pp. 157–158.

8. Franklin, *La Vie privée,* p. 155.

9. Bricheteau, Chevallier, and Furnari, "Note," 48.

10. Corbin, *The Foul and the Fragrant,* pp. 93–94.

11. Boudriot, "Essai sur l'ordure," 521. Bricheteau, Chevallier, and Furnari, "Note," 47. Mercier, *Tableau de Paris,* 11:36 (1789 ed.). A decree by the city of Paris early in 1792 criticized the unsafe practices of individual cesspool cleaners and affirmed the company's monopoly in the name of the public

interest. *Arrêté concernant la salubrité et la vidange des fosses d'aisances, puits et puisards* (Paris: Municipalité de Paris, 1792).

12. Bernardini Ramazzini, *Diseases of Workers,* trans. Wilmer Cave Wright (Chicago: University of Chicago Press, 1940), p. 95. Ramazzini was Italian, but his work was translated into French and strongly influenced students of occupational health in France.

13. Ibid., p. 97.

14. A.-J.-B. Parent-Duchâtelet, "Les Chantiers d'équarrissage de la ville de Paris" in *Hygiène publique,* 2 vols. (Paris: J.-B. Baillière, 1836), 2:135.

15. Mercier, *Tableau de Paris,* 7:139.

16. Lacordaire, *Histoire secrète,* p. 179.

17. Jean-Noël Hallé, *Recherches sur la nature et les effets du méphitisme des fosses d'aisances* (Paris: Ph.-D. Pierres, 1785), pp. 33–34.

18. Ibid., pp. 1–72. De Marcorelle, *Réflexions historiques et critiques sur quelques moyens indiqués pour neutraliser les fosses d'aisances servant de réponse aux injustes imputations de M. Janin de Combeblanche, médecin oculiste à Lyon* (Narbonne: Veuve Besse, 1785), p. 8. (quoted) Corbin recounts this experience in *The Foul and the Fragrant,* pp. 2–3.

19. Baron des Genettes, *Eloge de M. Hallé* (Paris: Didot le Jeune [1822]), p. 14.

20. Ramazzini, *Diseases of Workers,* p. 105.

21. Franklin, *La Vie privée,* pp. 15, 57–58.

22. Roger Picard, *Les Cahiers de 1789 et la classe ouvrière,* quoted in Charles Benoist, *La Crise de l'état moderne. L'Organisation du travail,* 2 vols. (Paris: Plon, 1905–1914), 2:215.

23. Ramazzini, *Diseases of Workers,* p. 105.

24. Mercier, *Tableau de Paris,* 1:78.

25. Franklin, *La Vie privée,* pp. 15, 57–58.

26. Cynthia J. Koepp, "The Alphabetical Order: Work in Diderot's *Encyclopédie*" in Steven Kaplan and Koepp, eds., *Work in France: Representation, Meaning, Organization and Practice* (Ithaca: Cornell University Press, 1986), pp. 229–257.

27. Jean-Henri Marchand, "Le Vuidanger sensible" (Paris: Le Moniteur du Bibliophile, 1880 [originally published in 1777]), pp. 25–26 ("Dissertation sur le drame").

28. Ibid., p. 59.

29. Mathieu Géraud, *Essai sur la suppression des fosses d'aisances, et de toute espèce de voiries, sur la manière de convertir en combustibles les substances qu'on y renferme, etc.* (Amsterdam, n.p., 1786), p. 111n1.

30. Charles Kunstler, *Paris souterrain* (Paris: Flammarion, 1953), p. 189.

31. Ramazzini, *Diseases of Workers,* p. 97. The scientists Laborie, Cadet le Jeune, and Parmentier reported that Parisian cesspool cleaners resorted to the same remedy. *Observations sur les fosses d'aisances, et moyens de prévenir les inconveniens de leur vuidange* (Paris: Ph.-D. Pierres, 1778), p. 11.

32. Géraud, *Essai,* p. 39.

33. Mercier, *Tableau de Paris,* 1:78.

34. Laborie, Cadet le Jeune, and Parmentier, *Observations sur les fosses,* p. 12.
35. Ibid., pp. 5–6.
36. Hallé, *Recherches,* pp. 2 (quoted), 126–127.
37. Mercier, *Tableau de Paris,* 1:77. See Antoine Laurent Lavoisier, *Œuvres de Lavoisier* (Paris: Imprimerie nationale, 1868), 4:323–324.
38. R. H. Guerrand, *Les Lieux* (Paris: La Découverte, 1987), p. 70.
39. Mercier, *Tableau de Paris,* 1:79.
40. Lacordaire, *Histoire secrète,* p. 149.
41. Georges Verpraet, *Paris. Capitale souterraine* (Paris: Plon, 1954), p. 145.
42. Parent-Duchâtelet, "Essai sur la cloaque ou égouts de la ville de Paris" in *Hygiène publique,* 1:232.
43. Ibid., 1:158–159.
44. Ibid., 1:161.
45. François Leuret, "Notice historique sur A.-J.-B. Parent-Duchâtelet" in ibid, 1:xii.
46. Ibid.
47. Parent-Duchâtelet, "Essai sur la cloaque," 1:159–160.
48. Ibid., 1:248n1.
49. Parent-Duchâtelet, "Rapport sur les améliorations à introduire dans les fosses d'aisances, leur mode de vidange, et les voiries de la Ville de Paris" in *Hygiène publique,* 2:380.
50. Ibid., 2:386.
51. Parent-Duchâtelet, "Essai sur la cloaque," 1:160–161. Surveying the work done in the sewers in the decade after he had completed his research, Parent-Duchâtelet sniffed that although the engineers had not seen fit to consult him about changing the sewer system, they had probably recognized the merit of his suggestions for they had followed *avec fidélité* the advice in his reports. *De la Prostitution dans la Ville de Paris,* 2 vols., 2nd. ed. (Paris: J.-B. Baillière, 1837), 1:21. For his work on prostitution, Parent-Duchâtelet was altogether more successful and less suspicious in assembling and analyzing written documentation than he had been for the sewers.
52. Parent-Duchâtelet, "Essai sur la cloaque," 1:252. Corbin, *The Foul and the Fragrant,* p. 212.
53. Parent-Duchâtelet, "Essai sur la cloaque," 1:250.
54. Ibid., 1:251–252. Later students of occupational health accused Parent-Duchâtelet of downplaying the dangers of various professions. See Bernard-Pierre Lecuyer, "Les Maladies professionnelles dans les *Annales d'hygiène publique et de médecine légale* ou une première approche de l'usure au travail," *Mouvement social* 124 (July-September 1983):45–69.
55. Sewermen today still use the term *le plomb* to describe the "generalized anemia" which years of work in the sewers produces. Archives Sarrazin, *La Vie mutualiste* (March 1977), p. 49.
56. Parent-Duchâtelet, "Essai sur la cloaque," 1:250.
57. Ibid., 1:166.
58. Ibid., 1:158.

59. Ibid., 1:259.
60. Ibid., 1:256–258. "Rapport sur le curage des égouts: Amelot, de la Roquette, Saint-Martin et autres" in *Hygiène publique,* 1:349–353n1.
61. For a brief introduction to Corbin's pathbreaking work on prostitution, *Les Filles de noce* (Paris: Aubier Montaigne, 1978), see his "Commercial Sexuality in Nineteenth-Century France: A System of Images and Regulations" in Catherine Gallagher and Thomas Laqueur, eds., *The Making of the Modern Body* (Berkeley: University of California Press, 1987), pp. 209–219.
62. Parent-Duchâtelet, "Essai sur la cloaque," 1:305.
63. Ibid., 1:304.
64. Ibid., 1:284–285.
65. Ibid., 1:248, 253, 280.
66. Ibid., 1:293–294.
67. Parent-Duchâtelet, "Rapport sur le curage," 1:309.
68. Parent-Duchâtelet made this lone critique of sewermen in a comment on their failure to keep manholes open. "Essai sur la cloaque," 1:285–286.
69. Parent-Duchâtelet, "Rapport sur le curage," 1:367.
70. Ibid., 1:315.
71. Ibid., 1:410.
72. Ibid., 1:355–361.
73. Ibid., 1:353.
74. Ibid., 1:313.
75. Ibid., 1:315, 376–378n1.
76. Ibid., 1:373–374.
77. Parent-Duchâtelet, "Essai sur la cloaque," 1:285–286.
78. Parent-Duchâtelet, "Rapport sur le curage," 1:354, 362–367.
79. Ibid., 1:354.
80. Ibid., 1:353. In 1822 the Inspecteur général de la salubrité criticized this practice because the city's failure to replace a sewerman on sick leave left his workmates short-handed and could encourage the ill sewerman to return to work early, with potentially mortal consequences. ADS VO³17, "Observations touchant la mort de plusieurs ouvriers égoutiers," 18 June 1822.
81. Parent-Duchâtelet, "Rapport sur le curage," 1:412.
82. Ibid., 1:353–354.
83. Ibid., 1:432.
84. Parent-Duchâtelet, "Essai sur la cloaque," 1:261n1, 305–306.
85. Victor Hugo, *Œuvres complètes,* ed. Jean Massin (Paris: Club Français du Livre, 1969), 11:884.
86. Parent-Duchâtelet, "Essai sur la cloaque," 1:258–259.
87. Jean Starobinski, *Jean-Jacques Rousseau, la transparence et l'obstacle* (Paris: Plon, 1957).
88. Parent-Duchâtelet, "Essai sur la cloaque," 1:306.
89. Ibid., 1:304.
90. Ibid., 1:307. Henry Mayhew had a similar reaction to the sewermen of London: "The flushermen are well-conducted men generally, and, for the most

part, fine stalwart good-looking specimens of the English labourer; were they not known or believed to be temperate, they would not be employed. They have, as a body, no benefit or sick clubs, but a third of them, I was told, or perhaps nearly a third, were members of general benefit societies. I found several intelligent men among them." *London Labour and the London Poor,* 3 vols. (London: Griffin, Bohn, 1861), 2:428.

91. Jill Harsin has captured Parent-Duchâtelet's defensive attitude toward his objects of study and his sense that work in places like sewers was "a test of courage and endurance." She comments that "he saw both himself and the sewers as doing the unheralded but necessary work of society." *Policing Prostitution in Nineteenth-Century Paris* (Princeton: Princeton University Press, 1985), pp. 111, 107. My reading of Parent-Duchâtelet is different: he identified with the sewermen—those charged with knowing the sewers and making them function properly—rather than the sewers themselves.

92. Parent-Duchâtelet, "Rapport sur le curage," 1:386n1.

93. Ibid., 1:349n1. Is it any surprise that Parent-Duchâtelet himself died of exhaustion in his mid-forties?

94. ADS VO³41, "Etat de payement des employés à la Visite des Egouts de Paris depuis y compris le 1er janvier 1812 jusqu'au 31 inclusivement."

95. APP D^9, Note to Préfecture de Police, 18 January 1839.

96. ADS VO³17, "Observations touchant la mort."

97. Parent-Duchâtelet, "Essai sur la cloaque," 1:305.

98. Another visitor to the sewers was struck by the periodic "cry of joy" of sewermen who had found coins or objects of value. Emile de La Bédollière, *Les Industriels. Métiers et professions en France* (Paris: Louis Janet, 1842), p. 182. The sewermen who explored and cleaned the sewers under Bruneseau's direction were spurred on by the promise that they could keep coins they uncovered. On ascending each day, sewermen had to strip and hand over everything they had found to a clerk who distributed the booty equally among all workers. Lacordaire, *Histoire secrète,* pp. 154–155. See also Hugo, *Œuvres complètes,* 11:880.

99. Parent-Duchâtelet, "Essai sur la cloaque," 1:261.

100. Ibid., 1:261n1.

101. François Ewald, "La Condition du mineur" in André Théret, *Parole d'ouvrier* (Paris: Grasset, 1978), pp. 7–60. Marc Lazar, "Ouvrier, histoire et littérature du parti. L'Exemple du mineur," *Revue des sciences humaines* 190 (April-June 1983):101–111. Bruno Mattéi, "Portrait du mineur en héros" in Evelyne Desbois, Yves Jeanneau, and Mattéi, *La Foi des charbonniers* (Paris: Editions de la Maison des sciences de l'homme, 1986), pp. 83–101. Mattéi, *Rebelle, rebelle! Révoltes et mythes du mineur* (Seyssel: Champ Vallon, 1987), esp. pp. 260–273. Lion Murard and Patrick Zylberman, "Le Petit Travailleur infatigable ou le prolétaire régénéré," *Recherches* 25 (1976):7–287.

102. See Donald Reid, "Introduction" to Jacques Rancière, *The Nights of Labor: The Workers' Dream in Nineteenth-Century France* (Philadelphia: Temple University Press, 1989), pp. xv-xxxvii.

8. Disorder Above and Order Below

1. Bricheteau, Chevallier, and Furnari, "Note sur les vidangeurs," *Annales d'hygiène publique et de médecine légale* 28 (1842): 46–55 (quote on p. 50). See also François Joseph Victor Broussais, *Le Catéchisme de la médecine physiologique* (Paris: Delauney, 1824), p. 67.

2. P. Giraud, *Mémoire et projet sur les voiries, les boyauderies, les ateliers d'écarissage, les manufactures de brique et de carreau, les fabriques de vernis gras, de colle forte, de minium, des nitrières artificielles* (Paris: n.p., n.d.), p. 11.

3. A.-J.-B. Parent-Duchâtelet, "Rapport sur les améliorations à introduire dans les fosses d'aisances, leur mode de vidange, et les voiries de la Ville de Paris" in *Hygiène publique*, 2 vols. (Paris: J.-B. Baillière, 1836), 2:379.

4. Chambre de commerce de Paris, *Statistique de l'industrie à Paris résultant de l'enquête faite par la Chambre de commerce pour les années 1847-1848* (Paris: Guillaumin, 1851), pp. 91–92.

5. Girard, Pelletier, d'Arcet, "De l'Assainissement de la vidange des fosses d'aisances," *Annales d'hygiène publique et de médecine légale* 3 (1830):359.

   The career of the worker-poet Louis Marie Ponty reveals the opposition drawn between the most exalted mental labor—poetry—and the most demeaning manual labor—cesspool cleaning. Ponty worked at a variety of trades before taking up cesspool cleaning in the 1830s because this occupation left him his days free to write poetry. The worker-poet Gabriel Gauny feared that this job would destroy his friend Ponty and urged him to quit. See Gabriel Gauny, *Le Philosophe plébéien,* ed. Jacques Rancière (Paris: La Découverte/Maspero, 1983), pp. 169–170. After Olinde Rodrigues identified Ponty as "ouvrier en vidanges" in his collection *Poésies sociales des ouvriers* (Paris: Paulin, 1841), pp. 97–122, shocked patrons of the arts got him a job working for the railways. "Louis Marie Ponty" in Jean Maitron, ed., *Dictionnaire biographique du mouvement ouvrier français* (Paris: Editions ouvrières, 1966), 3:242.

6. Bricheteau, Chevallier, and Furnari, "Note sur les vidangeurs," 48.

7. Jacques Rancière, *La Nuit des prolétaires* (Paris: Fayard, 1981), p. 18.

8. F. Liger, *Fosses d'aisances. Latrines, urinoirs et vidanges* (Paris: J. Baudry, 1875), pp. 13–14.

9. Francisque Sarcey, *Les Odeurs de Paris,* 2nd series (Paris: Grande Imprimerie, 1882), p. 14.

10. Parent-Duchâtelet, "Rapport sur les améliorations," 2:365. See also A. Alphand, *Note du directeur des travaux de Paris. La Situation du service des eaux et égouts. Les Mesures à proposer au conseil municipal* (Paris: A. Chaix, 1879), pp. 63–65.

11. [Jules Burgy], *Observations sur le vidange de Paris et son transport à Bondi* (Paris: Schneider and Lengrand, 1842), p. 8.

12. Richer, *A Monsieur le Préfet de la Seine, M. le Préfet de Police et Messieurs les membres du Conseil-général du département* (Paris: Everat, 1835), pp. 2–3.

13. APP D⁸157, Tribunal de Police municipale to Procureur impérial, 27 November 1867; "Note à Monsieur le Préfet de Police" from cesspool contractors in Paris and environs [1867]; Report of Tribunal de Police municipale, 2 May 1868.

14. Ministère de l'Agriculture et du Commerce. Commission de l'Assainissement de Paris, *Rapports et avis de la Commission* (Paris: Imprimerie nationale, 1881), p. 63.

15. Gustave Flaubert, *Correspondance* (Paris: L. Conard, 1926–1954), 3:249 (Flaubert to Louise Colet, 25–26 June 1853). Cited in Mario Vargas Llosa, *The Perpetual Orgy: Flaubert and Madame Bovary,* trans. Helen Lane (New York, Farrar, Straus and Giroux, 1986), p. 213. My thanks to Peter Filene for bringing this to my attention.

16. Gustave Flaubert, *Correspondance supplément* (1864–1871), ed. René Dumesnil, Jean Pommier, and Claude Digeon (Paris: L. Conard, 1954), pp. 33–34 (Flaubert to Jules Duplan, 26 May 1865).

17. The Préfecture de Police's "Cahier des charges du nettoiement de la ville de Paris, pour la rive gauche de la Seine" (29 December 1830) includes the contract governing sewer cleaning and the penalties for failure to meet its provisions. A. Chevallier, "Notice historique sur le nettoiement de la ville de Paris, depuis 1184 jusqu'à l'époque actuelle," *Annales d'hygiène publique et de médecine légale* 42 (1849): 299–300. A.-J.-B. Parent-Duchâtelet, "Essai sur la cloaque ou égouts de la Ville de Paris," *Hygiène publique,* 1:235. Emile de La Bédollière *Les Industriels. Métiers et professions en France* (Paris: Louis Janet, 1842), pp. 179–180.

18. Chevallier, "Notice historique," 299–300. La Bédollière, *Les Industriels,* p. 180. M. Boudin, "Etudes sur le pavage, le macadamage et le drainage," *Annales d'hygiène publique et de médecine légale* 45 (1851):270–271.

19. La Bédollière, *Les Industriels,* p. 183.

20. ADS VO³17, Bruneseau, "Renseignements sur la situation actuelle des égouts de Paris," 27 December 1806.

21. APP DᴬS no. 19, Conseil de Préfecture du Département de la Seine. Nettoiement de la Ville de Paris. *Pour M. le Préfet de Police contre la liquidation de MM. Savalete et Cie. Défense à la réplique de la Compagnie* (Paris: Imprimerie de Lottin de Saint-Germain, 1840), pp. 52–54, 57; no. 29, "Rapport. Chef de comptabilité," 27 April 1849.

22. Jules Janin, "Les Egouts," *Revue de Paris* 34 (1836):232.

23. Edmond Texier, *Tableau de Paris,* 2 vols. (Paris: Paulin and Le Chevalier, 1852–53), 2:234.

24. Edmond and Jules Goncourt, *Journal,* ed. Robert Ricatte (Paris: Fasquelle/Flammarion, 1956-), 1:1228–29 (9 February 1863).

25. Texier, *Tableau de Paris,* 2:234.

26. E. and J. Goncourt, *Journal,* 1:1294 (2 July 1863).

27. Texier, *Tableau de Paris,* 2:234.

28. La Bédollière, *Les Industriels,* p. 183.

29. Charles Augustin Sainte-Beuve, *Les Cahiers* (Paris: Alphonse Lemerre, 1876), p. 97.

30. H. C. Emmery, "Statistique des égouts de la ville de Paris (année 1836)," *Annales des ponts et chaussées* 7 (1837):270.

31. H. C. Emmery, "Egouts et bornes-fontaines," *Annales des ponts et chaussées* 4 (1834):256. Georges Bechmann, *Salubrité urbaine. Distributions d'eau et as-*

sainissement, 2 vols. (Paris: Ch. Béranger, 1899), 2:112–113. See also Parent-Duchâtelet, "Essai sur la cloaque," 1:280; and Georges Eugène Haussmann, *Mémoires du Baron Haussmann,* 3 vols. (Paris: Victor-Havard, 1893), 3:109.

32. "The fateful process of civilization would thus have set in with man's adoption of an erect posture." Sigmund Freud, *Civilization and its Discontents,* trans. James Strachey (New York: W. W. Norton, 1961), p. 46n1.

33. Maxime du Camp, *Paris. Ses organes, ses fonctions et sa vie dans la seconde moitié du XIX^c siècle,* 6 vols. (Paris: Hachette, 1869–1875), 5:458. Emile Gérards, *Paris souterrain* (Paris: Garnier Frères, 1908), pp. 489, 506.

34. A. Wazon, *Principes techniques d'assainissement des villes et habitations suivis en Angleterre, France, Allemagne, Etats-Unis et présentés sous forme d'études sur l'assainissement de Paris* (Paris: J. Baudry, 1884), pp. 284–285. P. Pignant, *Principes d'assainissement des habitations des villes et de la banlieue* (Dijon: Imprimerie Darantière, 1890), p. 171.

35. E. Imbeaux, "Evacuation des immondices liquides: égouts et vidanges" in A. Calmette, E. Imbeaux, and H. Pottevin, *Egouts et vidanges* (Paris: J.-B. Baillière, 1911), p. 403. Will Darvillé, *L'Eau à la ville, à la campagne et dans la maison* (Paris: Librairie de la Construction moderne, n.d.), pp. 492–493.

36. Philippe Audebrand, "Courrier de Paris," *L'Illustration* 62 (9 August 1873):90–91.

37. Eugène Belgrand, *Les Travaux souterrains de Paris,* 5 vols. (Paris: Dunod, 1887), 5:196–197. Bechmann, *Salubrité urbaine,* 2:112–113, 224. Ch. Rouchy, *Les Eaux d'égout de Paris* (Paris: Jules Rousset, 1907), p. 30.

38. Lucy Hooper, "A Visit to the Sewers of Paris," *Appleton's Journal* 13 (3 April 1875):429.

39. Benjamin Ward Richardson, "A Whitsuntide Sanitary Pilgrimage, with the Lessons," *Longman's Magazine* 21 (December 1892):193.

40. Pierre Larousse, *Grand Dictionnaire universel du XIX^c siècle* (Paris: Administration du *Grand Dictionnaire universel,* 1870), 7:263 (Ratier). London sewermen enjoyed the same reputation for exemplary health. H. Jenner-Fort III, "The Human Mole: The Strange Life and the Stranger Perils of the Men who Work in the London Sewers," *Royal Magazine* 9 (December 1902):121.

41. A. Mille, *Assainissement des villes par l'eau, les égouts, les irrigations* (Paris: Dunod, 1885), p. 143.

42. Georges Bechmann, *Notice sur le Service des eaux et de l'assainissement de Paris* (Paris: Ch. Béranger, 1900), p. 333.

43. Darvillé, *L'Eau,* p. 480.

44. Wazon, *Principes,* p. 260.

45. Paul Wéry, *Assainissement des villes et égouts de Paris* (Paris: Dunod, 1898), p. 395. At the end of the century the American sanitary engineer George Waring dressed the more than two thousand street cleaners in New York in white uniforms—they were known as "White Wings"—and organized them in military fashion. Martin V. Melosi, *Garbage in the Cities. Refuse, Reform, and the Environment, 1880–1980* (College Station: Texas A & M University Press, 1981), pp. 65–66.

46. Hooper, "A Visit," 429–430.

47. A. Gastinel, *Les Egouts de Paris. Etude d'hygiène urbaine* (Paris: Henri Jouve, 1894), p. 32.

48. Henry Haynie, *Paris Past and Present*, 2 vols. (New York: Frederick A. Stokes, 1902), 2:300.

49. J. J. Waller, "Under the Streets of Paris," *Good Words* 35 (July 1894):493.

50. Du Camp, *Paris*, 5:459.

51. *Le Réveil de l'Assainissement*, 26 August 1900, p. 2.

52. Emile Beaule, "Les Victimes de l'Egout" (poem) in *L'Echo des Travailleurs municipaux*, 10 November 1896, p. 3.

53. Belgrand, *Les Travaux souterrains*, 5:186.

54. Ibid., 5:204–205. La Bédollière, *Les Industriels*, p. 182.

55. Bechmann, *Salubrité urbaine*, 2:219.

56. Hooper, "A Visit," 431.

57. Nadar [Gaspard Félix Tournachon], *Quand j'étais photographe* (Paris: Flammarion, 1899), p. 118.

58. Charles Kunstler, *Paris souterrain* (Paris: Flammarion, 1953), p. 229. This observation continued an earlier rhetorical tradition.

59. *L'Illustration*, 10 January 1874, p. 27.

60. *Le Temps*, 1 July 1899, pp. 2–3.

61. L. Lalanne, "Notice sur la vie et les travaux de M. E. Belgrand," *Annales des ponts et chaussées* 6th series 2 (1881):366. Belgrand was not the first sanitary reformer to see sewermen as a potential bulwark of public order. In April 1848 Chadwick suggested to Scotland Yard that the sewermen of London could help foil any Chartist attempt to take over the city. "The Chartists might throw up barricades in the streets, from which it would be difficult to dislodge them. But, suggested Chadwick, a band of two or three hundred sewer men might be sworn in as special constables, to creep unsuspected along the sewers and emerge at manholes in the rear of the startled revolutionaries." R. A. Lewis, *Edwin Chadwick and the Public Health Movement 1832–1854* (London: Longmans, Green, 1952), p. 90n4.

62. Harold Clunn, *The Face of Paris: The Record of a Century's Changes and Developments* (London: Simpkin Marshall, 1933), p. 314.

63. E. and J. Goncourt, *Journal*, 3:1017 (27 July 1889).

64. X. Feyrnet, "Courrier de Paris," *L'Illustration* 44 (10 December 1864):371.

65. Edwin Chadwick, *Report on the Sanitary Condition of the Labouring Population of Great Britain* (Edinburgh at the University Press, 1965), p. 165. Proponents of alternatives to both the current mode of cesspool cleaning and the *tout-à-l'égout* trumpeted their systems in similar terms. "In a word, the most delicate of men will be able to handle the products of *le vidange*, whereas nowadays they are handled only by robust, strong-stomached (*peu dégoûtés*) men who, in any case, are not paid enough to do this ignoble and degrading work." F. A. Bonnefin, *Rien à l'égout ou contre-projet du tout à l'égout* (Paris: Schmidt, 1883), pp. 9–10.

66. Ministère de l'Agriculture et du Commerce, *Rapports*, p. 69. Alphand, *Note du directeur*, p. 67.

67. M. Humblot, *Les Egouts de Paris à la fin de 1885* (Paris: Imprimerie Chaix, 1886), p. 57.
68. Ministère de l'Agriculture et du Commerce, *Rapports,* pp. 43–45, 84–87.
69. A. Durand-Claye, *Observations des ingénieurs du service municipal au sujet des projets de rapport présentés par MM. A. Girard et Brouardel* (Paris: Imprimerie Chaix, 1881), pp. 44–48.
70. Ann-Louise Shapiro, *Housing the Poor of Paris 1850–1902* (Madison: University of Wisconsin Press, 1985), pp. 81–82.
71. Gastinel, *Les Egouts de Paris,* pp. 32–35. Humblot, *Les Egouts de Paris,* pp. 57–59.
72. In 1880 Emile Raspail reflected on the accident that killed several sewermen that year. He blamed noxious odors which "menace the existence of the courageous workers who traverse the capital's gigantic network of sewers and the lives of all who approach the infinite number of [sewer] orifices." *Des Odeurs de Paris,* 2nd ed. (Paris: n.p., 1880), pp. 9–10.
73. And, in turn, the representations of workers in the nuclear power industry are about the most split among occupations in contemporary America, from the martyr Karen Silkwood to the moron Homer Simpson.
74. Such representations are social constructions which tell us more about the society in which they flourished than about occupational groups themselves. The danger in exploring such characterizations is that the historian will replicate the power relationships which produced them in the text. Here, for instance, within the "other" of sanitary labor, cesspool cleaners become a subordinate "other," as seemingly necessary for me, the historian, as for the society about which I write. The representation of Second Empire sewermen has special attraction to the historian charged with the measured, disciplined handling of the residue of past societies. Yet a little reflection reveals that the nineteenth-century representation of cesspool cleaners incorporates a vital—even appealing—amalgam of autonomy, independence, and liberation which challenges the plotting historian. (Dominick La Capra is on to something in his defense of cats. "Chartier, Darnton, and the Great Symbol Massacre," *Journal of Modern History* 60 (1988):95–112). And if that historian stoops too often for the reader's taste to the lowest form of humor, threatening the sober, unitary vision the monograph shares with the *tout-à-l'égout,* one can always put it down to unsettling traces of the representations which cesspool cleaners have left behind.

9. The World Turned Upside Down

1. While cleaning the cesspools and sewers of Paris has always been men's work, the socialist idea that a true revolution would require the valorization of waste removal is akin to the feminist argument that such a revolution would have to address in a direct and radical manner the issues of who does housework and how it is valued in society.
2. Pliny reports the use of convict labor to cleanse the sewers. Alex Scobie, "Slums, Sanitation, and Mortality in the Roman World," *Klio* 68 (1986):408.

For Roman legislation on sewer cleaning, see Léon Homo, *Rome impériale et l'urbanisme dans l'antiquité* (Paris: Albin Michel, 1951), pp. 470–473.

3. Natalie Zemon Davis, *Culture and Society in Early Modern Europe* (Stanford: Stanford University Press, 1975), pp. 46–47. The passage to which Davis is apparently referring is less explicit. Thomas More, *The Complete Works of Saint Thomas More,* ed. Edward Surtz and J. H. Hexter (New Haven: Yale University Press, 1965), 4:77. My thanks to John Headley for his assistance in tracking down references to sewers in More's works.

4. Alain Corbin, *The Foul and the Fragrant: Odor and the French Social Imagination,* trans. Miriam L. Kochan (Cambridge: Harvard University Press, 1986), p. 93. A. Tournon, *Moyens de rendre parfaitement propres les rues de Paris* (Paris: Lesclapart, 1789), p. 32n1.

5. Mathieu Géraud, *Essai sur la suppression des fosses d'aisances et de toute espèce de voiries, sur la manière de convertir en combustible les substances qu'on y renferme, etc.* (Amsterdam: n.p., 1786), pp. 50–61, 91.

6. More, *The Complete Works,* 4:224–227.

7. Louis-Sébastien Mercier, *L'An Deux Mille Quatre Cent Quarante. Rêve s'il en fût jamais,* ed. Raymond Trousson (Paris: Editions Ducros, 1971), pp. 173–174.

8. Frank E. Manuel and Fritzie P. Manuel, *Utopian Thought in the Western World* (Cambridge: Harvard University Press, 1979), p. 663.

9. Jonathan Beecher, *Fourier* (Berkeley: University of California Press, 1986), pp. 286–287. Fourier does not discuss sewermen specifically. Jonathan Beecher to Author, 20 November 1986. However, at least some contemporaries understood Fourier's "hordes" to be cleaning sewers. Jacques Rancière, *La Nuit des prolétaires* (Paris: Fayard, 1981), p. 232.

10. Auguste Blanqui, *Critique sociale,* 2 vols. (Paris: Félix Alcan, 1885), 1:191–193. One is reminded of Parent-Duchâtelet's outburst against doctors. See p. 76 above.

11. Jean Jaurès, "L'Organisation socialiste" in *Œuvres de Jean Jaurès,* 9 vols., ed. Max Bonnafous (Paris: Rieder, 1931), 3:340.

12. Peter Kropotkin, *The Conquest of Bread* (London: Penguin Press, 1973), p. 178.

13. Pierre Hamp, *Les Métiers blessés* (Paris: Editions de la *Nouvelle Revue Française,* 1919), pp. 191–192.

14. Ibid., p. 190.

15. See Pierre Hamp, *People,* trans. James Whitall (New York: Harcourt, Brace, 1921), pp. 175–176.

16. Jules Romains, *La Douceur de la vie* (Paris: Flammarion, 1939), p. 240.

17. Jacques Prévert, *Paroles* (Paris: Editions du Point du Jour, 1947), pp. 84–85.

18. Ibid., pp. 142–143.

19. Ibid., pp. 264–265.

20. The Madwoman is mentally and emotionally trapped by a broken romance in the Paris of the late nineteenth and early twentieth centuries: it is appropriate that she call on a sewerman in this period of their greatest public prominence.

21. Jean Giraudoux, *Pleins pouvoirs* (Paris: Gallimard, 1939).

22. Jean Giraudoux, "La Folle de Chaillot" in *Théâtre complet,* ed. Jacques Body (Paris: Gallimard, 1982), pp. 962–963 (henceforth "La Folle de Chaillot" [Pléiade]). There are several versions of "La Folle de Chaillot." I also refer to the version in *Le Théâtre complet de Jean Giraudoux* (Paris: Ides et Calendes, 1945), vol. 15 (henceforth "La Folle de Chaillot" [Ides et Calendes]).

23. Giraudoux, "La Folle de Chaillot" [Ides et Calandes], p. 69.

24. Léon Bonneff and Maurice Bonneff reported that sewermen loved flowers. *La Vie tragique des travailleurs* (Paris: J. Rouff, 1908), p. 214.

25. Giraudoux, "La Folle de Chaillot" [Pléiade], pp. 990–991.

26. Ibid., p. 991.

27. Marthe Besson-Herlin, "Notes et variantes" to "La Folle de Chaillot" [Pléiade], p. 1778.

28. Giraudoux, "La Folle de Chaillot" [Pléiade], p. 991.

29. Ibid., p. 992.

30. Ibid., p. 993.

31. Gaston Leroux's *La Double Vie de Théophraste Longuet* (in Leroux, *Romans fantastiques*, vol. 3, Paris: Robert Laffont, n.d.), is the story of Théophraste Longuet—the reincarnation of Cartouche. He and the police commissioner who is pursuing him are trapped in the Catacombs where they stumble upon the land of Talpas, populated by people speaking perfect fourteenth-century French but with snouts and no eyes. In Talpas society there is no private property, no laws, no police or criminals, and complete sexual freedom. The Talpas live in fifty groups of four hundred; except for the construction of a bridge or a sewer every two hundred years there are no "public affairs" (3:458).

32. Giraudoux, "La Folle de Chaillot" [Pléiade], p. 992.

33. Hervé Hamon and Patrick Rotman, *Génération,* 2 vols. (Paris: Seuil, 1987), 1:489.

34. A sanitation worker from Mali interviewed in Paris in the 1970s turned typical French criticisms of African workers on their head with his comment that Parisians' habits in the matter of trash disposal revealed what pigs they were. Jean Anglade, *La Vie quotidienne des immigrés en France de 1919 à nos jours* (Paris: Hachette, 1976), p. 146.

35. Raphaël-Emile Verhaeren, Michèle Bonnechère, Maryse Trippier, and Marius Apostolo, *Questions de l'immigration et syndicat* (Paris: Centre Confédéral d'Etudes Economiques (CGT), 1981), pp. 14, 19.

36. Jean Benoit, *Dossier E . . . comme Esclaves* (Paris: Alain Moreau, 1980), p. 81. See also Françoise Pinot, *Les Travailleurs immigrés dans la lutte de classes* (Paris: Cerf, 1973), p. 52.

37. Jacques Barou, *Travailleurs africains en France* (Grenoble: Presses universitaires de Grenoble, 1978), p. 10.

38. Benoit, *Dossier E,* pp. 223–224.

39. Tewfik Allal, Jean-Pierre Buffard, Michel Marie, and Tomaso Regazzola, *Situations migratoires. La Fonction-miroir* (Paris: Editions Galilée, 1977), p. 12.

40. Ibid., pp. 293–294.

10. In the Public Service

1. Felix Target, *On the Main Drainage of Paris and the Utilisation of Its Sewage* (London: W. Clowes, 1878), p. 6.

2. London sewermen complained of private contractors as well. Henry Mayhew wrote, "To contractors, the comforts or health of the labouring men must necessarily be a secondary consideration to the realization of a profit." *London Labour and the London Poor*, 3 vols. (London: Griffin, Bohn, 1861), 2:486.

3. Ministère de l'Agriculture et du Commerce. Commission de l'Assainissement de Paris, *Rapports et avis de la Commission* (Paris: Imprimerie nationale, 1881), pp. 84–87n1. Eugène Belgrand, *Les Travaux souterrains de Paris*, 5 vols. (Paris: Dunod, 1887), 5:195.

4. Belgrand, *Les Travaux souterrains*, 5:195–196n1. E. Deligny, president of the Commission des eaux et égouts of the Paris city council, responded to critics of the *tout-à-l'égout* in 1881: "I affirm that the city council will vote all the funds necessary for the sewers to be continuously washed and cleaned like the courtyard of a good house." *Observations du Président de la Commission des eaux et égouts au sujet des rapports de MM. Aimé Girard et Brouardel* (Paris: Imprimerie Chaix, 1881), p. 27.

5. Louis Gauthier, *Le Tout-à-l'égout et l'assainissement de la Seine par l'utilisation agricole des eaux d'égout de Paris* (Paris: Georges Chamerot, 1888), p. 31.

6. Maxime du Camp, *Paris. Ses organes, ses fonctions et sa vie dans la seconde moitié du XIXᵉ siècle*, 6 vols. (Paris: Hachette, 1869–1875), 5:458.

7. Information on 89 sewermen was taken from *Le Réveil de l'Assainissement*, 17 August 1902, p. 1; and from the columns, "Nos Morts pour la défense de la République," in the incomplete runs of *Le Réveil* in the Bibliothèque nationale-Versailles Annex and AN F⁷13834.

   The usual sources for a prosopography of the popular classes are insufficient for the study of sewermen in the late nineteenth and early twentieth centuries. Employment records have not been preserved (Jacques Chèze to Author, 29 July 1988). Sewermen lived in a variety of working-class *quartiers*, so the possibilities for using census lists are restricted. Because many sewermen did not take up the trade as youths, a study based on marriage records would generate limited (and skewed) data. Finally, one faces legal restrictions on use of the *état civil* for much of the period under study.

8. Adrien Weber, "Les Conditions de travail de la ville de Paris," *Revue socialiste* 148 (April 1897): 401–402. Gérard Noiriel places in its context the introduction of discrimination by nationality in the workplace at the end of the nineteenth century in *Le Creuset français. Histoire de l'immigration XIXᵉ–XXᵉ siècles* (Paris: Seuil, 1988), pp. 282–283 and *passim*.

9. AN F⁷13833, clipping from *Journal des débats*, 3 September 1908.

10. Lenard Berlanstein, *The Working People of Paris 1871–1914* (Baltimore: The Johns Hopkins University Press, 1984), p. 45. Sewermen continued to work more than eight-hour days when necessary, but received overtime pay for their efforts. G. M. A. Cadoux, "Les Salaires et les conditions du travail des ouvriers et employés des entreprises municipales de Paris," *Bulletin de l'Institut International de Statistique* 19 (1911), 1:337n1.

11. The union reported indignantly that the medical examination for work in the sewers was more strict than that for entrance into the military. *Le Réveil de l'Assainissement,* 25 March 1917, pp. 1–2.

12. *Le Réveil de l'Assainissement,* 12 May 1901, p. 1.

13. Léon Bonneff and Maurice Bonneff, *La Vie tragique des travailleurs* (Paris: J. Rouff, 1908), p. 213.

14. *Le Réveil de l'Assainissement,* 4 June 1916, p. 1.

15. Jules Larminier, "La loi de 21 mars 1884 et les travailleurs municipaux," *Mouvement socialiste* 150 (1 March 1905):315–329.

16. *Le Réveil de l'Assainissement,* 25 May 1902, p. 1.

17. *Le Réveil de l'Assainissement,* 27 September 1903, p. 2.

18. *Le Réveil de l'Assainissement,* 30 November 1899, p. 4.

19. *Le Réveil de l'Assainissement,* 28 January 1917, p. 1.

20. *Le Réveil de l'Assainissement,* 25 March 1900, p. 2.

21. *Le Réveil de l'Assainissement,* 9 June 1899, p. 1; 7 January 1900, p. 2. The union also provided swimming instruction to members in an effort to reduce the number of drownings. Léon Bonneff and Maurice Bonneff, *Les Métiers qui tuent* (Paris: Bibliographie sociale, 1900 [sic]), p. 115.

22. Bonneff and Bonneff, *La Vie tragique,* p. 213.

23. A. Daverton, *Assainissement des villes et égouts de Paris* (Paris: Dunod, 1922), pp. 343–344, 505. During the periods of budgetary constraint in the early 1870s, the number of sewermen was reduced and they were temporarily divided into "flying brigades" which were dispatched where work needed to be done. Du Camp, *Paris,* 5:458.

24. *Le Temps,* 1 July 1899, pp. 2–3. Earlier, sewermen had met each day at the rue des Bernardins and gone from there to their places of work. Larminier claimed that under this system, sewermen had worked only five hours per day in the sewers. Once there were more changing areas, the men worked longer hours in the sewers with deleterious effects on their health. *Le Réveil de l'Assainissement,* 11 December 1898, p. 4. Recently, the administration has given the romantic sounding *chambres de rendez-vous* the sober name of *lieux d'appel.*

25. Bonneff and Bonneff, *La Vie tragique,* p. 206.

26. AN F⁷13833, clipping from *La Nouvelle,* 22 March 1909. Such antibureaucratic fervor characterized *allemaniste* socialism. On Larminier's *allemaniste* connections, see *Le Réveil de l'Assainissement,* 24 February 1901, p. 2. One socialist sewerman, Jean-Baptiste Sémanaz, achieved some prominence as mayor of Pré-St. Gervais from 1904 until his death in 1914. See *Le Réveil de l'Assainissement,* 11 February 1917; and Jean Maitron, ed., *Dictionnaire biographique du mouvement ouvrier français 1871–1914* (Paris: Editions ouvrières, 1977), 15:151–152.

27. *Le Réveil de l'Assainissement,* 16 December 1917, pp. 1–2.

28. Du Camp, *Paris,* 5:459.

29. *Le Réveil de l'Assainissement,* 16 February 1902, p. 3.

30. *Le Réveil de l'Assainissement,* 27 March 1898, p. 1; 24 April 1898, p. 1.

31. *Le Réveil de l'Assainissement,* 15 January 1899, p. 1.
32. *Le Réveil de l'Assainissement,* 19 February 1899, pp. 1–2.
33. Du Camp, *Paris,* 5:444–446. Georges Bechmann, *Notice sur le service des eaux et de l'assainissement de Paris* (Paris: Ch. Béranger, 1900), p. 300.
34. Bonneff and Bonneff, *La Vie tragique,* p. 183.
35. Will Darvillé, *L'Eau à la ville, à la campagne et dans la maison* (Paris: Librairie de la Construction moderne, n.d.), p. 484.
36. *Le Réveil de l'Assainissement,* 28 April 1901, p. 1.
37. *Le Réveil de l'Assainissement,* 16 July 1899, p. 2. Georges Verpraet reports another occasion on which sewermen protested before the Hôtel de Ville with big rats tied to their poles. *Paris. Capitale souterraine* (Paris: Plon, 1954), p. 147.
38. *Le Temps,* 5 July 1891, p. 1; 16 February 1892, p. 3.
39. Larminier, "La loi de 21 mars," 315–329.
40. See, for instance, Jean Jaurès, "L'Organisation socialiste" in *Œuvres de Jean Jaurès,* 9 vols., ed. Max Bonnafous (Paris: Editions Rieder, 1931), 3:331–337. Could the public sector improve on the forms of management employed in the private sector? The Third Republic sought ways to manage labor in state enterprises without relying on either the arbitrary brutality of the foreman or the ponderous bureaucracy of the state. See Donald Reid, "The Third Republic as Manager: Labour Policy in the Naval Shipyards, 1892–1920," *International Review of Social History* 30 (1985): 183–206.
41. Georges Cahen, *Les Fonctionnaires. Leur action corporative* (Paris: Armand Colin, 1911), pp. 71–72.
42. Ernestine A. Durand-Claye, *Alfred Durand-Claye 1841–1888* (Paris: Imprimerie Chaix, n.d.), p. 52.
43. *Le Réveil de l'Assainissement,* 27 September 1903, p. 2.
44. *Le Réveil de l'Assainissement,* 30 December 1900, p. 3.
45. D. R. Watson, "The Nationalist Movement in Paris, 1900–1906" in David Shapiro, ed., *The Right in France 1890–1919* (Carbondale: Southern Illinois University Press, 1962), pp. 49–84. The conservative city council was more anti-socialist than anti-labor.
46. *Le Réveil de l'Assainissement,* 1 May 1904, p. 1. Bonneff and Bonneff, *Les Métiers,* p. 108. (I could not locate this particular motif in the *Journal officiel.* To what extent was it a projection of how sewermen thought they were viewed?)
    The myth of the card-playing sewermen has great appeal. Ed Norton, the New York City sewerman of "The Honeymooners," told of sitting on the banks of the sewer, playing poker ("wet cards wild")—a feat theoretically possible in Paris but not in New York, where sewers lack the necessary ledges. Robert Daley, *The World beneath the City* (Philadelphia: J. B. Lippincott, 1959), p. 193.
47. *Le Réveil de l'Assainissement,* 29 January 1902, p. 2; 29 March 1902, p. 1.
48. *Le Réveil de l'Assainissement,* January 1898.
49. APP BA896, "Corporation des travailleurs municipaux," 12 February 1911. This criticism periodically generated dissension within the sewermen's union.

It would be interesting to know more about these debates as a way of probing Larminier's construction of an identity for sewermen based on their solidarity in the face of an unsympathetic world.

50. *Le Réveil de l'Assainissement*, 19 February 1899, pp. 3–4.
51. *L'Eclair*, 10 November 1901, pp. 2–3.
52. *Le Réveil de l'Assainissement*, 19 July and 26 July 1903. Judith Wishnia places the municipal workers' struggle for the right to organize into a larger context in "French Fonctionnaires: The Development of Class Consciousness and Unionization, 1884–1926" (Ph.D. diss., State University of New York at Stony Brook, 1978), p. 19 and *passim*.
53. *Le Réveil de l'Assainissement*, 20 April 1902, p. 2; 15 June 1902, p. 3.
54. *Le Réveil de l'Assainissement*, 9 November 1902, p. 2.
55. See, for example, *Le Réveil de l'Assainissement*, 22 November 1903, p. 2.
56. AN F⁷13876, clipping from *Le Journal*, 15 August 1910.
57. AN F⁷13876, clipping from *La Petite République*, 7 February 1910.

11. The Body of Sewermen

1. For a recent examination of the psychological consequences of falls in the sewers (as well as the frequency of phobias concerning enclosed spaces, rats, dirty water, and so on) among sewermen, see Archives Syndicat, "Travail dans les égouts," prepared by Médecins inspecteurs régionaux du travail and the Ingénieur en chef des égouts de Paris, January 1982.
2. *Echo des travailleurs municipaux*, 10 April 1897, p. 2.
3. Archives Syndicat, "Maladies. Accidents professionnels."
4. *L'Humanité*, 29 October 1977, p. 4.
5. Léon Bonneff and Maurice Bonneff, *La Vie tragique des travailleurs* (Paris: J. Rouff, 1908), pp. 190–199.
6. *Le Réveil de l'Assainissement*, 29 July–4 August 1900, p. 2.
7. A.-J.-B. Parent-Duchâtelet, "Essai sur la cloaque ou égouts de la Ville de Paris" in *Hygiène publique*, 2 vols. (Paris: J. B. Baillière, 1836), 1:281.
8. *Le Réveil de l'Assainissement*, 29 March 1903, pp. 1–2. Foveau de Courmelles was typical of many early doctors whose interest in occupational health reflected a general trajectory on the margins of medical science. Foveau de Courmelles was, for instance, quite interested in hypnotism and had been vice-president of the International Magnetic Congress in 1889. See his *Hypnotism*, trans. Laura Ensor (Philadelphia: David McKay, n.d.), p. vi.
9. Léon Bonneff and Maurice Bonneff, *Les Métiers qui tuent* (Paris: Bibliographie sociale, 1900 [sic]), pp. 110–111. Calculations from figures in Paul Wéry, *Assainissement des villes et égouts de Paris* (Paris: Dunod, 1898), pp. 645, 650, confirm these statistics for 1887–1897.
10. Henry Haynie, *Paris Past and Present*, 2 vols. (New York: Frederick A. Stokes, 1902), 2:307. Haynie's credulity had its limits. "There is, however, reason to doubt the claim that those who work down in the Paris sewers are more healthy, or longer lived than other labourers"; ibid.

11. Bonneff and Bonneff, *Les Métiers*, p. 111.
12. Roger Price, *A Social History of Nineteenth-Century France* (New York: Holmes and Meier, 1987), p. 63. See Pierre Guillaume, *Du désespoir au salut: les tuberculeux aux XIXᵉ et XXᵉ siècles* (Paris: Aubier, 1986).
13. Bonneff and Bonneff, *Les Métiers*, p. 104.
14. Georges Bechmann, *Notice sur le service des eaux et de l'assainissement de Paris* (Paris: Ch. Béranger, 1900), p. 302.
15. Ibid., p. 301. Daniel Bellet and Will Darvillé, *Ce que doit être la Cité moderne* (Paris: Bernard Tignol, n.d.), pp. 122–124.
16. *Le Réveil de l'Assainissement*, 15 February 1903, p. 1.
17. Alain Cottereau, "La Tuberculose: maladie urbaine ou maladie de l'usure au travail? Critique d'une épidémiologie officielle: le cas de Paris," *Sociologie du travail* 78 (1978):192–224.
18. Wéry, *Assainissement*, calculations from data on pp. 645, 649, 650.
19. Haynie, *Paris*, 2:308. Bonneff and Bonneff, *La Vie tragique*, p. 185.
20. *L'Eclair*, 10 November 1901, pp. 2–3.
21. Bonneff and Bonneff, *Les Métiers*, pp. 111–12. Bonneff and Bonneff, *La Vie tragique*, p. 200.
22. *Le Réveil de l'Assainissement*, 1 January 1899, p. 3.
23. Bonneff and Bonneff, *Les Métiers*, pp. 111–112.
24. *Le Réveil de l'Assainissement*, 3 July 1916, pp. 1–3.
25. *Le Réveil de l'Assainissement*, 18 March 1906, p. 1.
26. Bonneff and Bonneff, *Les Métiers*, p. 114.
27. *Le Réveil de l'Assainissement*, 22 May 1898, p. 1.
28. *Le Réveil de l'Assainissement*, 5 March 1899, p. 1.
29. See Jacquelyn D. Hall et al., *Like a Family: The Making of a Southern Cotton Mill World* (Chapel Hill: University of North Carolina Press, 1987).
30. Bonneff and Bonneff, *La Vie tragique*, pp. 205–206.
31. Ibid., pp. 201, 206.
32. Ibid., p. 208.
33. Jules Larminier, "La Colonie des ouvriers égoutiers et de l'assainissement de la ville de Paris à la Ville-sous-Orbais (Marne)," *Revue Socialiste* 273 (September 1907) and 274 (October 1907), 274:355.
34. Bonneff and Bonneff, *La Vie tragique*, p. 208.
35. *Le Réveil de l'Assainissement*, 12 March 1916, pp. 1–2.
36. *Le Réveil de l'Assainissement*, 22 May 1898, p. 1.
37. Larminier, "La Colonie," 273:278–279. For an overview of welfare services in Paris, see J. H. Weiss, "Origins of the French Welfare State: Poor Relief in the Third Republic, 1871–1914," *French Historical Studies* 13 (1983):47–78.
38. Bonneff and Bonneff, *La Vie tragique*, p. 209.
39. *Echo des travailleurs municipaux*, 25 September 1896, p. 2. *Le Réveil de l'Assainissement*, 6 April 1902, p. 1. Larminier, "La Colonie," 273:273–274.
40. In 1903, three thousand attended the Fête. *Le Réveil de l'Assainissement*, 22 November 1903, p. 2.
41. *Le Réveil de l'Assainissement*, 9 December 1900, p. 1. On the care provided children by the Assistance publique, see Rachel Fuchs' fine study, *Abandoned*

Children: Foundlings and Child Welfare in Nineteenth-Century France (Albany: State University of New York Press, 1984).

42. *Le Réveil de l'Assainissement,* 24 December 1899, p. 2; 28 December 1919, p. 3.

43. Larminier, "La Colonie," 273:280–281.

44. Ibid., 281.

45. *Le Réveil de l'Assainissement,* 24 April 1904, p. 1.

46. *Le Réveil de l'Assainissement,* 23 February 1902, p. 2.

47. Larminier, "La Colonie," 273:280.

48. Bonneff and Bonneff, *La Vie tragique,* p. 208.

49. *Le Réveil de l'Assainissement,* 6 January 1901, p. 2; 18 November 1917, p. 1. Larminier, "La Colonie," 273:281.

50. *Le Réveil de l'Assainissement,* 16 January 1916, p. 2.

51. *Le Réveil de l'Assainissement,* 17 March 1901, p. 1. Joan Scott has pointed out the related familial imagery of contemporary socialist municipalities: "Like a working-class family, but on a larger scale, the socialist commune was depicted as a shelter against the ultimate alienation and impoverishment of capitalism." See "Mayors versus Police Chiefs: Socialist Municipalities Confront the French State" in *French Cities in the Nineteenth Century,* ed. John Merriman (London: Hutchinson, 1982), p. 242.

52. APP BA896, "Corporation des travailleurs municipaux," 23 April 1910.

53. Bonneff and Bonneff, *La Vie tragique,* p. 209.

54. *Le Réveil de l'Assainissement,* 27 January 1901, p. 2.

55. *Le Réveil de l'Assainissement,* 21 April 1901, p. 3.

56. *Le Réveil de l'Assainissement,* 9 June 1901, p. 1. The Palais du Travail was a failed effort to create a syndical and cooperative center in Paris (1897–1905). Jean Gaumont, *Histoire générale de la coopération en France,* 2 vols. (Paris: Fédération nationale des coopératives de consommation, 1923), 2:361n43.

57. The idea of the colony also differed significantly from the short-lived anarchist communities started around Paris at the turn of the century. See Georges Narrat, *Milieux libres. Quelques essais contemporains de vie communiste en France* (Paris: Félix Alcan, 1908).

58. Larminier, "La Colonie," 273:275–276.

59. Ibid., 273:282–283.

60. Ibid., 273:272–273.

61. Ibid., 274:340–359. In his "Historique de la Colonie" (Archives Sarrazin), Sarrazin states that a sewerman who spent several days in the region of la Ville-Sous-Orbais saw the land and brought it to the attention of the union.

62. *Le Réveil de l'Assainissement,* 28 November 1920, pp. 2–3.

63. Larminier, "La Colonie," 274:358–359.

64. *Le Réveil de l'Assainissement,* 6 May 1917, p. 2.

65. *Le Réveil de l'Assainissement,* 29 August 1915, p. 1.

66. Bonneff and Bonneff, *La Vie tragique,* p. 213.

67. *Le Réveil de l'Assainissement,* 3 July 1916, p. 1.

68. *Le Réveil de l'Assainissement,* 15 August 1915, p. 3.

69. Bonneff and Bonneff, *La Vie tragique* p. 212.

70. *Le Réveil de l'Assainissement,* 15 August 1915, p. 3.
71. Larminier, "La Colonie," 274:345.
72. Archives départementales de la Marne, Secrétaire du Syndicat des Egoutiers de Paris to Inspecteur de l'Assistance publique (Marne), 18 September 1922.
73. *Le Réveil de l'Assainissement,* 18 November 1917, p. 1.
74. *Le Réveil de l'Assainissement,* 16 December 1917, p. 3.
75. Larminier, "La Colonie," 274:353.
76. Cottereau, "La Tuberculose," 224. For a much more developed contemporary syndicalist experience in health care, see Alan Derickson, *Workers' Health, Workers' Democracy: The Western Miners' Struggle, 1891–1925* (Ithaca: Cornell University Press, 1988).
77. Jean-Pierre Frey, *La Ville industrielle et ses urbanités. La Distinction ouvriers/employés 1870–1930* (Brussells: Pierre Mardaga, 1986), p. 120.
78. For an excellent study of the housing problem in late nineteenth-century Paris, see Ann-Louise Shapiro, *Housing the Poor of Paris* (Madison: University of Wisconsin Press, 1985).
79. The sewermen's union split briefly over this issue. AN F⁷13833, report of Paris Préfecture de Police, 12 July 1911. On joining the central, see ibid., clipping from *La Voix du peuple,* 17–24 September 1911.
80. AN F⁷13833, report of Paris Préfecture de Police, 3 November 1913.
81. AN F⁷13834, clipping from *L'Humanité* (October 1916).
82. *Le Réveil de l'Assainissement,* 16 July 1916, p. 3.
83. *Le Réveil de l'Assainissement,* 2 January 1916, p. 2.
84. *Le Réveil de l'Assainissement,* 17 December 1916, p. 2.
85. *Le Réveil de l'Assainissement,* 6 May 1917, p. 2.
86. *Le Réveil de l'Assainissement,* 16 December 1917, p. 4.
87. *Le Réveil de l'Assainissement,* 13 January 1918, p. 2.
88. *Le Réveil de l'Assainissement,* 13 October 1918, p. 3; 11 April 1920, p. 4.
89. In 1912, an aging Larminier had asked to be relieved of his position as union secretary. Léon Bonneff and Maurice Bonneff, *La Vie tragique des travailleurs* (Paris: J. Rouff, 1914), p. 220n1. (Other references are to the 1908 edition of this book.)
90. *Le Réveil de l'Assainissement,* 16 December 1917, pp. 1–2.
91. AN F⁷13834, report of Paris Préfecture de Police, 13 June 1921.
92. After the war, the sewermen's union took advantage of new legislation which gave unions the right to own property. It sought to purchase the shares it had sold in the colony before the war and in 1921 took over direct control of the operation. *Le Réveil de l'Assainissement,* 25 April 1920, p. 1. Archives Syndicat, agreement between the Colonie and the Syndicat des Egoutiers, 15 July 1921.
93. Guillaume, *Du désespoir,* pp. 203ff.
94. AN F⁷13835, report of Paris Préfecture de Police, 23 October 1926. Archives Sarrazin, statutes of "Colonies de repos et de vacances du personnel égoutier et des services municipaux et départementaux (Paris et Seine)," 9 November 1935.
95. Archives Sarrazin, Sarrazin, "Histoire de la colonie." Most sewermen today

have only a vague idea of the colony. Those hostile to the union suspect that *les gros* within it have somehow benefited from the colony.

96. Why are the projects of Larminier and his union—the sewermen as family, etc.—shielded from the ironic glance accorded so many other undertakings in this work? Is lack of sources a sufficient explanation? Perhaps the insistent use of familial metaphors, the occasional evidence of disharmony in the prewar union, and the short life of the colony could be made to reveal Larminier's disappointments with his moral proletarians. While the historical judgments and political sympathies of the author should not be ignored in answering this question, the inner workings of the text offer an alternative way of explaining the anomalous treatment of the union experience. Like sewage farming, the largely uncontested culmination of the first part of this book, the colony offers an irresistible closure—Chadwick's ouroborus—in which the ideologies of social programs and the imperatives of textual practice align.

97. Bonneff and Bonneff, *La Vie tragique,* p. 205.

98. Bonneff and Bonneff, *Les Métiers,* pp. 115–116. The prominent labor movement journalists brothers Léon and Maurice Bonneff penned two glowing essays on the sewermen in the years before World War I. Specialists on alcoholism and work-related health and safety issues, they wrote reports on dozens of occupational groups. The workers the Bonneffs admired the most were the sewermen, whose solidarity and creative union policies they praised highly. On the Bonneffs, see Michelle Perrot, "Préface" to Léon Bonneff and Maurice Bonneff, *La Vie tragique des travailleurs* (Paris: E.D.I., 1984), pp. vii-xxvii.

99. Foveau de Courmelles, "Impôts nouveaux et prolétariat cérébral" in *Moniteur medical* (2 January 1917) reprinted in *Le Réveil de l'Assainissement,* 28 January 1917, p. 2.

100. Jacques Donzelot, *L'Invention du social. Essai sur le déclin des passions politiques* (Paris: Fayard, 1984). Judith Stone, *The Search for Social Peace: Reform Legislation in France 1890–1914* (Albany: State University of New York Press, 1985); and "The Radicals and the Interventionist State: Attitudes, Ambiguities and Transformations, 1880–1910," *French History* 2 (1988):173–186. François Ewald, *L'Etat providence* (Paris: Grasset, 1986). Sanford Elwitt, *The Third Republic Defended: Bourgeois Reform in France. 1880–1914* (Baton Rouge: Louisiana State University Press, 1986).

101. The Colony can be seen as a particular variant of what Stephen Yeo refers to as "associationism" in "Notes on Three Socialisms—Collectivism, Statism and Associationism—Mainly in Late Nineteenth- and Early Twentieth-Century Britain" in *Socialism and the Intelligentsia,* ed. Carl Levy (London: Routlege and Kegan Paul, 1987), pp. 219–270.

12. Sewermen Today

1. Archives Sarrazin, M. Sentenac, "Section des égouts," p. 9.

2. Archives Sarrazin, Sarrazin, "Les Conditions de travail" (late 1970s); Ar-

chives Gauchet, Lucien Gauchet, "Les Egouts de Paris," 5 December 1983. Catherine Levy, "Les Conditions de travail des égoutiers parisiens et la grève d'automne 1977," (report for Laboratoire de sociologie du travail et des relations professionnelles, 1978), p. 30.

3. Archives Sarrazin, *La Vie mutualiste* (March 1977), p. 49.
4. Archives Sarrazin, Sarrazin, "Aspects sociologiques du métier."
5. Archives Gauchet, Gauchet, "Les Egouts de Paris."
6. Jacques Chèze to Author, 29 July 1988.
7. Archives Sarrazin, Sarrazin, "Aspects sociologiques du métier."
8. Ibid.; Sarrazin, "Les Conditions de travail."
9. Archives Sarrazin, Sarrazin, "Aspects sociologiques du métier." As a union official, Sarrazin considered the city's attacks on the illegality of "double-dipping" sewermen hypocritical since the practice served management's interests by dividing and demobilizing workers.
10. Archives Sarrazin, Sarrazin, "Les Conditions de travail."
11. Archives Syndicat, "Sous le pavé, le monde terrifiant des égouts de Paris" (undated clipping).
12. Archives Sarrazin, *La Vie mutualiste* (March 1977), p. 49.
13. *L'Humanité,* 29 October 1977, p. 4.
14. Ibid.
15. Archives Gauchet, Gauchet, "Les Egouts de Paris."
16. Archives Syndicat, "La Vie des égoutiers." (c. 1946)
17. Jacques Chèze to Author, 29 July 1988.
18. Levy, "Les Conditions de travail," p. 33.
19. Archives Syndicat, Médecins inspecteurs régionaux du travail and Ingénieur en chef des égouts de Paris, "Travail dans les égouts" (January 1982). Some doctors maintain that the sewermen's repeated contacts with small doses of infected materials give them greater immunity to a variety of diseases. P. Gros, J. C. Mahieu, J. F. Ulysse, *Projet de guide. L'Hygiène et la sécurité des personnels d'exploitation des réseaux d'assainissement* (Paris: Service technique de l'urbanisme. Division des equipements urbains, 1983), p. 33.
20. Archives Sarrazin, *La Vie mutualiste* (March 1977), p. 42. Archives Syndicat, "Maladies. Accidents professionnels."
21. Archives Syndicat, "Sous le pavé"; "Travail dans les égouts."
22. Levy, "Les Conditions de travail," p. 22.
23. Archives Sarrazin, Sarrazin, "Aspects sociologiques du métier."
24. Levy, "Les Conditions de travail," p. 37. Lucien Gauchet to Author, 29 September 1988.
25. Archives Syndicat, "Un peu d'histoire syndicale sur l'application journalière des 6 heures de travail"; "La Vie des égoutiers."
26. Levy, "Les Conditions de travail," pp. 5–8. This work provides the only detailed account of the strike.
27. Ibid., pp. 17–18.
28. Ibid., pp. 38–51.
29. *L'Humanité,* 7 November 1977, p. 5. Lucien Gauchet to Author, 20 April 1988.

30. Lucien Gauchet to Author, 29 September 1988.
31. Archives Sarrazin, Sarrazin, "Aspects sociologiques du métier."
32. Jacques Chèze to Author, 29 July 1988.
33. Ibid.
34. Levy, "Les Conditions de travail," p. 30. Archives Sarrazin, Sarrazin, "Les Conditions de travail"; "Aspects sociologiques du métier."
35. Jacques Chèze to Author, 29 July 1988.
36. Work is under way on developing a small robot which could be used to clean the most dangerous and difficult-to-reach areas, but even such a device would alter the sewermen's job little. Archives Syndicat, clipping from *Le Parisien*, 2 March 1987.
37. "Réseau d'assainissement de la Ville de Paris" (report prepared by the city of Paris in early 1980s).
38. Concern over control of information about the sanitary system was not new. At the beginning of the July Monarchy the engineer H. C. Emmery, author of books on both the sewer and water systems of Paris, had explained in the latter study that private individuals always tried to keep a knowledge of the water system to themselves. Without studies like the one he was undertaking, future generations would be "at the mercy of a workers' tradition." *Statistique des eaux de la ville de Paris (année 1839)* (Paris: Carilian-Gœury et Dalmont, 1840), pp. 1–2.
    New York City experienced the most extreme case of individual control of knowledge about the sewers. Robert Daley wrote of Teddy May, Superintendent of Sewers in New York for twenty-nine years, "From 1903 when Teddy made the first survey of the sewer system until about 1940, the only map of the network was the one Teddy carried in his head . . . This knowledge Teddy held like a cocked revolver at the head of the city, protecting his power. Thus for half a century no new sewers were laid in New York, nor old ones condemned, without the approval of Teddy May." *The World beneath the City* (Philadelphia: J. B. Lippincott, 1959), p. 175.
39. "Réseau d'assainissement de la Ville de Paris."
40. Such changes had taken place long before in other municipal services. Among *cantonniers*, for example, the number of workers had been reduced one-quarter between 1914 and 1922. An engineer explained at the time that the service "had to lose the quasi-familial feeling that it had before the war, at a time when each *atelier* constituted a virtually isolated domain functioning under the initiative of the *chef cantonnier*. It must take on the pace of an industry aiming at savings and in which *lost time* is, as much as possible, eliminated." M. L. Girard, *Le Nettoiement de Paris* (Paris: Librairie de l'enseignement technique, 1923), p. 32.
41. "Réseau d'assainissement de la Ville de Paris."
42. Ibid. For background on the introduction of computerization into sewer management, see Ministère de l'Urbanisme, du Logement et des Transports. Service technique de l'urbanisme. Division des equipements urbains, *Gestion automatisée des réseaux d'assainissement* (Paris: Ministère de l'Urbanisme, du Logement et des Transports, 1986). Computerization of data relating to sea-

sonal garbage production and periods of traffic congestion in Paris have allowed significant improvements in the efficiency of garbage collection in recent years. Catherine de Silguy, *La Saga des ordures du Moyen Age à nos jours* (Paris: Editions de l'Instant, 1989), pp. 30–31.

43. Le Service technique de l'assainissement, "Le Métier d'égoutier" (1986).

44. High national unemployment rates, wage increases, and improved working conditions have transformed the composition of the labor force engaged in street-cleaning in Paris since the early 1970s. In 1972, 72% of street-cleaners were foreign; the figure had fallen to 38% by 1986. de Silguy, *La Saga des ordures*, p. 31.

45. Archives Sarrazin, Sarrazin, "Aspects sociologiques du métier."

46. Archives Syndicat, clipping from *Le Parisien*, 6 May 1985.

Conclusion

1. Jerrold Seigel, *Bohemian Paris: Culture, Politics, and the Boundaries of Bourgeois Life, 1830–1930* (New York: Viking Penguin, 1986), pp. 140–142. A study of the ragpickers' place in social thought would complement the examination of cesspool cleaners and sewermen in this work. See Alain Faure, "Classe malpropre, classe dangereuse? Quelques remarques à propos des chiffonniers parisiens au XIXᵉ siècle et de leurs cités," *Recherches* 29 (December 1977): 79–102; Catherine de Silguy, *La Saga des ordures du Moyen Age à nos jours* (Paris: Editions de l'Instant, 1989), pp. 49–71; and Catherine Kudlick, "Disease, Public Health and Urban Social Relations: Perceptions of Cholera and the Paris Environment, 1830–1850" (Ph.D. diss., University of California at Berkeley, 1988), pp. 196–201.

The nineteenth-century *chiffonnier* (*Lumpensammler* in German) is kin to Marx and Engels' lumpenproletarian (or proletarian in rags, although *Lump* and its compounds possess more general derogatory connotations than *chiffon*). In his stay in Paris in the 1840s, Marx must have encountered the city's famed ragpickers. Their ambiguous social origins (some were said to be fallen aristocrats), their reputed involvement in shady dealings, and their symbiotic relationship to the rich—who had more valuable rubbish to dispose of than the poor—endowed them with characteristics not unlike those of the Marxist lumpenproletariat. And the diverse jumble of things ragpickers collected make them a suitable embodiment of the confused catch-all category of lumpenproletariat in Marxist thought. Jacques Rancière makes some very perceptive comments on this subject in *Le Philosophe et ses pauvres* (Paris: Fayard, 1983), pp. 143–44.

Ragpickers conveyed significant meanings for others as well. On the eve of the Haussmannization of Paris, Alexandre Privat d'Anglemont touted the "spontaneous urban renewal project" of the Villa des Chiffonniers in which, like the sewermen of Parent-Duchâtelet and Larminier, "the poor developed virtues of fraternity and self-help" (Seigel, *Bohemian Paris*, p. 142). Frédéric Le Play and his followers allocated ragpickers a special place in their typology of social life. Some writers even claimed ragpickers as their own special proletariat because the rags collected went to make the paper they used. Walter Benjamin's thoughts on ragpickers (and on Baudelaire's famous "Le Vin des chiffonniers") offer another interesting avenue of study. See Irving Wohlfarth, "Et Cetera? The Historian as Chiffonnier," *New German Critique* 39 (1986):143–168. Kudlick is currently engaged in an important study of Parisian ragpickers in the nineteenth century.

In the twentieth century, various institutionalized forms of urban gleaning and recycling of refuse have been interpreted in terms of the simultaneous reclamation of souls and restoration of bodies. See the account of the renowned Abbé Pierre Grouès and his flock in Boris Simon, *Abbé Pierre and the Ragpickers of Emmaus,* trans. Lucie Noël (New York: P. J. Kenedy, 1955).

2. In so doing the union exhibited a greater sense of foresight than it is customary to attribute to French workers of the period. Peter N. Stearns, *Old Age in European Society: The Case of France* (London: Croom Helm, 1977), pp. 42–79. My thanks to Michael Hanagan for suggesting this idea.

Index

Achères, 62, 63, 65, 66, 69, 83
Alphand, Adolphe, 65, 78, 194n6
Amelot sewer, 22, 26, 100–102, 103, 104, 105, 111
Animals in the sewers: dogs, 114, 119; rats, 130, 150–153, 165, 174, 178, 184n5, 194n2, 221n37, 222n1; alligators, 184n6; turtles, 184–185n6
Ariès, Philippe, 15
Assistance publique, 158, 159, 162
Aubriot, Hugues, 12
Augustine of Hippo, 15, 23

Bechmann, Georges, 32, 44, 62, 81, 82, 113, 116–117, 141, 147–148, 154, 163, 167, 171
Belgrand, Eugène, 29, 30, 35, 58, 59, 62, 78, 116, 117, 163, 171, 205n46, 215n61
Benjamin, Walter, 44, 229–230n1
Berlanstein, Lenard, 139
Bertholon, Pierre, 122
Blanqui, Auguste, 19–20, 21, 124, 125, 127, 144, 148, 175
Bloy, Léon, 50, 196n47
Bondy, 58, 76, 77–78, 97
Bonneff, Léon and Maurice, 167, 226n98
Boussingault, J. B., 79
Brouardel, Paul, 81, 110, 118
Bruneseau, Pierre-Emmanuel, 21, 22–23, 48, 57, 58, 111, 189n8, 190n19, 191n27, 211n98
Burges, George, 197n6
Buttes-Chaumont, 11, 65

Cadet Le Jeune, 94
Cartouche, 190nn12, 17, 218n31
du Camp, Maxime, 41, 48, 54, 65, 116, 138
Catacombes of Paris, 16–17, 44, 52
Cemeteries of Paris, 15–17, 65
Cesspool cleaners, 78, 87–88, 96, 107, 117, 121, 123, 124, 126, 179, 180, 212n5; in the Old Regime, 12, 88–95, 207nn7, 11; debate over tout-à-l'égout, 79, 80, 118–120, 146; health and safety, 89–95, 109, 120; drinking, 89, 94, 109, 120; guild, 89, 90, 95, 207n7; in the nineteenth century, 108–110; number, 108; wages, 108, 109; See also Cesspools of Paris; Representations of sanitary labor
Cesspools of Paris, 10, 57, 71, 74, 79, 81, 82, 88, 91, 118, 122, 205n40
Chadwick, Edwin, 27–29, 56–57, 59, 63, 79, 118, 198n22, 200n68, 215n61, 226n96
Charpian, 98, 104, 105, 116
Chauvet, 122
Chevalier, Louis, 3, 18
Chirac, Jacques, 173, 174, 175, 176, 177, 178
Cholera, 3, 18, 23–24, 25, 26, 35, 51, 82, 107, 119, 178, 204n28
City and countryside, 54, 56, 65, 103, 162–165
Civilization and barbarism, 1–2, 50, 73, 78, 80, 82, 123, 183n2; and sewers, 3, 9, 20, 24, 36, 113, 114; and sewage farming, 55, 58, 60, 66; and sewermen, 103, 114, 117, 147

Claudel, Paul, 55
Clichy, 57, 58, 60, 62, 82
Cluacina, 15, 81
Colbert, 96
Colony of the sewermen's union, 162–167, 168, 224n57, 225n92, 225–226n95, 230n2
Communists in France, 68, 106
Confédération Française des Travailleurs Chrétiens, 173, 174, 175
Confédération Générale du Travail, 68, 132, 165, 166, 170, 172, 173, 174, 175, 178
Corbel, Théophile, 160–161, 164
Corbin, Alain, 44, 82, 89, 99
Cottereau, Alain, 154, 164

Dante, 21, 45
D'Arcet, Jean-Pierre, 77
Darnton, Robert, 4
Darvillé, Will, 144
Davis, Natalie Zemon, 122
Deloncle, Eugène, and the Cagoule, 51, 196n50
Demography: of Paris, 18; and sewers, 22, 55; and sewage farming, 56–57
Doctors, 74, 76, 103, 114–115, 125, 126, 204n28: and cesspool cleaners, 90–92, 93, 94–95. See also Sewermen and occupational medicine
Dorgères, Henri, 202n94
Douglas, Mary, 2, 21
Drabble, Margaret, 185n7
Dumps, 10–11, 78–79, 80. See also Bondy; Montfaucon; Poudrette
Durand-Claye, Alfred, 59, 60, 62, 80, 83, 119, 146
Durand-Claye, Léon, 59

Egotism and sanitary practice, 14, 15, 24, 76, 82, 95, 103, 124, 144, 148, 167
Ellison, Harlan, 184n6
Emmery, H. C., 22, 26, 27, 113, 228n38
Engels, Friedrich, 1–2, 4, 229n1
Engineers: ideology and aspirations, 18, 21–23, 29, 36, 50–51, 53, 58, 72, 82, 109, 113–117, 120, 148, 179, 180, 202n97. See also Sewermen's union and engineers
Ewald, François, 106

Flachat, Stéphane [Stéphane Mony], 24
Flaubert, Gustave, 110
Force Ouvrière, 173, 174, 175
Fourier, Charles, 54, 123, 125, 127, 217n9
Foveau de Courmelles, 153, 167, 222n8
Freud, Sigmund, 2, 4, 50, 214n32

Garnier, Jules, 74, 78
Gauchistes, 106, 132–133
Gennevilliers, 58, 60–65, 66, 81, 83, 107
Geismar, Alain, 131
Géraud, Mathieu, 54, 93, 94, 122, 123, 126
Girard, Aimé, 78
Giraud, Pierre, 73, 74, 77
Giraudoux, Jean, 4, 128–131, 132, 217n20
Gisquet, Henri Joseph, 72, 74, 75, 76
Goncourt, Edmond and Jules, 112, 117
Greene, Graham, 185n7
Guillerme, André, 10
Guizot, François, 183n2

Hallé, Jean-Noël, 24, 74–75, 77, 91, 94–95, 96
Hamp, Pierre, 125–126, 127, 131, 148
Haussmann, Georges Eugène, 29–30, 32, 36, 39, 48, 49, 51, 65, 80, 131, 196n48
Himmelfarb, Gertrude, 5
Hugo, Victor, 3, 14–15, 18, 20–22, 30, 35, 36, 41, 45, 47, 48, 50, 55, 57, 59, 66, 73, 79, 81, 97, 102, 128, 129, 185n7, 189nn7, 8, 197n9, 198n10
Huizinga, Johan, 15

Janin of Lyon, 91
Janin, Jules, 76, 112
de Jaucourt, 15
Jaurès, Jean, 124, 125, 131, 175

Kerr-McGee Corporation, 69
King, Stephen, 185n7
Kings of France: François I, 12; Henri II, 12; Louis XII, 12; Louis XIII, 12, 13; Louis XV, 14; Louis XVI, 91; Louis XIV, 95–96
Kropotkin, Peter, 68, 125

de La Bédollière, Emile, 39, 112–113
Laborie, 94
Larminier, Jules, 141, 143, 144, 148, 154,

157, 158, 160, 162, 163, 164, 165, 166, 167, 222n49, 225n89, 226n96
Lavoisier, Antoine Laurent, 91, 122
Legien, Karl, 143
Leneveux, Henri, 109
Lenoir, 90, 95
Le Play, Frédéric, 229n1
Leroux, Gaston, 3, 130, 190n17, 218n31
Leroux, Pierre, 54–55, 56, 57, 59, 66
Lesser, Wendy, 2
Leuret, François, 96
Lévi-Strauss, Claude, 4
Liebig, Justus, 55, 56, 79

Malaparte, Curzio, 51
Malthus, Thomas, 54, 197n6
Marat, Jean-Paul, 19–20, 21
Marchand, Jean-Henri, 92–93
Marx, Karl, 1–2, 4, 57, 92, 229n1
Massiet, Raymond, 52
Mattéi, Bruno, 106
Mayer, Alfred, 47
Mayhew, Henry, 21, 210n90
Mephitism and mephitic odors, 91, 98, 120
Mercier, Louis-Sébastien, 14, 15, 26, 91, 92, 94, 95, 120, 122–123, 126
Miasmas, 16, 24, 68, 74, 82, 90, 91, 92, 94, 122, 123, 178
Michels, Robert, 143
Mille, A., 36, 58–60, 80, 115
Millerand, Alexandre, 162
Miron, François, 13
Monfalcon, J.-B., 24
Montfaucon, 11–12, 17, 23, 54, 58, 65, 72–77, 78, 81, 82, 88, 103, 203nn6,7,8, 204n22. *See also Poudrette*
Moral proletarians, 95, 100, 102–104, 106, 148, 226n96
More, Sir Thomas, 122, 126
Mumford, Lewis, 65
Murard, Lion, 106

Nadar [Gaspard Félix Tournachon], 44, 117
Nadaud, Martin, 62
Napoleon III, 25, 28, 29, 36, 47, 48, 57, 59, 60, 196n37
de Nerval, Gerard, 26
Nuclear power industry, 53, 69–70, 120, 185n6, 216n73

Odors, 56, 77, 188n28; in Paris, 10, 16, 29, 37–38; of excrement dumps, 11–12, 72, 76, 78; in sewers, 12, 14, 28–29, 44, 81, 97, 118–119, 216n72; of sewage farming, 66, 69; of 1880, 78, 81, 138, 205n48; of cesspool cleaning, 90, 92, 108, 109, 207n4. *See also* Mephitism and mephitic odors
Organisation Armée Secrète, 52

Parent-Duchâtelet, Alexandre-Jean-Baptiste, 3, 13, 25, 28, 30, 58, 72, 74–77, 78, 79, 81, 82, 83, 108, 109, 110, 112, 115, 116, 117, 120, 137, 167, 180, 209n54, 217n10; study of sewers and sewermen, 4, 27, 44, 95–106, 111, 149, 209n51, 210n68, 211n91; study of prostitution, 23, 35–36, 41, 97, 99, 153, 191n29, 209n51, 211n93
Paris municipal government, 12, 13, 14, 60–62, 75, 80, 82, 138, 145–147, 162–163, 173, 175, 204n22, 205n48, 219n4, 221n45. *See also* Chirac, Jacques; Polity as employer
Parlement of Paris, 13, 89
Parmentier, Antoine, 94
Pasteur, Louis, 81
Pelloutier, Fernand, 143
Pinkney, David, 3
Pliny, 15, 47
Plomb (illness), 94, 98, 104, 209n55
Police of Paris, 29, 41, 76, 89, 90, 91, 111, 148, 161
de Polinière, A.-P. I., 24
Polity as employer, 111, 137, 145, 148, 180, 221n40
Poudrette, 11–12, 54, 72, 76, 77
Prévert, Jacques, 127–128
Public visits: to the sewers, 5, 39–47, 49, 50, 51, 52, 54, 83, 111, 115, 116, 117, 120, 129, 144, 155; to the Catacombes, 16–17; to the irrigation fields, 62, 66; to the Canal Saint-Martin, 194n6
Pynchon, Thomas, 184n6

Ragpickers, 53, 117, 125, 128, 131, 132, 179, 180, 206n48, 229–230n1
Ramazzini, Bernardini, 15, 90, 91, 92, 94, 98, 108, 208n12
Rambuteau, Claude, Comte de, 192n2

Rancière, Jacques, 106
Representations, 5, 186n14; of sanitary labor, 87–88, 95, 106, 107–108, 111, 114, 119, 120–133, 144, 145, 153, 155, 167, 168, 169, 172, 177–178, 179–180
Restif de la Bretonne, Nicolas-Edmé, 13, 54, 89, 93
Richer, 79, 108, 109, 110
Rol-Tanguy, 52
Romains, Jules, 127
Rome: sewers, 15, 19, 29, 36, 47–48, 55; catacombs, 16; aqueducts, 29; Louis Veuillot on comparison to Second Empire, 49–50; convict labor in sewers, 92, 98–99, 121, 216n2; Gustave Flaubert on comparison to Second Empire, 110. *See also* Cluacina
Rousseau, Jean-Jacques, 11, 75, 89, 93, 103
Roux, Louis, 73

Saint-Simonianism, 24, 29, 116, 148
Sainte-Beuve, Charles Augustin, 113
Sarcey, Francisque, 60, 63, 66
Sarrazin, 169, 170, 175
Seine, sewage flow into, 12, 26, 57–58, 60, 78, 79, 82, 89, 206n57
Sewage: and social thought, 54–55, 56–57, 65–69, 82; value, 198n10, 200n58
Sewage farming, 80, 129; Chadwick's conception, 56–57; outside Paris, 58–66, 68–69, 226n96; outside Berlin, 66–67; outside other cities, 201n85, 202n91. *See also* Achères; Gennevilliers
Sewermen of London, 210–211n90, 214n40, 215n61, 219n2
Sewermen of Paris: and the norm for labor, 4, 87–88, 107, 121; military metaphor, 4, 115–116, 117, 137, 144, 145, 146, 176; debate over *tout-à-l'égout*, 4, 118–120; number, 26, 96, 102, 105, 111, 114, 119, 137, 138, 141, 147, 155, 169, 176, 220n23; before the Second Empire, 26–27, 95–106, 111–113; work, 26–27, 30–35, 115, 142–143, 156, 171, 176–177, 228n36; sand extraction, 27, 32, 143, 171, 175, 176; Second Empire and Third Republic, 35, 44, 112–120, 137–140; the public visit, 39–41, 144; health and safety, 47, 97, 98, 101, 104, 105, 111, 112, 114–115, 118–119, 149–155,

172, 209n55, 210n80, 220n21, 222nn1,10, 227n18; moral behavior, 98–100, 144, 157, 160; drinking, 99, 101, 146, 157; avarice, 99, 105, 211n98; length of workday, 100, 138, 139, 143, 144, 146, 147, 155, 170, 219n10, 220n24; management, 100–102, 105–106, 111–112, 116–117, 137, 141–143, 147; wages, 101–102, 105, 111, 125, 139; pension, 111, 139, 140, 147, 155–156, 157, 158, 159, 164, 173; idealized images, 112, 113, 117, 129–130; protests and strikes, 113, 144, 172–173, 174–175, 221n37; medical screening, 114, 115, 118, 139, 156, 220n11; tuberculosis, 119, 154, 156, 160, 164–165, 166; geographical origins, 132, 138–139, 140, 169, 170; endogamy, 139, 140, 158, 169–170, 175; occupational background, 139, 163, 170; secondary occupations, 140, 170, 227n9; sick leaves, 155, 156–157, 172; vacation, 155, 163; orphans, 156, 158, 159–161, 162, 163–164, 165, 166, 168; widows, 156, 158, 159, 162, 163, 164, 165, 166; occupational medicine, 156–158, 172, 220n11; retirees, 158–159, 162, 166; World War I, 165–166; Fifth Republic, 168–177. *See also* Charpian; Colony; Parent-Duchâtelet, A.-J.-B.; *Plomb;* Polity as employer; Representations; Sewermen's union; Sewers of Paris
Sewermen's union, 4, 127, 140–148, 149, 155–167, 168, 180; hiring and promotion, 141; relations with engineers, 141, 144, 145, 146, 147–148, 171–172; on bureaucracy, 143, 145, 148, 159, 168; moral discourse, 144, 148; familial metaphor, 158, 161, 162, 224n51; Fête de la Caisse des Veuves, 159, 163, 223n40; dissension, 221–222n49, 225n79; Bonneffs on, 226n98. *See also* Colony; Larminier, Jules; Sewermen of Paris; Unions, 1884 law
Sewers of New York City, 221n46, 228n38
Sewers of Paris: length, 12, 13, 26, 30, 35, 184n5; Old Regime, 12–15, 95–96; Revolution of 1789, 14–15, 18–19, 22, 48; sedition, 18–20, 48, 49–50, 51–52, 178, 189n5; crime; 20, 41, 52; contents, 20–21, 30, 48, 53, 172; First Empire,

21–22, 25; map, 22, 228n38; Restoration Monarchy, 25–26; July Monarchy, 26–27; Second Empire, 27–35, 47, 48, 49–50, 107, 115, 130; secondary functions, 30, 35, 51, 194n30, 196n48; and cloaca, 35–36; siege and Paris Commune of 1870–71, 48; Occupation, 51–52, 131; privatization, 147, 175; Fifth Republic, 171, 175–177. *See also* Amelot sewer; Animals in the sewers; Cartouche; Demography and sewers; Odor in sewers; Sewermen of Paris; Public visits to the sewers; Rome
Société philanthropique, 103, 104, 167
Solidarism, 148, 167–168
Stallybrass, Peter, 2
Street cleaners and garbage collection, 11, 54, 125, 126, 130, 139, 170, 177, 205n48, 228n40, 228–229n42; foreign labor, 132–133, 174, 218n34, 229n44; trash removal, 205n46, 205–206n48
Sue, Eugène, 20

Talleyrand, Charles Maurice, 109, 192n2
Taves, 52
Taylor, Frederick Winslow, 102
Texier, Edmond, 112
Therapeutic encouters with refuse, 4, 51, 52, 55, 66, 75, 77, 82–83
Thiers, Adolphe, 62
de Tocqueville, Alexis, 19, 124
Tournon, 122
Tout-à-l'égout, 80–82, 129, 154, 172, 207n60; alternate proposals, 81, 206n52, 215n65; and representations of labor, 118–120, 146; municipal council support for, 138, 205n48. *See also* Cesspool cleaners; Sewermen of Paris
Trollope, Frances, 37–38, 48, 49, 55
Trotsky, Leon, 51
Turgot, Anne-Robert-Jacques, 90
Turgot, Michel-Etienne, and the Turgot sewer, 14, 15, 91

Unions, 1884 law, 145, 147, 162, 225n92

Verne, Jules, 68
Veuillot, Louis, 49–50
Villermé, Louis-René, 23, 24, 28
La Villette, 58, 78, 80
Voltaire, 16, 93

Waldeck-Rousseau, René, 162
Waring, George, 185n7, 214n45
White, Allon, 2
Williams, Rosalind, 2
Women and the feminine: and sewers, 23, 54, 184n6; and Saint-Simonian Paris, 29; and the public visit, 41; women underground, 130, 218n31; and Montfaucon, 203n6; and valorization of waste removal, 185n7, 207n2, 216n1

Zola, Emile, 2, 50, 51, 103
Zylberman, Patrick, 106